Lifting the Burden

Lifting the Burden

Reading Matthew's Gospel in the Church Today

Brendan Byrne, S.J.

LITURGICAL PRESS
Collegeville, Minnesota

www.litpress.org

1	2	3	4	5	6	7	8	9

Library of Congress Cataloging-in-Publication Data

Byrne, Brendan (Brendan J.)
    Lifting the burden : reading Matthew's Gospel in the church today / Brendan Byrne.
        p. cm.
    Includes bibliographical references.
    ISBN 0-8146-3026-X (alk. paper)
    1. Bible. N.T. Matthew—Commentaries. I. Title.

BS2575.53.B97   2004
226.2'07—dc22

2004000333

Contents

Introduction

With respect to Matthew's gospel, for me it is a case of "late have I loved thee." Though I value all four gospels, Matthew was far from my favorite. One missed Mark's sharp eye for detail and Luke's gift for narrative. In contrast, the First Gospel appeared moralizing and didactic, with rather too much talk of punishment and hellfire. Moreover, the Church seemed over-exposed to the gospels of Matthew and John; people needed to hear the independent voices of Mark and Luke (especially the former), as well as Paul.

Then a colleague's absence on study leave a few years ago led to my teaching a scheduled course on Matthew. Reading in preparation for that course—especially J. Andrew Overman's *Matthew's Gospel and Formative Judaism*[1]—worked something of a conversion. The rekindled debate regarding Matthew's relationship to Judaism caught my interest. Jesus emerged as interpreter of the Torah in a fresh and liberating way. In particular, Overman drew my attention to the significance for Matthew of a text from the prophet Hosea, "What I want is mercy, not sacrifice" (Hos 6:6), a text Jesus twice cites in defense of his approach to religious law and tradition (Matt 9:13; 12:7).[2]

In Matthew I discovered a gospel that teaches us to look at humanity through the eyes of Jesus and see it as afflicted and weighed down with all manner of burdens. Far from adding to humanity's burdens, Jesus comes to bear and lift them. Hence Matthew's frequent portrayal of him in the guise of the "Servant" figure in Isaiah.

[1] J. Andrew Overman, *Matthew's Gospel and Formative Judaism: the Social World of the Matthean Community* (Minneapolis: Fortress, 1990).

[2] Matthew both times quotes Hos 6:6 according to the LXX, which uses *eleos* ("mercy") to translate the Hebrew *hesed*. The *NRSV* translation "steadfast love" would seem to reflect more accurately than "mercy" the sense of the Hebrew original of Hos 6:6. However, in connection with Matthew it is appropriate to translate the prophetic text according to the lead given by the Evangelist; cf. the *NRSV* translation in Matt 9:13; 12:7 ("mercy" in both cases).

This approach to Matthew's gospel seemed to find ready acceptance when put forward in courses, workshops, occasional lectures and the like. Of all the four gospels it is Matthew that has contributed most to Christian identity and self-understanding. At a time when much soul-searching is going on regarding what it means to be Church, it is fitting to look again at the image of Church emerging from Matthew. The Second Vatican Council left the Catholic communion with a marvelous vision of the Church, but fifty years on we find ourselves still grappling with the unfinished business of the Council. For many, the hopes raised by that remarkable gathering in the mid-1960s have been dashed. Oppressive structures and habits of mind linger or have been reimposed. The Church's relationship to a wider world, steadily becoming more and more pluralistic, remains problematic and unsure. One significant area of human life neglected by the Council— human sexuality—has come back to haunt the Church in a devastating way. In the early years of this new millennium we find ourselves a very burdened community—burdened from within by the weight of our own sinfulness and institutional failure, burdened from without through sharing the common lot of humankind in a fearful and unsettled time.

How can a reading of Matthew's gospel address this situation? I am not for one moment suggesting that it be done in a simplistic way—by taking the various prescriptions and commendations in the gospel and applying them literally to life in the Church today. The community responsible for the gospel lived in a situation totally different from our own. A knowledge of its historical setting, its likely issues and challenges, greatly aids interpretation. But there is no sense in attempting to recreate that pattern now. That is to take the path of religious fundamentalism—a road to death rather than life, as we know all too well at the present time. We read and venerate the gospels because of their witness to the power and presence of the risen Lord in our community. We attempt to be captured by their vision, not that we may be drawn back to the world from which they spring but rather that we may be drawn into the narrative world that each of them projects and into the values of that world, which are those of the crucified and risen Lord.

I have subtitled this book "A Reading of Matthew's Gospel." "A Reading" is meant to suggest one interpretation among several that could be offered. In presenting my personal interpretation from a particular point of view I in no sense wish to imply that it is the only valid reading or even the most obvious or the best grounded. I do believe it to be a valid interpretation, well founded in the text of the gospel. However, I shall for the most part simply allow its own developing logic to commend it, without detailed argumentation or constant discussion with other scholarly points of view. Technical details and disputed points requiring further treatment I relegate to the notes. The work is similar to a commentary in that I do move through the gospel continuously from beginning to end. It is unlike a commentary in that I do not feel obliged to comment on everything in detail. I shall linger on areas of the text where the approach I am taking seems notably prominent, paying less attention to those where it is not.

To keep the book within reasonable size and expense I have not, save in very few places, set out the text of the gospel in English translation. The translation to which I adhere most closely is that of the *New Revised Standard Version.* I would urge readers to have this by them as they consult or work their way through the book. Of great assistance to more serious students will be a synopsis of the three synoptic gospels, such as Burton H. Throckmorton's *Gospel Parallels,* the most recent edition of which uses the *NRSV.*[3] But, of course, the first and most essential resource is the Old or First Testament, the "fulfillment" of which Matthew is time and time again at pains to point out.

I hope the book will be accessible for the general reader as well as useful for the student. While the tone is not overtly devotional, this interpretation of Matthew stems from a faith commitment and a conviction that the Evangelist writes out of a distinctive vision of the God revealed by Jesus and with the aim of commending a pattern of personal and community life coherent with that vision.

"Difficult" Matthew

Despite my "conversion" to Matthew, I remain acutely aware that the gospel presents interpreters and preachers with particular challenges today. One has to do with the whole area of relationship to Judaism; this I take up in the following chapter. The other is that the teachings of the Matthean Jesus reflect not only the moral seriousness of Judaism in general but also encapsulate that teaching within the eschatological worldview of Jewish apocalypticism, in which the prospect of final judgment and accountability is never far from view. Matthew, for whom the Church of his time was very much a mixed body containing weeds among the wheat, is not slow to hold a threat of judgment, which originally had wider reference, before the

[3] *Gospel Parallels: A Comparison of the Synoptic Gospels* (5th ed. Nashville: Nelson, 1992).

community itself. The view of Jesus as Emmanuel ("God with us" [1:23]) who comes to lift humanity's burden sits in considerable tension with that of the Son of Man due to come on the clouds of heaven to judge the world (24:39-41; 25:31-46; 26:64). Invitations of welcome into the final kingdom (25:21, 23, 35, 46) are matched by threats of hellfire (5:22; 18:9; 25:41) and castings out into exterior darkness where there will be "weeping and gnashing of teeth" (8:12; 13:42, 50; 22:13; 24:51; 25:30).

I shall attempt to deal with such material in places where it is more particularly prominent. For the present I simply observe more generally that contemporary Christian theology, while retaining the moral serious-ness and challenge of this gospel, is not committed to a literalistic under-standing of such matters. Indeed, to ignore the symbolic cast of such expressions would falsify their original intent, which is not to provide information about the future state but to summon people to a responsible pattern of life here and now—an aim hardly achieved by paralyzing people with fear. As with all biblical documents, the crucial thing, I believe, is to place all such statements within their proper context in the unfolding cumulative message of the gospel, which is unmistakably that of a God who desires to heal, gather, and save rather than to condemn.[4] Even in the more difficult areas I hope to show how that essential positive message never really falls from view.

Some Presuppositions

In developing this approach to Matthew's gospel I would like to make clear certain things I am presupposing with little or no further justification.

First of all, I take the gospel in its final canonical form, paying little attention to issues concerning its likely sources or what might have been the process of its composition. Along with most scholars, I take it to be written by a third-generation Christian in the closing decades of the first century C.E. The place of composition was probably somewhere in Syria, perhaps in the great city of Antioch, but certainly somewhere where there was opportunity for both continuing interaction with Jewish synagogues and contact of a missionary nature with the surrounding non-Jewish (Gentile) world. In line with tradition I shall refer to its author as "Matthew," while recognizing that the traditional identification of the gospel with the tax collector of that name called by Jesus (9:9; the character named "Levi" in

---

[4] Cf. Ulrich Luz, *Das Evangelium nach Matthäus* (see following note) 4:555.

Mark 2:14 and Luke 5:27) lacks historical verification. It is in fact improbable, granted that the narrative reflects the use of sources rather than direct, eyewitness memory. Readers wishing to follow up such matters can do so by consulting the standard commentaries. Here I acknowledge those which have been particularly influential in my own understanding of Matthew and whose scholarship stands behind much of the interpretation proposed here both in detail and overall understanding: Ulrich Luz,[5] W. D. Davies and Dale Allison,[6] M. Eugene Boring,[7] Daniel J. Harrington,[8] John P. Meier,[9] and Rudolf Schnackenburg.[10]

Again, along with the majority of scholars I accept the "Two-Source" theory of the relationship among the three synoptic gospels. According to this theory both Matthew and Luke, in addition to using sources of their own, drew independently on Mark's gospel and also upon a source, consisting largely of teachings and sayings, that scholars reconstruct and call "Q." Without wishing to be as definite about the nature of this source as some scholars are, I think it is necessary to postulate some such fount of tradition, whether in written or rather fixed oral form, in order to account for the large amount of non-Markan material Luke and Matthew have in common. In the light of this theory and to bring out the First Evangelist's distinctive preoccupations I shall at times point out places where Matthew appears to have embellished his Markan source or departed from its order.

Encounter with the Living Lord

Last but by no means least, readers have to be aware that the interpretation offered here proceeds entirely from a distinct view of what the

---

[5] Four volumes in the original German: Ulrich Luz, *Das Evangelium nach Matthäus* (EKK 1) Vol. 1: *Mt 1–7;* Vol. 2: *Mt 8–17;* Vol. 3: *Mt 18–25;* Vol. 4: *Mt 26–28* (Zürich: Benziger; Neukirchen-Vluyn: Neukirchener Verlag, 1985–2002). Two volumes of a projected three-volume English translation have appeared: *Matthew 1–7: A Commentary.* Translated by Wilhelm C. Linss (Minneapolis: Augsburg, 1989); *Matthew 8–20: A Commentary.* Translated by James E. Crouch. Hermeneia (Minneapolis: Fortress, 2001).

[6] W. D. Davies and Dale Allison, *A Critical and Exegetical Commentary on the Gospel According to Saint Matthew.* ICC. 3 vols. (Edinburgh: T&T Clark, 1988–97).

[7] M. Eugene Boring, "The Gospel of Matthew," in Leander E. Keck, ed., *The New Interpreter's Bible 8* (Nashville: Abingdon, 1995) 87–505.

[8] Daniel J. Harrington, *The Gospel of Matthew.* SP 1 (Collegeville: Liturgical Press, 1991).

[9] John P. Meier, *Matthew* (Wilmington: Michael Glazier, 1980).

[10] Rudolf Schnackenburg, *The Gospel of Matthew* (Grand Rapids: Eerdmans, 2002). Translation of *Das Evangelium nach Matthäus.* 2 vols. (Würzburg: Echter, 1985, 1987).

gospels are and what they are not. First, what they are not: Though cast in a form that follows the pattern of Jesus' life they are in no way biographies in the modern sense. They certainly record memories about Jesus and give a fair indication of the basic shape of his life. But their primary purpose is not to pass on accurate historical information concerning things Jesus of Nazareth said and did in his historical life.

Matthew's account of Jesus, no less than those of Mark, Luke, and John, is shot through with a vision of faith. The essential core of what Christians believe about Jesus—that his death on the cross under Pontius Pilate was followed by his resurrection and exaltation to the right hand of God—colors the entire account from beginning to end. It forms a thick "lens" through which any details of his historical life have to be discerned. It determined what details were remembered and how such memories were embellished and extended when passed on down the decades in a context of faith and worship. Very influential in this process, especially for Matthew, was the understanding of Jesus as the fulfillment of hopes and promises embedded in the scriptures of Israel (for Christians the Old Testament). A scriptural aura in this sense hovers around the stories about Jesus, contributing color, detail, and language, and also, to some extent, content.

Thus the Jesus portrayed in the gospels is the risen Lord active in the community today. The aim of the narrative is to engage the reader in the drama in such a way as to communicate the sense of being a participant, not a spectator, in what is going on. *I* share in the terrible dilemma facing Joseph as he becomes aware that Mary is pregnant (1:18-19); *I* bring my gifts to the newborn King along with the wise men from the East (2:1-12); *I* sit among the crowd listening to Jesus' authoritative teaching on the mountain (chs. 5–7); *I* am the Canaanite woman whose wit and faith overcome Jesus' reluctance to heal her child (15:21-28). This is not make-believe. Behind it lies the reality for the believer that Jesus really is alive and that those whom his Spirit touches undergo an experience of salvation that is just as immediate and real as it was for those who saw him, heard him, and felt his touch in Galilee and Judea.[11]

So the gospel may appear to be a story about "back there." But it is not really about "back there" at all. It is about *now*—and about a future for the Church and the world. I shall on occasion comment upon the extent to

[11] For a development of this understanding of the gospel, especially in relation to prayer in the Ignatian tradition, see further Brendan Byrne, "'To See with the Eyes of the Imagination . . .': Scripture in the Exercises and Recent Interpretation," *Way Supplement* 72 (Autumn 1991) 3–19.

which a particular tradition in the Gospel of Matthew may or may not reflect what Jesus said or did in his historical life. But my concern is not to
take the reader "back" to this Jesus—something not usually possible save
in a speculative and limited degree. Some readers may find this lack of
concern for history disappointing or even disturbing. I can only ask them to
enter upon the journey for a while. What they have lost of "history" will,
I hope, be more than compensated for by the sense of being grasped by the
power of the risen Lord that the Matthean narrative, with great dramatic
power, conveys.

We would not read the Gospel of Matthew at all if we did not recognize
that it is in some sense "our story" too. Standing as we do at a moment of
great change and turmoil in Christian understanding and community, we
very much need to be people who, like the master of a household described
in Matt 13:52, know how to bring out of their treasure chest what is new
and what is old. This book aims to play a part in that process.

Matthew's Gospel and Judaism

From its earliest days Matthew's gospel has been recognized as the "Jewish gospel," the one most reflective of Christianity's Jewish background. At the same time and somewhat ironically in view of this, it is chiefly in relation to Matthew that the issue of New Testament anti-Semitism arises most keenly. Only in the Matthean Passion narrative do we hear from the crowd the fearful cry, "His blood be on us and on our children" (27:25), a cry that has unleashed torrents of murderous Christian anti-Judaism and provided legitimacy for persecution and pogroms, culminating in the Nazi Holocaust of the last century. Likewise, it is only Matthew who records Jesus as saying to the chief priests and scribes, "Therefore I tell you, the kingdom of God will be taken away from you and given to a people that produces its fruits" (21:43), a statement that has fed the sense of Christianity as "superceding" Judaism as the people of God. As I hope to explain when discussing these and other sensitive areas of the gospel, such understandings are neither true to the original thrust of the narrative nor, even if they were, would they be ethically responsible. Nonetheless, recalling them points to the high importance of sorting out from the start the relationship of the First Gospel to Judaism in regard to both history and interpretation.

To spend some time on the historical question first: A significantly creative area in recent scholarship on Matthew has been a reconsideration of its historical position *vis-à-vis* the Judaism of its time. This has been part of a wider appreciation of the nature of Judaism as a whole in the centuries immediately before and after the time of Jesus. Before the destruction of the Jewish state and the sacking of Jerusalem, at the end of the First Jewish Revolt, 66–70 C.E. (the period for which scholars now prefer the less value-laden term "Second Temple Judaism") Judaism in Palestine presented a very pluriform face, with various movements and sects vying for influence and allegiance. Besides the Sadduccees and Pharisees well known from the gospels, we can list the Essenes (among whom the people responsible for

1

the scrolls found at Qumran are probably to be numbered), more radical groups such as those who in the years immediately before the revolt became the "Zealots," disciples of John the Baptist, and, as I think we have to call them at this point, "Jesus messianists"—that is, those Jews who, without separation from the broad mass of the Jewish commonwealth, believed that Jesus of Nazareth, crucified in the early 30s by the Roman procurator, Pontius Pilate, was the appointed Messiah, raised by God from the dead and destined soon to return in glory as Son of Man to complete his messianic work.

Let us linger for a moment on the Pharisees—the group that bulks largest in the Gospel of Matthew. The members of this movement were united in the belief that God had communicated to Moses not only the written Torah, making up the first five books of the Bible (Pentateuch) but also an oral law preserved and passed down in a body of codified traditional rulings, of which they in particular were the guardians. The rulings, chiefly focused on Sabbath observance and determination of what was "clean" and "unclean," enabled the Pharisees and those they sought to guide to live as God's people, holy and set apart, in the mixed society in which Jews now lived—mixed in the sense that Palestine contained Jewish and non-Jewish population in almost equal measure. While Pharisaism, like any religious practice, could degenerate into the kind of legalism attacked by Jesus in the gospels, at its best it represented a serious attempt to create for the people at large the possibility of living out, in a mixed society, the ideal of the book of Leviticus, that Israel should be a holy people, a nation of priests before the Lord (Lev 20:26; cf. Exod 19:6). The Pharisaic rituals of washing and cleanliness served to preserve and foster that distinct sense of identity.

The trouble was—and this is the view of Jesus, as presented in the gospels—that the "holiness" net could be drawn too tightly. Not only pagans but also some classes of *Jews* could be considered more or less permanently outside the pale because social disadvantage or occupation (for example, tax collecting for the Roman occupying power) rendered them permanently unclean. Taking up earlier tradition (cf. Mark 7:1-23), Matthew presents Jesus as severely criticizing Pharisees for disenfranchising their fellow Israelites in the name of what for him is not the God-given Torah but purely human tradition.

The destruction of the Temple in 70 C.E. largely swept away the power of those groups, especially the Sadduccees and priestly class in general, that depended on it for influence. Two groups stood to be less affected by this otherwise cataclysmic event. One was the Pharisees, for whom Torah rather than Temple had long been the chief focus. The other group was the Jesus messianists, who had long since come to believe that the atoning function of the Temple and its sacrifices had been superceded once and for all by the shedding of Jesus' blood on Calvary (Matt 26:28; cf. Rom 3:25).

The stage was set, then, in the years following 70 C.E. for the ever-increasing ascendancy in Jewish religious and national life of the heirs of the Pharisees: the rabbis. The next hundred years or so represent the period known in scholarly parlance as the era of "Formative Judaism": Judaism on the way to becoming (around 200 C.E.) full-blown Rabbinic Judaism, the ancestor of all forms of Judaism that have survived to this day. During this time the leading rabbis sought to recreate the national life by gathering a shattered people around the Torah and the body of interpretive traditions that, as explained above, they held to be a separate fount of revelation derived from Moses. In the synagogues and circles of disciples that leading rabbis gathered around themselves this body of tradition, endlessly developed by intense study and discussion, showed how the Torah should be lived out in the conditions in which Jews found themselves at the time.

It is widely agreed today that Matthew's gospel and in particular its decidedly Jewish character reflect intense interaction, much of it hostile, with leading representatives of Judaism undergoing this transformation. A struggle to preserve the heart of Israel in difficult times was under way. Groups bitterly contested the terms upon which that was to be achieved. The intensity of the polemic against the scribes and Pharisees in the First Gospel reflects, then, not so much the practice of Jesus during his public life (ca. 30–33 C.E.), but these struggles of a later period. The Jesus messianists behind this gospel, who also had no cause to lament the loss of the Temple, found themselves under pressure from an ascendant Synagogue increasingly intolerant of groups who deviated from the vision of Israel they were trying to recapture and impose.

Lurking here is a central issue much exercising Matthean studies today. With respect to the community responsible for the gospel, should we have in mind a group that, however deviant and in dispute with other authorities, would still consider itself—and be considered—as existing within the broad Jewish commonwealth? Or, by the time of the composition of the gospel, is this group of Jesus messianists now so cut off and separate—though still engaged in polemics—that we really have to speak of a separate religion? *They* might have considered themselves to be still part of Israel, indeed to be the *true Israel* in continuity with the covenant people of old. But did the rest of the Jewish commonwealth still recognize them as Jews?—or, on the contrary, had there already taken place so genuine a "parting of the ways" as to make it appropriate to speak now of two distinct entities: Judaism and Christianity?[1]

Much in Matthew's gospel supports the former view. First, there is the immense sense of continuity with the Jewish tradition—in particular the insistence on the validity of the Torah and the "righteousness" it requires (5:17-20). Then there are the instructions from Jesus that appear to restrict the mission to the "lost sheep of the house of Israel," forbidding going to the Gentiles (10:5-6; cf. 15:24). At one point (23:2-3) the gospel seems to recognize the authority of the scribes and Pharisees who "sit upon Moses' seat," though their behavior is not to be imitated. Even the warning about being dragged "before councils" and beaten "in synagogues" (10:17) suggests ongoing submission to the discipline of Jewish religious authorities.

On the other hand, there is also much to suggest a final, definitive breach. References to "their synagogues" (4:23; 9:35; 10:17; cf. 23:34) and to "the Jews" as though to an alien, outside group (28:15) convey a very distancing impression. Despite the isolated injunction in 10:5-6, the all-important exit-line of the gospel, 28:19-20, makes clear that the missionary focus of the community now rests upon the Gentile world (28:16-20).[2] The most significant factor, however, is the one that is most obvious: the absolute centrality of what this community believed about Jesus—his personal status and his role in the design of God. Matthew's gospel makes clear from its very opening pages that the status and role of Jesus go far beyond conventional Jewish expectation concerning the Messiah. Jesus is the Messiah, son of David, yes, but he is also God's Son in a unique, transcendent sense, as established by the miraculous nature of his birth (1:20-25) and attested by various divine interventions (3:17; 17:5), culminating in his being raised from the dead. For the Matthean community Jesus, both in his lifetime and as risen Lord, is "Emmanuel" ("God with us") in a transcendent sense never dreamed of by the prophet who formulated the relevant text (Isa 7:14; Matt 1:23). Conventional Jewish expectation has yielded to hope for his return as the Danielic "Son of Man" (7:13-14), who will institute universal judgment and definitively establish the "kingdom" or "rule"

---

[1] For a recent survey see Douglas R. H. Hare, "How Jewish Is the Gospel of Matthew?" *CBQ* 62 (2000) 264–77; also M. Eugene Boring, "The Gospel of Matthew," in Leander E. Keck, ed., *The New Interpreter's Bible*. Vol. 8 (Nashville: Abingdon, 1995) 97–101; Daniel J. Harrington, *The Gospel of Matthew*. SP 1 (Collegeville: Liturgical Press, 1991) 20–22.

[2] See Brendan Byrne, "The Messiah in Whose Name 'the Gentiles Will Hope' (Matt 12:21): Gentile Inclusion as an Essential Element of Matthew's Christology," *AusBR* 50 (2002) 55–73.

of God on earth (Matt 16:27-28; 24:29-31). A final indicator of separation is the community's designation of itself as "church" (Greek *ekklēsia*), a usage with no precedent in Judaism save as the Greek translation (LXX) of the Hebrew *qahal,* used of the community of Israel during the period of Sinai wandering.

For these reasons I believe and will presume in this reading of the gospel that the community responsible for it regarded itself as independent of the leadership currently ascendant in the Jewish world. At the same time it existed in a state of rivalry and competition with "the synagogue across the street," and so disputed intensely the claims of the ascendant group to be the true Israel, gathered around the legitimate and valid interpretation of the Torah.

For both parties, the Pharisaic-Rabbinic and the Matthean Jesus Messianist, the Torah is central. For both it is probably true to say, as I once heard a rabbi say with passion: "Israel is Torah and the Torah is Israel." The issue between them concerns *interpretation.* For what was now becoming mainstream Judaism, the key to interpreting Torah and establishing the true Israel on that basis is the body of tradition handed down in oral form from Moses and guarded by the rabbis. The Matthean community, on the contrary, believes that it has the key to interpreting the Torah in the person of Jesus. For them Jesus is *the* interpreter of the Torah, enjoying as unique Son of God an authority far beyond that of Moses or any oral tradition purported to derive from him. Jesus is more than a "new Moses." He is the Interpreter *par excellence,* authorized to challenge and in places to set aside rulings from Moses, even when formulated in the written Torah. Situated at the beginning of his public career, the Great Sermon (Matthew 5–7) irrevocably enshrines this claim.

We must be careful, however. Matthew does not present the community of the kingdom as the "replacement" of Israel or even as a kind of "New Israel" discontinuous with the old. Rather, in direct continuity with biblical Israel the community would see itself as having the key to bringing about the Israel that God intends for the era of the kingdom, a divine intent indicated in the Scriptures, which numerous events in the life of Jesus have already "fulfilled." The "key" of course is the Torah authoritatively and definitively interpreted by Jesus, not only in his historical life, the memory of which they preserve, but also in the rulings he continues to impart to the community through his presence among them as risen Lord (18:20; 28:20). The quarrel of Matthew's community as reflected in its gospel is not with Judaism as such but with the Pharisaic-Rabbinic leadership that has vigorously contested its claims for the messianic status of

Jesus and sought to foster among the people at large an alternative view of the Israel that God wants, one based on Torah interpreted according to the "tradition of the fathers," whose guardians they assume themselves to be. Polemical statements such as that in Matt 21:43, "the kingdom of God will be taken away from you and given to a people that produces its fruits," do suggest a belief that the rival leadership has really forfeited any claim to foster the people of God. The Matthean community appears to see in these leaders the lineal descendants of the "chief priests and scribes" who had clamored for the execution of Jesus and brought down upon themselves and their children the calamity of 70 C.E. (the true meaning of the "blood" charge of 27:25; see below).

Even as regards the ordinary populace, the gospel seems to reflect a stage when a mission to the Jews as such has been abandoned—its memory preserved only in earlier elements of the tradition. While treasuring its Jewish heritage and still seeing itself as "Israel," the community now seems to have its energy entirely directed to the Gentile mission. In other words, what we have in the gospel is the reflection of a community, Jewish in origin and character, that would now more readily identify with the Gentile churches who share its faith in Jesus as Messiah rather than with the Jewish groups to whom, through lack of success, it has virtually ceased to appeal. It is in fact very likely that the impetus to compose the gospel—in effect to commission a talented scribe among their number for the task—came from a desire to state in writing the understanding of themselves at which they had now arrived—probably in the mid-80s: that is, as comprising an inclusive Israel that it had always been God's intention to bring about, an Israel being gathered from the nations of the world preliminary to the return of Jesus as Son of Man to institute judgment and the consummation of the kingdom.

Adopting the course taken already by the author of Mark's gospel, this community or its selected scribe chose to make this statement of identity through the genre of a gospel: a narrative cast in the shape of a biography of Jesus that would portray his deeds and actions, even his eventual fate, as prefiguring and legitimating its own hopes, self-understanding, and mission. The greatest task—and achievement—of the Evangelist was to show that the inclusion within Israel of great numbers from the nations of the world was not an aberration, as their opponents might claim, but in fact the fulfillment of what God had intended all along and indicated clearly in the Scriptures. Hence the need of a scribe, "discipled for the kingdom of heaven" (13:52), who knew how to bring out of his store things new (Gentile) and things old (continuity with Israel).

In this sense neither Christianity as a whole nor Matthew's community in particular should be seen in relation to Judaism as child to parent. If we look to the decades immediately after the fall of Jerusalem in 70 C.E. we can say that both Formative Judaism (that is, Judaism on the way to becoming Rabbinic Judaism, as explained above) *and* the Jesus Messianist communities (that is, the communities gathered around the gospel who were to become "Christianity") were the legitimate "children" of the pluriform phenomenon known as Second Temple Judaism (Judaism prior to 70 C.E.).[3] Thus, rather than being related as parent to child, the two movements are more like siblings, children of the same parent (which makes Rabbinic Judaism and mature Christianity "cousins" in a subsequent generation). Behind Matthew's gospel, then, and imprinted clearly upon it are the struggles and hopes of a group of believers engaged in an adolescent-like struggle to establish and clarify their identity as the nucleus of "true Israel" over against the claims of their rival and more numerous siblings. It is not surprising, then, that the gospel should reflect much of the love-hate relationship characteristic of adolescence.

This reconstruction of the likely historical circumstances of the community that produced Matthew's gospel goes a long way to accounting for the elements in the narrative that lead to its being seen as anti-Jewish. What the gospel reflects is the kind of struggle for the heart of Israel that many groups within the wider Jewish commonwealth were engaged in during an era of change and conflict. The writings of other groups totally *within* Israel, such as those of Qumran, exhibit polemics against rival leadership just as intense and rejecting as any to be found in Matthew—even more so in some cases. There is a sense, then, that the gospel reflects an *intra*-Jewish debate, which renders the charge of its being *anti*-Jewish untenable.

At the same time the gospel does clearly reflect a community distancing itself from the forms of Judaism gaining ascendancy. As that process continued in the following century and Christianity became a separate religion it was all too easy for the polemical statements in the gospel to lose their original reference and be employed as accusations against Judaism as such, a path taken with tragic frequency in the subsequent Christian tradition. Belatedly but increasingly strongly in recent decades awareness of the

---

[3] A view formulated by the Jewish scholar Alan Segal: see *Rebecca's Children: Judaism and Christianity in the Roman World* (Cambridge, MA: Harvard University Press, 1986) 1, 142, 162, 179–81; also James A. Charlesworth, "Exploring Opportunities for Rethinking Relations among Jews and Christians," in idem, ed., *Jews and Christians: Exploring the Past, Present and Future* (New York: Crossroad, 1990) 35–53, especially 41–42.

calamitous ethical consequences of this development has become wide-spread in Christian circles. It is incumbent upon Christian interpreters to make sure that in reading the "good news" out of Matthew they are not reading very bad news out of it for Jews. Interpretation that is responsible will not only work from a sense of the location of Matthew in its original historical setting but also appreciate that, more than any other of the gospels, it most unambiguously shows the rootedness of Christianity in Judaism and the utter impossibility of understanding the gospel without sympathy for that essential matrix. In dealing with particular passages of Matthew, especially those that are problematic in this respect, I hope to be able to point to ways of interpretation that are sensitive to this concern.

The Design of Matthew

Almost all studies of Matthew's gospel agree that it is one of the most carefully structured documents in the New Testament. Determining its precise shape is less easy. Several models are on offer.

One Suggestion: the Fivefold Narrative + Discourse Structure

The Evangelist has left signposts that many consider indicative of structure in the shape of a phrase that five times forms a concluding comment on a discourse Jesus has given: "And it happened when Jesus had finished these words/instructions/parables" (the first seven words [six in Greek] are invariable). The phrase occurs:

- at the end of the Great Sermon (7:28);

- at the end of the missionary instruction to the disciples (11:1);

- at the end of the instruction given in the form of parables (13:53);

- at the end of the instruction on life in the Church (19:1);

- at the end of the long discourse on the future (26:1).

In each case the phrase marks a transition from the discourse just given to a narrative section less concerned with Jesus' teaching and more with his actions. Setting aside the infancy story (Matthew 1–2) on the one hand, and the Passion-Resurrection account (Matthew 26–28) on the other, and regarding the prelude to the public ministry (3:1–4:25) as an opening narrative section, then for the whole central body of the gospel we have a pattern in which, five times over, a narrative block is followed by a discourse concluded with the formula indicated above. This means that the body of the gospel (Matthew 3–25) consists essentially of five main sections or "books":

9

Book 1: 3:1–7:29
>   Narrative: Jesus' early public life in Galilee: 3:1–4:25
>   Discourse: Great Sermon: 5:1–7:29

Book 2: 8:1–10:42
>   Narrative: Jesus as healer and proclaimer of forgiveness: 8:1–9:37
>   Discourse: Missionary instruction of the disciples: 10:1-42

Book 3: 11:1–13:53
>   Narrative: Jesus encounters controversy and rejection: 11:1–12:50
>   Discourse: Instruction in parables: 13:1-52

Book 4: 13:53–18:35
>   Narrative: Final stage of Jesus' ministry in Galilee: 13:53–17:27
>   Discourse: Instruction on life in the Church: 18:1-35

Book 5: 19:1–25:46
>   Narrative: Jesus' ministry in Judea and Jerusalem: 19:1–23:39
>   Discourse: Discourse on the Future: 24:1–25:46

This "Five-Book" (Pentateuchal?) understanding gives a "handle" on the long central block of the gospel. Matthew did perhaps intend to allow the narrative to pause five times in order to communicate forcefully through the discourses a sense of Jesus as teacher and interpreter of the Torah. The schema is most convincing in regard to the five discourse sections, but less so in respect to narrative, since not everything reported in these sections clearly falls into that category, and in some cases the narrative section seems to look *back* rather than forward. (For example, the narrative of Jesus as healer and reconciler in chs. 8–9 seems to complement the presentation of him as interpreter and teacher in chs. 5–7.) Moreover, concentration on the schema obscures what in terms of the narrative flow appear to be important moments of transition. The description in 4:12-17 of the beginning of Jesus' public preaching in Galilee is clearly one of these, as is also the episode at Caesarea Philippi, 16:13-23, when, hard upon Peter's confession of faith, Jesus reveals his destiny to go up to Jerusalem to suffer and die.[1] We should not allow a rigid adherence to the fivefold narrative-plus-discourse pattern to obscure such features.

---

[1] Both passages feature the phrase "from that time on Jesus began . . ." (4:17; 16:21).

Another Suggestion:
Tracking the Unfolding Narrative Line

With considerable debt to Francis J. Matera[2] I would argue that running along with this recurring pattern of discourse and indeed carrying the whole structure is a more significant narrative line focusing on the nature and direction of Jesus' messianic role. Behind this issue, and indeed pervading the gospel as a whole, is the bitter truth that the One whom the members of the early communities believed to be Israel's God-sent Messiah experienced, for the most part, rejection from his own people. The early believers who took up the proclamation of the Gospel in his name found that their experience matched that of Jesus: where he experienced rejection from the leaders of the people and acceptance from those on the margins, they experienced similar rejection from Jewish communities, along with increasing acceptance in the non-Jewish world beyond.

To a very large degree the gospel seems designed to state this issue and address it theologically. The narrative does this, first of all, by bringing out that the pattern—rejection from the Jewish world, acceptance by the Gentile—was foreseen in the redemptive design of God laid out in the Scriptures. Of key significance here are Matthew's distinctive "fulfillment" quotations: places where the narrative pauses ten times to state explicitly how some event connected with Jesus "fulfills" what had been written "by the prophet," an indication of God's intent for the messianic age.[3]

The narrative further parallels the experience of Jesus and that of the later Church (10:17-42; 24:9-14) by the use of a recurrent phrase drawing attention to the rejection-acceptance pattern in the life of Jesus. Several times, we are told, in the face of hostility from Jewish sources he (or others "on his side": Joseph; the magi) "withdraw(s)" (Greek *anachōrein*) into some secure region, usually Galilee, where the saving events proceed along another track. In the face of Herod's hostility the magi "withdraw" to their own country (2:12, 13). To escape Herod's massacre Joseph "withdraws" with the child and his mother to Egypt (2:14), whence, on returning, to avoid Herod's son (Archelaus), he "withdraws" to Galilee (2:22). Jesus himself "withdraws" four times: to Galilee, following John's arrest (4:12); in the face of hostility from Pharisees (12:15); in response to the

---

[2] Francis J. Matera, "The Plot of Matthew's Gospel," *CBQ* 49 (1987) 233–53.

[3] Matt 1:22-23; 2:15; 2:17-15; 2:23; 4:14-16; 8:17; 12:18-21; 13:35; 21:4-5; 27:9; very similar quotations occur also in 2:5; 3:3; 13:14-15. See the Excursus: "Matthew as Interpreter of Scripture," in M. Eugene Boring, "The Gospel of Matthew," in Leander E. Keck, ed., *The New Interpreter's Bible*. Vol. 8 (Nashville: Abingdon, 1995) 151–54.

report of John's death (14:13); to the district of Tyre and Sidon following criticism from Pharisees (15:21).[4] This "withdrawal" pattern occurs too frequently in the gospel to be merely accidental.[5] Through it the Evangelist indicates the way in which the experience of Jesus himself foreshadows the Gospel's going to the Gentiles in the face of rejection from its original hearers. As Jesus "withdraws" into "Galilee of the Gentiles," so the Gospel will "withdraw" to a more receptive Gentile world.

In respect to the playing out of this pattern the gospel narrative falls into three major blocks:

1. Prologue to Jesus' messianic ministry to Israel: 1:1–4:11

2. The Messianic Ministry of Jesus to Israel: 4:12–28:15

3. The Messianic Ministry extended to the World: 28:16-20.

The central block may appear to bulk disproportionately large, especially in comparison with the last. But this final section, while slight in content, is vast in ambit: a missionary program extending to the end of time.

I propose now a "walk" through the narrative, noting the more significant signposts and turning points in these stages.

1. Prologue to Jesus' Messianic Ministry: 1:1–4:11

The account of Jesus' origins and childhood (1:1–2:23) introduces us to the person of Jesus and begins to hint at the mysterious path his messianic career will take. An intense concentration of Matthew's distinctive "fulfillment" quotations in this section (1:22-23; 2:15; 2:17-18; 2:23) makes clear that everything, even the checks and threats, unfolds according to a divine redemptive plan traceable in the Scriptures. The circumstances of Jesus' birth (following a virginal conception) show him to be God's Son in a unique and transcendent degree ("God with us" [Emmanuel]), far outstripping merely conventional expectation concerning the Davidic Messiah. The visit of the wise men (magi) from the East (2:1-23) foreshadows the pattern to be played out in his life and that of the Church: hostility/rejection from the Jewish leadership, acceptance/worship from the nations of the world.

Starting with the ministry of John the Baptist a series of scenes further indicates the direction Jesus' adult ministry will take (3:1–4:11). Following

---

[4] Two remaining occurrences of the Greek term *anachōrein*—9:24; 27:5—are not relevant. Mark uses the term once only: 3:7 (// Matt 12:13), Luke not at all (but cf. Acts 23:19; 26:31).

[5] Cf. Deirdre Good, "The Verb *anachōreō* in Matthew's Gospel," *NovT* 32 (1990) 1–12.

his submission to baptism from John, we readers are privileged witnesses to the descent of the Spirit and the heavenly acknowledgment of him as the beloved Son, in whom the Father is well-pleased (3:16-17). He is Messiah, but a Messiah filially related to God in a most intimate and unique way.

The temptation (4:1-11) reveals the fundamental source of hostility to Jesus' messianic mission: the devil (Satan), whose rule in the world Jesus has come to supplant with the rule ("kingdom") of God. It also makes clear once and for all Jesus' determination, cost what it may, to be the kind of Messiah his filial relationship with God requires.

2. The Messianic Ministry of Jesus to Israel: 4:12–28:15

2.1. Early Galilean Ministry: Jesus: Interpreter, Healer, and Reconciler on Behalf of Burdened Humanity: 4:12–10:42

With John's public ministry brought to a close (4:12a), Jesus takes over the summons to repentance in view of the onset of the rule of God (4:12-25). He does so by "withdrawing" to Galilee, which, the Evangelist points out, fulfills a hint in the prophet Isaiah that in the messianic age God would shed light upon the Gentiles who formerly sat in darkness (4:12-17).

In response to a vision of burdened humanity (4:23-25), Jesus ascends a mountain, calls his disciples to him, and then, with the unparalleled authority he enjoys as unique Son of God, promulgates an interpretation of the Torah definitive for the community of the kingdom (5:1–7:29).

Alongside the portrayal of Jesus as teacher and interpreter of the Torah a series of episodes, including nine miracle stories, depicts him as healer and reconciler with God (8:1–9:37). Jesus defends his association with "sinners" by pointing to the prophetic text, Hos 6:6, for an indication of what God wants for the last age: "mercy, not sacrifice" (9:13). His *exercise* of mercy complements his burden-lifting interpretation of Torah.

Having begun his Galilean ministry by calling disciples (4:18-22), Jesus concludes this phase of his activity by sending them out as apprentices of his mission. The instruction they receive (10:1-42) foreshadows the experience of the later Church and reinforces the pattern already established: difficulty with Israel prompting outreach to a wider world.

2.2. Later Galilean Ministry: Crisis: "Not the Messiah We Were Expecting!": 11:1–16:12

A question, conveyed by disciples, from the imprisoned John the Baptist (11:1) makes explicit the crisis Jesus' teaching, healing, and reconciling activity is bringing on. More and more he incurs hostility in the public arena, while in private he communicates to his disciples a deeper under-standing of the intimacy with the Father that underlies the direction of his messianic work (11:1–12:50).

The Parables Discourse, 13:1-52, with its central quotation from Isa 6:9-10 (13:13-15), shows that this divided response to Jesus' ministry was already foreseen by God.

In the context of growing hostility (13:53–16:12), the fate of John (14:1-12) prefigures what lies in store for Jesus. At the same time his ministry to the crowds (14:13-21; 15:32-39) and interaction with his own disciples (14:22-33) foreshadows the life and ministry of the Church, soon to emerge as the community of the kingdom. The wit and faith of a desper-ate Gentile woman compel Jesus to show himself, even at this stage, to be the Messiah ("Son of David") in whose "name the Gentiles will hope" (15:21-28).

2.3. The New Direction: The Messiah's Journey to Jerusalem: 16:13–20:34

The turning point of Jesus' messianic ministry to Israel comes in the scene at Caesarea Philippi (16:13-28). His wider ministry to the Galilean crowds now yields to the formation of the disciples, destined to become, on the rock-foundation of Peter, the "building" of the Church (16:13-20). "From this time on" (v. 21) he begins to make known to them the costly destiny awaiting him in Jerusalem (16:21-28). The beloved Son in whom the Father is well pleased (17:1-8) will fulfill his messianic mission through an obedient entry into the pain and suffering of the world.

These two intertwined themes—what lies ahead of Jesus in Jerusalem and the formation of the Church (cf. 18:1-35)—dominate this central section. As the journey to Jerusalem gets under way a series of episodes and instructions makes clear the costly values that must prevail in the community of the kingdom (19:1–20:34).

2.4. The Messiah's Ministry in Jerusalem: 21:1–25:46

At the end of the journey Jesus enters Jerusalem as its king but in a way—humble and riding on a donkey—that redefines messiahship (21:1-11). His reclaiming of the Temple as a base for teaching and healing rather than sacrifice (cf. 21:23) provokes a series of controversies with leading groups, in which he consistently gains the upper hand (21:12–23:39).

Finally, a remark from the disciples about the Temple (24:1) sparks a long discourse on the future (24:1–25:46). In a sequence of apocalyptic warnings and parables this communicates a double message to the disciples and the later Church: (1) the calamities that will occur should not cause them to lose hope; all have been foreseen by Jesus, who will return in glory to vindicate his suffering, persecuted followers and gather them for the kingdom. (2) But since he will come as judge as well as deliverer they must employ the time in between not in "sleeping" or inactivity but in pursuit of the good works that will earn his commendation, especially deeds of mercy done to him in the persons of "the least of his brothers and sisters" (25:31-46).

2.5. The Passion, Death, and Resurrection of the Messiah: 26:1–28:15

The rejection of the Messiah approaches its climax as, aided by Judas, the chief priests and elders set in motion a plot to bring about his death (26:1-59). These human machinations are, however, encompassed within a wider divine plan traced out in the Scriptures, which Jesus fulfills (26:31, 55-56). The alterations Jesus makes to the Passover ritual when instituting the Eucharist (26:26-29) bring out the true meaning: he goes to his death to save "many" from their sins (26:28; cf. 1:21).

As Jesus hangs upon the cross before dying at the ninth hour (27:26-50) he is mocked in terms of his claim to be God's Son. God, seemingly, has abandoned him and Elijah has not come to save him. But as soon as Jesus dies, nature itself erupts in a turmoil foreshadowing resurrection (27:51-52). This leads the (Gentile) Roman centurion and his cohort to become the first to confess the crucified Jesus as "truly the Son of God" (21:54).

Despite the best efforts of the authorities to seal the tomb (27:62-66), when Mary Magdalene and her companions arrive they find an explosion of life. First through an angel and then by an appearance of the risen Lord himself the women learn that Jesus has been raised and is going ahead of the disciples to Galilee, where they will see him (28:1-10).

3. The Messianic Ministry Extends to the World: 28:16-20

The account of Jesus' messianic mission to Israel reaches its goal in the final, open-ended scene in Galilee. Short in content but vast in scope, it provides the rationale for what the Church is and does until the end of time. Clad with his authority and assured of his continuing presence ("God with us" [Emmanuel]), it extends his messianic ministry to the nations of the world.

Conclusion

Throughout his life and ministry the gospel has told of Jesus "withdrawing" in the face of hostility from the leaders of his people to find fresh opportunity in another location (Galilee or a Gentile region). His Passion sets in motion the climactic instance of this pattern—even if it involves nonviolent submission to arrest and execution rather than actual physical withdrawal. His resurrection and appearance in Galilee completes the pattern. Through the mission of the Church his messianic power "withdraws" to the wider Gentile world, making him the Messiah in whose "name the Gentiles will place their hope" (12:21).

Matthew's gospel, then, is designed to help the Church understand how its identity, mission, and experience flow from those of Jesus. The divine redemptive plan that lay behind his life and transformed rejection into a wider bestowal of life reaches into the Church's story too and will continue to do so until the end of time. Rejection, failure, sinfulness do not have the last word as, again and again, the Church is summoned to "go to Galilee" to find her risen Lord.

PROLOGUE TO JESUS'
MESSIANIC MINISTRY: 1:1–4:11

Jesus' Origins and Childhood: 1:1–2:23

1. The Messiah's "Coming to Be": 1:1-25

Like all good writers Matthew captures the reader with an evocative opening sentence (v. 1). The first phrase in the Greek, *biblos geneseōs,* can go in several directions. It could be a title introducing the entire gospel ("The life-story of Jesus Christ, the son of David, son of Abraham"). More specifically, it could introduce the account of the mysterious origins of his life told in chapter 1 or, more narrowly still, just introduce the genealogy that follows ("a record of the ancestry of Jesus Christ . . ." [1:2-17]). *"Biblos geneseōs"* also evokes "Genesis," the first book of the entire Bible. Already we have a hint that what will occur in the life of Jesus Christ will be nothing less than the renewal of the entire creation—as the cataclysmic events (earthquake, opening of graves) following Jesus' death (Matt 27:51-53; cf. 28:2-3) will also attest. From the start, then, the narrative signals an intent to tell a story of overwhelming significance for humanity and the entire world.

What of the two titles that follow? In the New Testament era "Son of David" was the basic title for the Messiah, the longed-for ruler of David's line who, it was hoped, would free Israel from its current captivity and rule in peace and justice over a renewed people.[1] Applying the title to Jesus introduces here an issue that will run through the narrative, creating much of its drama. From now on we (readers) know that Jesus is the Messiah, Son of David. The question is, What kind of Messiah will he be? How will he conceive his messianic role and seek to discharge it? Will he follow conventional expectations of messiahship? Or will he, from the start, play the role very differently—evoking puzzlement, misunderstanding and hostility—because he will be following a divine agenda concerned for the rescue

---

[1] Apart from several references in the Qumran literature, the classic expression of this hope is found in the *Psalms of Solomon* 17:21-46; 18:1-9.

of humankind from forces that alienate it from God? "Son of David" is, then, a crucial title in this gospel, something that the genealogy itself will disclose.

The addition of a third title, "Son of Abraham," is a little more puzzling. Every Jew is a son or daughter of Abraham and the title could simply stress the Jewish credentials of Jesus. But around "Abraham" hovers an ambiguity that the gospel will also exploit. Besides being "father" of the Jewish people Abraham was also known in the tradition as the first "proselyte" or convert from the nations of the world (Gentiles) to the worship of the one true God. "Son of Abraham," then, signals an openness to the non-Jewish world (cf. Paul in Rom 4:1-25; Gal 3:1-29); it hints at a possibility that God can bring into the family of Abraham people beyond those Jewish by birth (cf. 3:9).

The Genealogy: 1:2-17

The genealogies of Jesus appearing in the gospels of Matthew (1:2-17) and Luke (3:23-38) are a preacher's nightmare. What scrap of inspiration is to be found in the list of unfamiliar—and largely unpronounceable—Hebrew names? I think there are riches to be drawn from the genealogy, but first a few remarks on what Matthew is and is not doing in placing such a list of ancestors at the head of his story.

To clear up the negative first: Matthew is not trying to be complete or accurate in a historical sense. Biblical genealogies aim to say something about the present status of the person whose ancestry they trace rather than to give information about history.[2] What Matthew's genealogy is chiefly attempting to do is to fill out the titles "son of David" and "son of Abraham," just given to Jesus (v. 1). Descent from Abraham weaves Jesus' story into that of his people; descent from David establishes his credentials as Messiah.

It is clear, moreover, that Matthew has constructed the list in a way that places particular stress on the Davidic aspect. At the end (v. 17) he pauses to do some sums, noting that there are fourteen generations from Abraham to David, fourteen again from David to the Exile ("deportation to

---

[2] For biblical models for the genealogy of Jesus in Matt 1:2-17 see Gen 4:17-22, 25-26; 1 Chronicles 2–3; Ruth 4:18-22. The last two of these passages seem to have provided the names for the descent from Abraham to the last ruler of the Davidic line, Zerubbabel. Matthew's source for the names after Zerubbabel is unknown. Luke and Matthew agree on the name of Jesus' great-grandfather (Matthan) but not on that of his grandfather or on any others in the generations back to Zerubbabel. The discrepancy undercuts the possibility that either list is historical.

Babylon") and fourteen from the Exile to "the Messiah" (Jesus).[3] The three consonants of the name "David" add up to fourteen in Hebrew reckoning. There were fourteen generations preparing for the beginning of the royal line of David, fourteen generations of kings who actually reigned, and for fourteen generations his family was deprived of rule. The arrangement strongly communicates the sense that, after a period of exile and the continuance of various conditions of captivity in the centuries that followed, the moment has come for the birth of a prince (the Messiah) who will truly restore to Israel the glories of David's reign. The genealogy is not, then, just a static list of ancestors. It conveys a dynamic sense that the time has at last arrived for God to send a Davidic savior to the people: "Unto us a child is born . . ." (Isa 9:6)!

Noteworthy also in the genealogy are the four places where women characters intrude, if that is the right word, into the otherwise relentlessly masculine list (Tamar, v. 3; Rahab, v. 5a; Ruth, v. 5b; the wife of Uriah [Bathsheba], v. 6b). In regard to these four women two things in particular stand out: (1) they are all non-Jewish in origin—or at least (in the case of Bathsheba) have a strong Gentile connection;[4] (2) an aura of sexual impropriety surrounds either their person (Rahab the prostitute) or the way they have been treated (Tamar, Ruth, Bathsheba). It is not clear which of these two aspects—the Gentile or the sexually improper—we are principally meant to note. Considering where the narrative will end (the mission to the nations in 28:18-20), it is highly appropriate that Matthew would want to note that the line of salvation reaching down to Jesus has not proceeded by a purely Jewish route, but brought in Gentiles as well. Second, the aspect of sexual impropriety provides a context for the situation, soon to be described (vv. 18-19), of Mary the mother of Jesus. The experiences of the four women offer biblical precedent for God's channeling the stream of salvation through an episode or relationship fraught with or *thought* to be

---

[3] As perceptive readers will note, Matthew actually gets his sums wrong at the end. There are only thirteen generations after the Exile, from Jechoniah to Jesus. On the other hand, Matthew may have intended the "error" to subtly communicate the sense that the generation gap between Joseph and Jesus was so complex (as vv. 18-25 will show) as to merit a double computation.

[4] While it is not absolutely clear that Tamar (Matt 1:3) is a non-Israelite, the text of Genesis 38 seems to associate her with the Adullamites. Rahab of Jericho (Matt 1:5) was certainly a non-Israelite (a Canaanite), as also was Ruth (a Moabite; cf. Ruth 1:4). The fact that the fourth woman is mentioned only as the wife of Uriah (1:6), though 2 Samuel 11 clearly identifies her as Bathsheba, suggests that she goes unnamed because her Gentile associations stem entirely from her husband, Uriah the Hittite.

fraught with sexual impropriety. Mary's pregnancy through the power "of the Holy Spirit" (1:18, 20) will then be the climactic instance of divine interventions bringing the line of salvation out of situations that appear at first sight morally deviant.[5] The Messiah Jesus may be Son of David and Son of Abraham. But he is also the descendant of Tamar and Rahab, of Ruth and the wife of Uriah. His ancestry already betrays an openness to the non-Israelite, Gentile world, conventionally considered unclean.

It may be, then, that the otherwise dry list of ancestors does contain some riches after all. The One believers own as Son of God and Savior did not just drop out of the sky, so to speak, without the mixed history—good and bad—that lies behind every human life. There are skeletons in his family closet just as there are in ours. Nor was his line "pure" in an ethnic sense or exempt from sexual scandal and exploitation. But it is through just such a human history that the thread of salvation runs. The invitation is there to trace in our own "ancestry," whether it be our family story or our individual life story, a similar working of grace and redemption, all to be woven into the wider pattern of salvation brought by Jesus.

The Birth of Jesus: 1:18-25

Matthew's account of Jesus' birth is sparse. All is shaped by the desire to bring out the extraordinary mode of Jesus' conception, what that entails for his identity and status, and how his birth in this way fulfills a divine script set out in Scripture. Other key details—place, date, and so forth—are missing. (Only at the beginning of the next episode [2:1] and then rather casually, do we learn that Jesus was born in Bethlehem.)

In general Matthew tells the story of Jesus' birth and childhood from the perspective of Joseph.[6] We should not fail to appreciate the sharpness of the dilemma that confronts him as soon as he becomes aware that Mary is pregnant. The statement that she "was found to be with child through the Holy Spirit" (v. 18) does not mean that he knew from the start that divine agency was operative. "Was found" does not mean "found by someone"; the Greek text echoes a Hebrew idiom where "was found" simply amounts more or less to "came to be."[7] We also need to understand that the relationship between Joseph and Mary at this stage is a fully marital one. It was

---

[5] Cf. W. D. Davies and Dale Allison, *A Critical and Exegetical Commentary on the Gospel According to Saint Matthew.* ICC. 3 vols. (Edinburgh: T&T Clark, 1988–97) 3:171–72.

[6] A notable point of contrast with Luke 1–2, where Mary is the leading character throughout.

[7] Rather like the French *se trouve;* Italian *si trova.*

custom at the time for women to be married at a very early age—when they were about twelve—and then, because of their youth, to remain a year or so longer in their own family home before moving to that of their husband. During this time, even though not living together, the couple were man and wife—not merely "engaged" in the modern sense.[8] Hence Joseph's conclusion at this point can only be that, since Mary has not become pregnant through relations with himself, her condition must be the result of sexual impropriety—that she is, in fact, guilty of adultery.

No false piety should make us shrink from this plain implication of the story.[9] From Joseph's point of view Mary is in a truly dreadful situation. If exposed to the full rigor of the Law, she is liable to be stoned as an adulteress (Deut 22:23-24). Even if such rigor no longer applied,[10] she is vulnerable to public shame and lifelong humiliation.

It is here that we learn something of Joseph's character—all contained in a single word of great importance for Matthew: "just/righteous" (Greek *dikaios*). The term characterizes a person who faithfully puts into practice the requirements of the Torah. We might expect, then, that Joseph would immediately set about doing what it tells him to do: publicly expose his wife's infidelity and divorce her. But what Joseph actually does—purposing to divorce her quietly so as to spare her open shame (v. 19)—shows him to be "righteous" in the way that Jesus' interpretation of the Torah will call for: an observance in which "mercy" functions as supreme criterion (Hos 6:6; cf. Matt 9:13; 12:7; 23:23). Joseph "models," in an anticipatory way, the fulfillment of the Torah that Jesus will promote (5:17-20).

With the appearance of an angel to apprise Joseph of the true situation (vv. 20-21), Matthew takes us into a biblical world of discourse where messages from the divine to the human realm regularly come by this means. The angel's words in fact fall into an "annunciation of birth" pattern well known from the biblical record.[11] Announcement and explanation in this form would be no surprise for the biblically instructed reader Matthew

---

[8] The rendering of the Greek *mnēsteutheis* as "engaged" in modern versions (e.g., *NRSV*) is seriously misleading.

[9] There is no ultimate suggestion that Mary *was* guilty of any fault; she was only *thought* to be in a compromised situation. The angel's explanation vindicates her completely.

[10] As appears to have been the case in Jesus' time—though John 8:1-11 presupposes otherwise.

[11] Gen 16:1-16 (Ishmael); Gen 17:1–18:15 (Isaac); Judg 13:2-7 (Samson); 1 Sam 1:1-28 (Samuel); cf. also Luke 1:5-25 (to Zechariah); 1:26-38 (to Mary); 2:8-14 (to the shepherds). See Raymond E. Brown, *The Birth of the Messiah: A Commentary on the Infancy Narratives in Matthew and Luke* (rev. ed. New York: Doubleday, 1993) 156.

presupposes. The miraculous conception of Jesus comes as the climax of all these earlier instances where the birth of a child in unusual circumstances (generally the overcoming of barrenness) heralds a new saving intervention of God.

But the mode of this birth outstrips any biblical precedents. Joseph's dilemma in regard to Mary's pregnancy is relieved when he learns what we readers already know (from v. 18): that it has come about through the agency of the Holy Spirit. He is to abandon any idea of sending Mary away; he is to take her to himself fully as wife. Through his lineage the child will be Son of David (v. 16). But conceived in the way described, the child will be, in a unique sense, *God's* Son, with a distinctive destiny indicated by the name he is to bear: "Jesus/Joshua."

Evoking a popular etymology of "Joshua" ("YHWH saves"), the name "Jesus" indicates that the child's role will be to "save the people from their sins" (v. 21). That the Messiah should be a saving figure introduces nothing new. What he would save from—not political and economic oppression, but sin and its consequences—is much more surprising. The phrase "from their sins" foreshadows the ministry of Jesus in which the lifting of the burden of sin will be so prominent; its full meaning will emerge as he gives his life "as a ransom for many" (20:28), his blood "poured out for the remission of sins" (26:28).

Matthew rounds off his account of Jesus' "coming to be" (*genesis* [v. 18]) by drawing attention to the fact that the birth of a Davidic child in this miraculous way fulfills something announced beforehand by God (vv. 22-23). For the New Testament writers generally the chief purpose of Scripture was not to give information about the past but to indicate God's intent for the messianic age. No other writer is more at pains to bring this out than Matthew, who, as noted earlier,[12] makes use of explicit "fulfillment" quotations for this purpose. We encounter the first of them here. Isa 7:14 comes from a passage in which the prophet tells King Ahab that he should interpret the pregnancy of a young woman—presumably a princess of the royal house—as a sign that the threat of foreign invasion is soon to be removed. In the Hebrew original there is no suggestion that the conception is virginal or that the sign points in any "messianic" sense beyond the current reign. But Matthew, reading the text in a Greek version (the Septuagint) that translates the Hebrew *almah* (= young woman) by *parthenos* (= virgin), finds in it a divine indication that the Messiah destined to arise

<hr>

[12] See above p. 11.

from the house of David will be born in this miraculous way: through virginal conception.

The second part of the text, "they will call his name Emmanuel, which means 'God is with us,'"[13] plays no less central a role in this gospel's presentation of Jesus. In the person of this child God will come among the people and remain with them in a uniquely close way. At the end of the gospel the last words of the risen Lord to his disciples, now becoming the community of the Church, will be an assurance of *his* remaining presence in much the same terms: "Behold, I am with you always, to the end of the age" (28:20). These two assurances of divine presence, at the beginning and at the end, "frame" the narrative in an open-ended way. The saving presence of God operative throughout the life of Jesus will continue in the life of the Church "to the end of the age": "For where two or three are gathered in my name, I am there among them" (18:20).

Obedient to the angel's instructions, Joseph takes Mary to be his wife (v. 24). He has no sexual relations with her until she gives birth to a son, who—again obediently—he names "Jesus" (v. 25).[14] Matthew is driving home the point that the child is not Joseph's natural son. But Joseph, by naming him, becomes his adoptive father and so brings him into the Davidic line (1:2-17), making him legally "Son of David," candidate Messiah. Thus Jesus emerges from the account of his birth as the Son of God, "Emmanuel," equipped to play the role of Messiah in a totally unforeseen, transcendent way.[15]

Before we move on, let us remind ourselves of the human circumstances in which this "invasion of the divine" came about: Mary's morally suspect and perilous situation and the acute dilemma Joseph faced as a result. A fraught and not unfamiliar human situation was the receptacle for

---

[13] The explanation "God is with us" actually comes not from Isa 7:14 but from Isa 8:10, again in the Septuagint (LXX) translation.

[14] Use of the Greek word *heōs* ("until") need not necessarily imply that Joseph and Mary had sexual relations *after* the birth of Jesus—which means that the Catholic tradition of Mary's perpetual virginity does not run counter to this text. The alternative does, however, represent the more natural reading, in which case Jesus' "brothers" and "sisters" mentioned in Matt 13:56 would be siblings, not "cousins" as traditionally supposed.

[15] The title "son of God" did not in itself connote divine status at the time of Jesus. The biblical tradition saw the king as God's "son" (cf. Ps 2:7) and indeed, in the same metaphorical sense, all Israelites enjoyed a filial relationship to God (e.g., Deut 14:1; Wis 12:7; etc.); see further Brendan J. Byrne, *'Sons of God'—'Seed of Abraham'* (Rome: Biblical Institute Press, 1979) 9–78, 223. In Matthew (also Luke) it is Jesus' virginal conception that lends transcendent depth to the title "Son of God."

the power of the Spirit and the emergence of salvation. No less than his subsequent obedience, Joseph's initial ignorance, anguish of mind, and basic human decency are all part of the story and help to make it a story we can enter and recognize as our own. God does not wait till all is right, ready, and perfect before entering the human scene. God enters it as it is, to heal it from within.

Excursus: The Virginal Conception Tradition

I have maintained that for Matthew (as indeed also for Luke) the truth that Mary conceived her child through divine power without any cooperation from a male parent is central to his presentation of Jesus' origins. The two gospel writers who treat of Jesus' infancy, while going separate ways on so many other details, are in plain agreement on this point. If, as I believe along with most scholars, they are working independently of each other, then both are passing on a belief derived from an earlier Christian tradition. What gave rise to such a belief? It is easy to answer, "a clear memory derived from the family of Jesus, ultimately Mary herself, that it was indeed historically the case that Jesus was so conceived." Granted the nature of the kind of literature we are dealing with in the case of the infancy stories, it is simply not possible to make such a historical judgment one way or the other. Christian belief in the virginal conception rests not upon historical, but upon theological truth.

The latter is not lightly to be dismissed. Jettisoning the tradition on the ground that it is simply a legend lacking historical foundation fatally undercuts the force of the Matthean (and I would maintain also the Lukan) infancy narrative. Jesus' conception in this mode is central to Matthew's portrayal of Jesus as God's Son. The theological objection to the tradition of Jesus' virginal conception stems from the sense that, without being conceived in the normal way, he cannot be truly human; the price exacted by the tradition is a derogation of his true humanity in the direction of Docetism. My sense, however, is that the two evangelists had no problems with the genuine humanity of Jesus; they could not have depicted his Passion and death with such unsentimental realism had they had doubts on this score. What they also make plain—as indeed does their forerunner Mark—is the sense of divine presence and power attending the human Jesus. They may not, as does the Fourth Gospel (and I would maintain Paul), explicitly present the Son as preexistent in some sense before his human history. But their narratives do reflect the *descendit de caelis* ("he came down from heaven") of the later creeds, holding together the two aspects of Jesus' person, the divine and the human, in a mystery beginning at his conception.

The tradition of the virgin *birth,* that is, that Mary remained a virgin in and after giving birth to Jesus, and that Joseph and she never lived together as husband and wife, is another question. While room can be found for such a tradition in the text (taking a certain understanding of *heōs* in 1:25 and understanding Jesus' "brothers" in 13:56 as "cousins"), the more natural sense of the narrative is that Joseph was "not afraid" to follow the divine instruction "to take Mary as your wife" (vv. 20, 24). Hesitation that grew up early in the Christian tradition concerning Mary and Joseph's living out their marriage may have owed more to a negative view of sexuality than to a reading of the biblical record. In any case it is not easy to disassociate the doctrine of Mary's perpetual virginity in giving birth *(in partu)* and afterwards *(post partum)* from a pessimistic attitude in this area. The doctrine sits in tension with more recent attempts to recapture a sense in which the sacramental aspect embraces the totality of married life, and one might ask what continuing usefulness in Christian devotion and spirituality it plays. It seems to lumber with excess baggage the more central and biblically well-founded truth of Jesus' virginal *conception.*

2. The Response to the Newborn Messiah: 2:1-23

Matthew has described the origins of Jesus, establishing his credentials as Messiah Son of David who is also, through the miraculous nature of his conception, Son of God and "Presence" ("Emmanuel") of God in an unparalleled degree. Now the issue is: What kind of response will the appearance of this infant King evoke? The second part of the infancy story, 2:1-23, outlines this response and does so in a way that foreshadows all that is to happen later in the gospel. Whereas Luke's account of Jesus' infancy is full of joy, with people bursting out into canticles of praise and admiration, the somber note already struck in Matthew continues. Murderous threats from Herod soon eclipse the moment of joy as the magi near the goal of their quest (2:10). The story ends in bloodshed and the rescue of the child only through divine intervention and, once more, faithful obedience on the part of Joseph. Opposition stalks Israel's Savior from the beginning of his life, replaying, in Matthew's presentation, Pharaoh's threats against an earlier infant savior of the people, Moses (Exod 1:8–2:10).

The Coming of the Magi: 2:1-12

The popularity of this story in Christian art and imagination stems from so many elements of immediate appeal: a long journey questing for something sensed from afar; the enterprise threatened by a ruthless king; a successful outcome and safe return outwitting his hypocrisy and guile. Precisely because of its appeal the journey of the magi has become in Christian tradition a central part of the Christmas story, attracting in the process all kinds of accretions that are not really part of Matthew's account, which is certainly rich enough to stand by itself. I shall take it simply as a story, leaving aside the question as to whether in whole or in part (the appearance of a star and so forth) it has any basis in history.[16]

Matthew begins by telling us at last where and when Jesus was born. The Son of David was born in Bethlehem in Judea,[17] David's own birthplace, in the days of King Herod (v. 1). The time marker sends a chill over the narrative. Apart from lavish building, Herod's chief characteristics as ruler were cruelty and viciousness, fed by paranoia stemming from his uncertain claim, as a non-Davidide, to the throne.[18] The magi walk into a minefield when they arrive innocently asking, "Where is the newborn King of the Jews?" (v. 2a).

Who are the magi? The story as Matthew tells it says nothing about their being kings, nor does it tell us their number.[19] The Greek word *magos* denotes people possessed of special and superior knowledge, experts in some field, especially—as would appear to be the case here—astronomy/ astrology. Though we do know of Jewish magi (cf. Acts 8:9), it seems clear that here we have to do with representatives from the non-Jewish (Gentile) world.[20] In line with a widespread belief that singular effects in the heavens marked the birth of great leaders, observation and calculation have led these wise ones to interpret the rising of a new star as signaling the birth of a Jewish king, to whom they wish to pay homage.[21]

---

[16] For this see the standard commentaries: e.g., Davies and Allison, *Matthew* 1:235, 252.

[17] Matthew is precise because there was another Bethlehem in Galilee, a short distance north of Nazareth.

[18] Herod was only half-Jewish, an Idumean by birth. Though favored by Rome, apart from his lack of Davidic credentials he faced constant threat from the previously ruling Hasmonean house, which he had supplanted.

[19] "Three kings" is a later deduction from the three kinds of gifts brought (v. 11).

[20] See Brendan Byrne, "The Messiah in Whose Name 'the Gentiles Will Hope' (Matt 12:21): Gentile Inclusion as an Essential Element of Matthew's Christology," *AusBR* 50 (2002) 60–61, n. 23.

[21] A messianic interpretation of the oracle of Balaam in Numbers 24 seems to be operative here (as also in Qumran literature: *CD* [Damascus Rule] 7:12-21 [Ms A]). The non-

In view of the (messianic) hope for a true Davidic ruler and Herod's questionable legitimacy, inquiries in Jerusalem about a newborn "King of the Jews" understandably cause "disturbance" in leadership circles, above all to the king himself (v. 3). They set in motion a challenge to the ruling authorities in Israel that will accompany the ministry of Jesus and come to a climax in the last days of his life. Herod, however, is experienced enough to move cautiously against this threat. In a false show of cooperation he summons the chief priests and scribes (later to be bitter foes of Jesus) to respond with their scriptural knowledge to both the visitors' and his own desire for further information.

The scriptural experts can supply a ready answer, "Bethlehem in Judea," because they have at hand a prophecy from Micah indicating that town as the place of origin of a ruler "who will shepherd my people Israel" (Mic 5:2). In the text as quoted in Matt 2:6 the "shepherding" clause comes not from Micah but from the address to David at the commencement of his reign in 2 Sam 5:2 (also 1 Chr 11:2). The combination ironically forces the scribes to concede that the ruler of whom the prophet spoke will, in sharp contrast to the one presently in power, exercise a "shepherd-like" rule over his people (cf. Matt 9:36).

Craftily, before he sends the magi on to Bethlehem to complete their quest Herod contrives to get from them accurate information as to when they first saw the star (vv. 7-8). That lets him know the upper age limit for the male children he has to include in a murderous sweep, should the magi fail to come back (as in fact they do [v. 12]) with a report on the exact location of the child.

Armed with the information they need, the magi emerge from the shadow of Herod and proceed on their way to Bethlehem.[22] Joy—a sure sign of being on the way to salvation—envelops them as they see once again the star going before them. The long journey reaches its climax as they enter the house, find the child with Mary his mother, and fall down in worship (vv. 9-11a).

The omission of any reference to Joseph, elsewhere the major player in Matthew's infancy story, reinforces what has emerged from the account of Jesus' "coming to be" *(genesis):* while Mary is the true mother of the child, Joseph is not his father. The one whom the magi have journeyed to

---

Israelite prophet Balaam, a practicer of divination, when summoned by a foreign king (Balak of Moab) to curse Israel (Numbers 22–24), found himself compelled to utter a blessing instead: "a star shall come out of Jacob, and a scepter shall rise out of Israel" (Num 24:17).

[22] In reality a very short journey: six miles (ten km)!

venerate is the Son of God. The "homage" (Greek *proskynēsis*) they pay him (v. 11a) is not simply the reverence due to any ruler but a genuine worship acknowledging "God with us" (1:23) in the person of this child.

The gifts these Gentile worshipers bring out of their "treasure chests" (v. 11b; cf. 13:52) suggest to a biblically informed reader the fulfillment of Ps 72:10-11 and Isa 60:6, two texts linked through a common reference to Sheba and the bringing of tributary gifts:[23]

> Ps 72:10b-11: may the kings of Sheba and Seba bring gifts.
> May all kings fall down (LXX [71:11] *proskynein*) before him,
> all nations give him service.
>
> Isa 60:6: all those from Sheba shall come.
> They shall bring gold and frankincense.

The echo of these texts suggests that the coming of this embassy from the East is a harbinger of the Messiah's role *vis-à-vis* the nations of the world. Through the mission of the Church (28:19-20) they too will worship him, fulfilling the prophecies of the pilgrimage of the nations to Zion (Isa 60:1-16; 66:20; cf. 45:15; also Paul in Rom 15:16).[24] As well as being Messiah of Israel, Jesus is also the Messiah "in whose name the Gentiles will hope" (Matt 12:21, quoting [LXX] Isa 42:4; cf. 11:1).

In this connection we may note how remarkably the whole episode affirms the value of the native wisdom of the magi. Their own natural gifts, the wisdom of their people, and their "scientific" investigations (astronomy) set them upon the quest that brought them to Jerusalem and eventually, when combined with the Jewish scribal information, to the discovery of the Savior in Bethlehem. Revelation sprang from a combination of natural wisdom and biblical prophecy—a valuable bequest of this episode to the Christian theological tradition.

---

[23] If Matthew intended an echo of these texts, it is odd that they are not made the subject of a "fulfillment" quotation (cf. David C. Sim, "The Magi: Gentiles or Jews?" *Hervormde Teologiese Studies* [Pretoria] 55 [1999] 980–1000, especially 996–98). An explicit quotation would have specified the magi as kings—something Matthew may not have found appropriate since the Gentiles targeted by the community's mission (28:19-29) at the time of writing hardly included rulers.

[24] The gifts are simply the kind of luxury items derived from the East (Arabia especially) that an embassy coming from that region would bring. They need not have the three separate meanings that later devotion ascribed to them: gold denoting royal status; incense divinity; myrrh destiny to suffer and die.

The Aftermath: Flight, Exile, Settlement in Nazareth: 2:13-23

Warned in a dream to avoid Herod, the magi return safely to their own country,[25] their journey and its goal achieved. But their coming has set in motion the first stirrings of the hostility that will dog the messianic ministry of Jesus, beginning with the murderous designs of Herod. This conflict between the divine power of salvation that has entered the world with the birth of Jesus and the authorities whose current grip on power it threatens now comes to the fore in a series of scenes that make the infant Messiah and his family refugees, exiles, returnees, and eventually settlers in a locality (Nazareth in Galilee) that was not their original home (Bethlehem in Judea).[26] The family of Jesus have to yield before the naked force of worldly power. Like refugees today, they have no control over where they may safely live but face constant uprooting as circumstances determined by those in power change.

Their safety is guaranteed, however, by divine guidance, which three times more intervenes in the shape of dream warnings to Joseph (2:13; 2:19; 2:22; cf. 1:20) to protect them from Herod's wrath and lead them in due course to settle in Nazareth. Without any forceful resistance on their part,[27] the king's plan is thwarted and the divine purpose goes through. The account, as Matthew tells it, looks back to Pharaoh's attempt to destroy in childhood Israel's first savior, Moses. It looks forward to the Passion and death of Jesus, when again the Messiah will not resist but submit to the violence of the authorities—but only "so that the scriptures may be fulfilled" (cf. 26:54). As the resurrection will show, it is through dying in obedience to the Father's will that Jesus will supremely fulfill his role as Savior (1:21) for his people and the world.

So the Messiah may be outwardly pushed around by hostile worldly power, but by tagging the various geographical moves made by the family of Jesus to three scriptural texts Matthew shows how all this has been

---

[25] In 2:12 and 2:13 we meet for the first time the verb "withdraw" (Greek *anachōrein*), which becomes for Matthew a stock usage to indicate withdrawal from hostility emanating from Jewish authorities and a removal to Gentile regions of greater security and receptivity (symbolized chiefly by Galilee); see pp. 11–12 above.

[26] Both Matthew and Luke agree that Bethlehem was Jesus' birthplace. For Matthew it was also the original home of his family, the transfer to Nazareth being a later necessity. For Luke Nazareth is the original home, to which they return after the temporary relocation to Bethlehem required by the census (Luke 2:1-5).

[27] Again we have Matthew's technical sense of "withdraw" in vv. 14 and 22; see pp. 11–12 above.

foreseen in Scripture and fulfills the saving plan of God. Herod in fact becomes a tool of that same divine purpose.

Thus the Messiah's sojourn in Egypt (2:13-15) makes the subsequent instruction to leave there and return to the land of Israel (v. 20) what the prophet Hosea really had in mind in writing (in God's name): "Out of Egypt I have called my Son" (Hos 11:1). Jesus relives the story of his people Israel by being called out of Egypt, though, as we readers understand, he is "called (God's) Son" in a far more personal and realistic way than was ever the case with Israel.

With the child safely in Egypt, the fate from which he has so narrowly escaped is made terribly clear through the report of Herod's murder, based on careful calculation (2:7), of all male children in Bethlehem and its vicinity up to two years old (2:16-18). A quotation from Jer 31:15 shows that this, too, has at least been foreseen by God.[28] Here Matthew's infancy story reaches its darkest note. The Son of God may personally be rescued from destruction, but violence and atrocity attend his life from its earliest moments. The world with which Matthew surrounds the Savior is the real world in which the lamentation of women for lost children and their refusal to be comforted because "they are not" is all too familiar. Nothing could portray more poignantly the need for the coming of a ruler who would "shepherd" rather than ravage the flock of Israel. In the face of brutal Herodian rule the Messiah for the time being can only "withdraw" (2:14; 2:22); later he too, like these little ones, will be put to death. But Scripture shows that their deaths, like his and those of all innocent victims of tyranny, are "precious in the sight of the Lord" (Ps 116:15). They too have their place in the wider pattern of salvation.

The third and final quotation (2:23) bears upon the location where Joseph brings his family finally to rest: Nazareth in Galilee. Obedient once more to a divine warning, Joseph takes "the child and his mother"[29] back to Israel (vv. 19-22). But learning that Herod's son Archelaus currently reigns

---

[28] In the case of this "fulfillment" quotation, to avoid the implication that the slaughter, even though foreseen, was directly willed by God, the Evangelist alters the customary introductory formula, omitting "in order that . . ." in favor of simply stating what the prophet said; cf. Davies and Allison, *Matthew* 1:266. M. Eugene Boring, "The Gospel of Matthew," in Leander E. Keck, ed., *The New Interpreter's Bible*. Vol. 8 (Nashville: Abingdon, 1995) 148–49, tackles head on the troubling issue as to why the parents of the remaining infants were not divinely warned about Herod's murderous intentions as Joseph was.

[29] "The child and his mother" is Matthew's circumlocution to avoid any suggestion that Jesus is Joseph's son; cf. also vv. 13, 14, 19.

in Judea (where Bethlehem is),[30] he is afraid to settle there. Warned for the final time, he "withdraws to Galilee" and settles in Nazareth, thus fulfilling "what was said by the prophets, 'He will be called a Nazorean.'"[31] Here we have the first instance of a pattern to be repeated in the gospel in which Jesus, in the face of opposition from Jewish authorities, "withdraws to Galilee," a region the gospel will later describe as "Galilee of the Gentiles" (4:15c).[32] The Messiah, originally—and appropriately—from David's city of Bethlehem in Judea, has become, through a strange combination of hostility from Jewish authorities and divine guidance, a resident of Galilee. Here he is well placed to become the Messiah "in whose name the Gentiles will place their hope" (12:21).

Looking back upon the total story we can see a pattern emerging. Israel's Messiah, who is also Son of God, "God with us," is already present in Israel as a child. Paradoxically, it is Gentile inquirers, schooled by their wisdom, who have detected his presence from afar and come in search of him, while the authorities of his own people are surprised and troubled at their report. The Gentile inquirers accord him the worship that is his due as Son of God, offering in tribute the riches of their lands. But the Jewish usurper king (Herod) plots to do away with this child whose birth so threatens his power. Foiled in his more subtle design, Herod unleashes violence, from which the child and his family escape only through divine warning and flight, until eventually, after a series of "withdrawals," they make their home in Galilee. So through the hostility of a king in Israel, Israel's Messiah is compelled to leave what ought be the primary locale of his ministry (Judea) and take up his residence in a locale where Gentiles will more readily have access to him.

---

[30] Archelaus, the son of Herod who inherited most of his father's brutality but little of his administrative ability, ruled as tetrarch in Judea, Samaria, and Idumea from 4 B.C.E. until his deposition by the Romans in 6 C.E.

[31] Notoriously, no such quotation can be found in either the Hebrew or Greek versions of the Old Testament. The unusual plural reference "prophets" may signal a "quotation" made up from a number of biblical texts combined on some basis presupposed by the Evangelist (or the tradition behind him). The basis would be the possibility of linking *Nazaraios* ("Nazarean") with the Hebrew word *nazîr*, designating a member of the ascetic class "Nazirite," set apart as particularly "holy" (cf. Judg 13:5-7 [Samson]). On this basis Isa 4:3 comes into view: "(he) will be called holy," with *Nazaraios* substituted for "holy." Another textual candidate is Isa 11:1, "A shoot will come forth from the stump of Jesse, and a branch will grow out of his roots," on the basis of a similar wordplay in regard to the Hebrew word for "branch" *(nezer)* and the (Davidic) messianic understanding of this text in Jesus' day (attested from Qumran: 4Q285). See further Davies and Allison, *Matthew* 1:274–81.

[32] See pp. 11–12 above.

This pattern emerging from the infancy story foreshadows what will happen on a much larger scale in Jerusalem at the climax of Jesus' ministry. Dramatically entering Jerusalem (21:1-11) as its Shepherd-King, the Messiah will threaten the Jewish authorities then in power (21:10). They will not only reject him but this time succeed in doing away with him. But God will raise him from the dead so that, clad with world authority as risen Lord, he can send his disciples to carry on his mission to the nations (28:19-20). Later still the Matthean church, conscious of its responsibility for this worldwide mission, will have its identity reinforced as it finds the pattern verified in its own experience: hostility and rejection from the Jewish side, welcome and response from the Gentile. It will have found comfort in discovering the pattern already present in the first days of their Lord's life.

We read the story today conscious of how soon in Christian history a reverse pattern set in, so that Jews experienced violence from Christians rather than the other way round. Interpretation and preaching sensitive to this development will seek to transcend the confines of the original Matthean setting and see in Herod and his associates not so much Jewish authorities of a particular time and place but symbols of that hostile "kingdom" that in so many times and places and in such a variety of forms (political, economic, social) retains an oppressive hold on human life. Seeking to reclaim the world for true humanity, God's saving presence ("Emmanuel"), itself manifested in all kinds of ministries and works, will always be in conflict with latter-day Herods and at times be compelled, like Jesus, to "withdraw" before them. The infancy story suggests that such moments are not aberrations, but elements of the ongoing story of salvation.

Prelude to Jesus' Public Ministry: 3:1–4:11

Without any warning the gospel transports us from the time of Jesus' childhood to the period just prior to the beginning of his adult public ministry. This time of preparation has three stages: John the Baptist's preaching and witness to Jesus (3:1-12); Jesus' own baptism (3:13-17); the testing of God's Son (4:1-11).

The Preaching and Witness of John the Baptist: 3:1-12

What are we to make of John? The question seems to have bothered the Christian community from the earliest days. John's appearance is forbidding, his message stark—he is a biblical character to admire from a distance but hardly one to win our hearts. Matthew, however, did warm to John and evidently considered that his stern warnings to Israel, especially the religious leadership, were something his own community might also usefully hear.

Matthew makes John, like Jesus, a proclaimer of the kingdom of heaven: "Repent, for the kingdom of heaven is very close" (3:2; cf. 4:17). "Kingdom of heaven" is Matthew's preferred circumlocution for the more usual "kingdom of God," which itself is better translated "rule of God," since the reference is not to an institution but rather to a state of affairs. To grasp what is meant by this phrase in the gospel tradition it helps to approach it via the negative background that is its essential presupposition. In most Jewish circles of Jesus' day there appears to have been a widespread conviction that the world as at present set up, including Israel, has largely fallen out of God's hand into the grip of Satan and a whole array of demonic forces. This captivity to evil manifested itself not only in the prevalence of sin but also in various kinds of sickness, including, of course, actual demonic possession. Even oppressive political structures such as the Roman occupation and the tyranny of local rulers like Herod were held to be outward manifestations of the rule of Satan in the world. In many circles, it seems, there was a belief that the Babylonian exile Israel underwent in the sixth century B.C.E. had not really come to an end. There may have been a physical return from Babylon and some measure of freedom in an outward political sense, but captivity under the Babylonians had simply been replaced by a far more basic enslavement to demonic powers.

In this situation it was natural to feel that the great promises of freedom and national restoration appearing in the prophet we know as "Second Isaiah" (Isaiah 40–66) were yet to come true. Around the time of Jesus devout Jews read these promises not with respect to their original reference—Israel's liberation from the Babylonian captivity in the sixth century B.C.E—but as applying to the captivity under which Israel presently labored: the rule of Satan in all its various manifestations. Passages from Isaiah evoked the hope that Israel's God, who is also the Creator of the entire universe, would break the grip of Satan and reassert divine rule in the world and particularly in Israel. That this "rule of God" ("kingdom of heaven") is soon to come to pass is the "good news" of which Isaiah speaks in several key texts, the "good news" or "gospel" that has become the center of Christian proclamation. A classic example of such a text is Isa 52:7:

> How beautiful upon the mountains
> are the feet of the messenger who announces peace,
> who brings *good news,*
> who announces salvation,
> who says to Zion, *"Your God reigns."*

Centuries after (Second) Isaiah pronounced such oracles with reference to freedom from Babylon, later generations heard them speaking of the longed-for liberation that *they* hoped for: the break of Satan's hold upon the world through the reassertion of God's rule (or "kingdom ").[1]

A significant element in the reassertion of God's rule was the institution of a great judgment in which the oppressive spiritual forces and the human agents who had been their accomplices would be cast down. The righteous, meanwhile, whom they had oppressed and shamed, would be vindicated and welcomed into full enjoyment of the blessings of salvation—the blessings that the Beatitudes (Matt 5:1-10; Luke 6:20-23) in particular list. We are less comfortable today with the idea of an end-time judgment that is so much part of the "eschatological package" early Chris-

---

[1] The fragmentary text known as the "Melchisedek" Scroll (11QMelch) shows that the Qumran community cherished a similar expectation based on Isaiah.

tianity derived from apocalyptic Judaism. However, we must remember that in its origins the judgment was something to be executed *on behalf of the righteous*—part of their liberation—rather than a threat hanging over them. God will institute judgment not to sort out everyone with grim impartiality, but to vindicate and free those who have been oppressed. The prospect of judgment is indeed an element of the proclamation of the kingdom, on the part of both John the Baptist and Jesus—an element Matthew is by no means inclined to play down. However, we should see it in its place within the overall perspective.

The early Christian tradition also reflects a development within apocalyptic Judaism in which the end-time judgment is not exercised directly by God but "delegated," so to speak, to an agent who will exercise it on God's behalf. In some Jewish texts this agent of judgment is an angelic figure or, if depicted in human form, one whose origins are heavenly rather than merely human. Daniel 7:14 accords this role to "one like a son of man" (that is, a human being), which gave rise to widespread expectation of a heavenly Son of Man who would come on the clouds of heaven with authority to execute judgment. In the early gospel tradition the more this-worldly role of the Davidic Messiah and the more transcendent nature and role of this Son of Man figure have fused together and coalesced around the person of Jesus. He has played the former (messianic) role—though with very considerable departure from the conventional "script"; he will play the latter, returning as Son of Man at the end of time to institute judgment preparatory to the full realization of God's rule. The crucified Messiah has risen from the dead and is now enthroned in messianic glory at God's right hand, whence he will come from heaven to judge the living and the dead.

All this should give some background for the portrayal of the appearance and preaching of John the Baptist in Matt 3:1-12. Because people were reading the (Second) Isaiah texts in the way described, it is not surprising that the tradition "slots" John into the role of the Isaiah's "voice crying in the wilderness" (Isa 40:3). A "wilderness" figure himself, whose appearance (v. 4) shows him to be playing the role of the returning Elijah (cf. 2 Kings 1:8; Mal 4:5; Sir 48:10), John is preparing in the wilderness a "way for the Lord" (Mal 3:1). The "Lord" is not now God himself but the coming messianic figure (Jesus) who will institute judgment on God's behalf. The "way" is no longer a physical road across the desert but a metaphorical "way" made up of repentant human hearts.

Thus the essence of John's message, as later that of Jesus, is "Repent!"—that is, undergo a "heart-change" (v. 3). This is not just a cleansing from whatever sins one may recently have committed. John calls for a deep-seated conversion of heart in view of the radical new state of affairs (the kingdom) that is at hand. He singles out "Pharisees and Sadducees" (v. 7) for warnings of particular severity.[2] Descent from Abraham (belonging to God's people) will not be sufficient. The only thing that will count at the judgment will be "bringing forth the fruits of repentance": good deeds issuing from a genuinely converted heart (vv. 8-9).

John also points to a coming "stronger One" from whose status and role he radically distinguishes himself (vv. 11-12).[3] Where he (John) offers water baptism as an outward sign of repentance, this coming stronger One will "baptize with the Holy Spirit and with fire." The reference is not to Christian baptism or to the coming of the Holy Spirit upon the disciples, as in the Lukan Pentecost (Acts 2:1-4). The vivid imagery (winnowing-fan, chaff) of the next verse (v. 12) makes clear that John is pointing to the coming One's role as eschatological judge.[4] The summons to repentance derives its urgency from the prospect of this strict judgment.

As we read on into the gospel we shall become aware that the role of eschatological judge that John here sketches out for Jesus is not necessarily one Jesus will carry out—at least not in his initial ministry, which will involve not simply a summons to repentance but also an authoritative assurance of forgiveness, something John could never give. Later the gospel narrative will tell of an "embassy" John sends to Jesus from prison, asking whether he *is* the One to come or "are we to wait for another?" (11:3). The incident suggests John's having doubts because, from what he has heard, Jesus is *not* fitting the role of fearsome eschatological judge that John himself had expected of him.

There is, then, a certain "gap" between John's description of Jesus' role and the "shepherding" tone that Jesus' messianic ministry eventually

---

[2] An association between these two groups is very unlikely in the actual time of John and Jesus. The hostility John is depicted as showing toward them here reflects more the conditions of Matthew's own time when the successors of the Pharisees were the leadership group in Judaism with which his community had to contend.

[3] Disciples or students customarily carried their master's sandals (v. 11). John is saying he is not worthy even to be the disciple of the coming One (cf. Matt 11:11).

[4] "Baptism" here has its biblical metaphorical meaning indicating the undergoing (as if through raging waters) of a severe ordeal (cf. Mark 10:38-39; Luke 12:50). To "baptize with the Holy Spirit" would then mean to subject people to a testing ordeal of judgment as one authorized by God's Spirit. "Fire" is a regular feature of judgment in the biblical tradition; see the references in W. D. Davies and Dale Allison, *A Critical and Exegetical Commentary on the Gospel According to Saint Matthew*. ICC. 3 vols. (Edinburgh: T&T Clark, 1988–97) 1:310.

takes. Nonetheless, as the perspective turns more to the future in the last weeks of Jesus' life, his role as eschatological judge comes to the fore, giving ultimate validity to John's depiction. Matthew presents Jesus as the One whose principal concern is to heal and lift the burdens of afflicted humanity but does not allow that perspective to eclipse his coming role as judge. The "slackers" in the community needed reminding of that prospect so that they might hear John's message as something applicable to themselves as well as to the Judean crowds.

Jesus' Baptism and Acknowledgment by the Father: 3:13-17

At last the adult Jesus appears on the scene (v. 13). The One whose coming role as eschatological judge has just been sketched in such formidable terms simply emerges from the mass of repentant Israelites coming for baptism. John, who sees in him the One whose status and role he has been describing, understandably demurs, protesting that a reversal of the process would be more appropriate (v. 14). But Jesus, in the first words he speaks in the gospel (v. 15), insists that this is how it is to be "for now,"[5] and adds as reason: "for it is proper for us in this way to fulfill all righteousness."

"Righteousness" is one of Matthew's distinctive concepts. It bears upon a central area of dispute with the Jewish synagogue with which he and his community are in conflict. In the biblical tradition "righteousness" denotes behavior in accordance with the requirements of a relationship. In Israel it applied particularly to the covenant relationship with God and to the Torah, which showed Israel how to live out the covenant requirements in everyday life. In this sense a righteous person is a person who keeps the Torah—not simply in a legalistic sense but because it represents the practical expression of God's will: what God wants. The great dispute between Jesus and those who become his principal adversaries as the narrative unfolds will concern precisely this point. Jesus will appeal back to the foundational sense of "what God wants" in order to make clear what "righteous" fulfillment of the Torah should mean.

For Jesus, "fulfilling all righteousness" is doing "what God wants," and "what God wants" of him here and now as he stands before John is to submit to baptism in the Jordan along with the rest of repentant Israel. His

---

[5] The same phrase (Greek *ap' arti*) will recur toward the end of the gospel when Jesus, standing before the High Priest, points to his coming role as eschatological judge (26:64).

submission to baptism at this point because that is "what God wants" anticipates his subsequent submission to suffering and death because that too will be "what God wants" (cf. 26:39, 42, 44), an entrance into even deeper solidarity with sinful humankind in order to fulfill the role of the Servant to "make many righteous" (Isa 53:11-12; cf. Matt 20:28; 26:28).

Jesus may be baptized along with repentant Israel, but what happens as he emerges from the water sets him apart from the rest (vv. 16-17). We have here a defining moment in the narrative of the gospel: a divine response to the "righteous" action of Jesus in submitting to baptism at the hands of John.

The "opening of the heavens" recalls the plea of Isa 64:1: "O that you would tear open the heavens and come down."[6] It signals the end of the long "drought" of communication from heaven of which Israel has been conscious in the period since the return from exile. The descent of the Spirit in the form of a dove takes us back further still: to Gen 1:2, where creation begins with the Spirit's "hovering" (as a dove hovers) over the face of the deep. Jesus' empowerment with the Spirit for his messianic role is the beginning of a renewal so profound as to amount to a new creation. His Spirit-empowered ministry will reclaim human lives for a new humanity to be lived out in a renewed people of God.

The high point of the scene comes with the divine address from heaven: "This is my Son, the Beloved, with whom I am well pleased" (v. 11b). What in Mark (1:11) and Luke (3:22) is more a private assurance to Jesus ("You are my Son . . ."), derived from the royal psalm, Ps 2:7, interpreted messianically, has become in Matthew a more "public" declaration: "This is my Son. . . ." That Jesus, as well as being Messiah, is also uniquely Son of God has been made clear in the infancy story (1:18-25; 2:15). Now, as he emerges from the waters of repentance he has obediently entered "to fulfill all righteousness," he is publicly acknowledged as God's Son, the status and title most significant for Matthew.[7]

Of the remaining elements of the address from heaven, "beloved" evokes the description in Gen 22:2 of the boy Isaac, whose obedient submission to God's apparent will for him became a celebrated theme in the post-biblical Jewish tradition. Above all, the echo in the final phrase ("in whom I am well pleased") of Isaiah's First Servant Song (Isa 42:1-4) intro-

---

[6] The entire passage beginning at Isa 63:7 provides a most illuminating background to Matt 3:16-17.

[7] See Jack Dean Kingsbury, *Matthew: Structure, Christology, Kingdom* (Philadelphia: Fortress, 1975) 40–127; *Matthew as Story* (rev. ed. Philadelphia: Fortress, 1988) 51–52.

duces something essential to Matthew's view of Christ and his mission: that he replays the role of the Servant.[8] Though not explicitly quoted here, the following line of the Song reads: "I shall put my Spirit upon him" (v. 1c). This is exactly what God has just done: empowered the Son with the Spirit to carry out the Servant's mission.

Let us stand back and reflect for a moment on what we know about the person of Jesus so far. The "bottom line," so to speak, of his identity is that he is the Messiah, Son of David. As well as Son of David, he is also Son of God—but not simply in the sense that any Israelite king (or any Israelite for that matter) could be dubbed "son (or daughter) of God." The mode of his conception has shown this Son of David to be God's Son in a transcendent sense; in his person God is "with us" (Emmanuel) in a unique, personal way.[9] The revelatory moment following his baptism has brought out the intimacy of this filial status ("the Beloved") and indicated the way in which this Messiah/Son of God will carry out his mission. As "Messiah" has been transformed by "Son of God," so "Servant" will indicate the direction Jesus' obedience as "beloved Son" will take: entrance into and solidarity with the burdened, sinful lot of humankind.

Moreover, because of that entrance and that solidarity, what Jesus experiences here following his baptism is something that all the baptized can claim. Each one, before any good work of which they may subsequently be capable and simply because of their union with Jesus, can take to themselves that same divine assurance: "This is my beloved son/daughter, with whom I am well pleased."[10]

The Testing of God's Son: 4:1-11

Jesus embraces and relives the experience of his people by undergoing a period of testing as the final element of his preparation for ministry. The essential background to the episode of the temptation is the forty-year-long wandering of Israel in the wilderness of Sinai. This was a time when God probed the hearts of the covenant people to see whether they would be

---

[8] Matthew will actually cite the entire Song later in the gospel, at 12:18-21.

[9] Cf. Ulrich Luz: "Next to 'God with us' (1:23; 28:20) it is the obedient Son of God who gives to the whole Gospel the christological frame" (*Matthew 1–7. A Commentary.* Translated by Wilhelm C. Linss [Minneapolis: Augsburg, 1989] 100).

[10] For this reason I hold that a reading of one of the gospel accounts of Jesus' baptism ought be part of every ceremony of Christian baptism.

faithful, in the long term, to the covenant just made. Israel failed the test by attempting to turn things around and test God. In chapters 6–8 of the book of Deuteronomy Moses reminds the people, now about to enter the Promised Land, of their previous failure in this regard and warns them against repeating it by putting God to the test once more.

These three chapters of Deuteronomy hold the key to understanding the testing of Jesus.[11] Recapitulating once more the history of his people (also called "God's Son" [Exod 4:22-33; Deut 14:1; Hos 11:1; etc.]), Jesus submits to testing after a forty-day sojourn in the wilderness. In line with the worldview of the time, the agent of the test is "the devil" (Satan), the leader of the malign spiritual forces who currently rule the world to the exclusion of the rule of God. Satan's aim is to nip in the bud the campaign to overthrow his rule by seeking to deflect from his preordained path the chief agent of that overthrow, Jesus. But for all his evil intent, Satan cannot escape being in some sense the instrument of God. Jesus will emerge from the test, his mission and his union with the Father more clearly set than ever.

As in the case of Israel, the test to which Jesus is put has to do with fundamental trust in God. Each of the three suggestions Satan puts to him cunningly contains a proposal that would seem to flow quite naturally from his just-affirmed status ("If you are the Son of God . . ." [v. 3; v. 6]). But each involves repeating Israel's failure: testing God's faithfulness to the relationship, something that must never be in question. (1) Jesus is hungry after his fast. Well, then, since God seems to be rather slow in getting around to providing him with food in the desert, as Israel was so provided (the manna [Exodus 16]), let him use his powers to force the issue: turn these stones into loaves of bread (v. 3). (2) Put to the test the divine pledge of protection to the Messiah contained in Psalm 91[12] by enacting the scenario the psalm seems to envisage: a reckless exposure to physical danger in the hope of angelic rescue. What better way to try this out than jumping from the "pinnacle" of the Temple (vv. 5-6).[13] (3) Instead of waiting for God to

---

[11] Along with almost all scholars, I am indebted here to the classic exegetical essay of Birger Gerhardsson, *The Testing of God's Son (Matt 4:1-11 & Par.)* (Lund: Gleerup, 1966).

[12] Since the Psalms were traditionally attributed to David, they were considered to be first and foremost the "book" of the Messiah, Son of David; they "scripted" the role he had to play.

[13] The "pinnacle" of the Temple, not otherwise known, seems to refer to some architectural feature jutting out at a height. The idea behind the temptation is not so much that of a public stunt designed to demonstrate messianic credentials as simply a personal testing of God's protection.

confer upon him, after costly obedience, the world authority that is right-fully his as Messiah, why not have it right away? Only one condition: wor-ship Satan instead of God (vv. 8-9).

Implicit in this last suggestion is the assumption mentioned earlier in connection with the rule or kingdom of God: that the world, including Israel, is currently in the grip of demonic powers. Those who exercise rule and authority in the world—Herod, the Romans—do so because they have given themselves over to the one who really pulls the strings, Satan. To hold such authority is to have made a pact with him, in effect to have "wor-shiped" him, as he bluntly suggests here.

It is not hard to see why this temptation is the climactic one for Mat-thew. Here the basic issue is out in the open. Will Jesus go along with Satan and seek world authority as his gift?—an easy path, but a deceptive one, because he would have such authority only as himself a slave of the one he has agreed to worship. Or will he "fulfill all righteousness" by going the way God wants: the way of an obedient and costly entry into the sinfulness and alienation of the world, in the guise of the Servant who "bears the sins of many" (Isa 53:11-12) and who, though brought to death, entrusts his cause to God? The final rebuttal of the devil's suggestion will come when, having obediently passed through the pangs of death, Jesus stands on a mountain in Galilee and claims in the glorious freedom of his risen life: "All power in heaven and on earth has been given to me" (20:18b)—given to him, that is, by the God whom he had refused, as obedient Son, to put to the test.

Jesus dismisses each suggestion, citing each time phrases from Deu-teronomy 6–8. (1) Bread may be the staff of life, but whether human beings live or die lies ultimately in the hands of God (v. 4, citing Deut 8:3). (2) When Satan takes up the scriptural challenge, citing Psalm 91, Jesus flings back the fundamental principle at stake: "You must not put the Lord your God to the test" (v. 7, citing Deut 6:16). (3) Finally, worship and service belong to none other than God alone (v. 10, citing Deut 6:13).

Jesus, then, heeds the warnings of Moses, succeeding where Israel failed. In each case he emerges from the trial with his status as God's "beloved Son" unscathed, the direction of his messianic mission set. In a gesture confirming that such is the case, he receives (v. 11) the angelic "service"—presumably the provision of food—that the devil had urged him to grasp. The "testing" episode thus makes a *theological* as well as a *christological* statement. Jesus will place his cause in the Father's hands right up to the obedience of the cross, because the Father he reveals and whose mission he serves is worthy of such trust.

THE MESSIANIC MINISTRY
OF JESUS: 4:12–28:15

1. EARLY GALILEAN MINISTRY: JESUS: INTERPRETER, HEALER, AND RECONCILER: 4:12–10:42

Jesus Begins His Ministry in Galilee: 4:12-25

News of John the Baptist's arrest[1] leads Jesus to "withdraw" to Galilee (4:12). The withdrawal is not a retreat or flight from danger but a further instance of a recurring pattern in the gospel: faced with hostility or threat from ruling authorities Jesus does not confront them on their own terms but moves on to where greater receptivity to his mission is likely to be found. If Judea is dangerous, a return to Galilee is called for—but not to the obscure village of Nazareth where he had grown up. From now on his base will be Capernaum, a sizeable city by the sea of Galilee, in the territory traditionally associated with the northernmost tribes of Israel, Zebulun and Naphtali.

The move to Capernaum provides Matthew with a chance to again signal fulfillment of Scripture:

> Land of Zebulun, land of Naphtali,
> on the road by the sea, across the Jordan,
> Galilee of the Gentiles—
> the people who sat in darkness have seen a great light,
> and for those who sat in the region and shadow of death
> light has dawned (4:15-16).

This attractive text from Isaiah (8:23–9:1) is programmatic for the ministry of Jesus now about to unfold. His appearance in Capernaum, the

---

[1] We will learn the sequel to the arrest in a flashback in 14:3-13.

city by the sea of Galilee, fulfills God's will that the Messiah's "light" should shine in the region the prophet dubs "Galilee of the Gentiles." Though basically Jewish, Galilee had a mixed population at the time of Jesus.[2] While his personal mission will be to "the lost sheep of the house of Israel" (15:24; cf. 10:5), the fact that he will conduct this in a region where his light will necessarily fall also upon "those who sit in darkness and in the region and shadow of death"—that is, the Gentiles—will on occasion (8:5-13 [the centurion]; 15:21-28 [the Canaanite woman]) make him already the Messiah in whose "name the Gentiles will hope" (12:21). Such contacts foreshadow the mission of the Church (28:19-20) to make the light of his presence shine in a receptive Gentile world, fulfilling the Servant's calling to be a "light to the nations" (Isa 42:6; 49:6; cf. 60:3).

The "light" that Jesus now begins to shine is the proclamation of the kingdom: "Repent; for the kingdom of heaven is at hand" (v. 17). As we have seen in connection with the identical proclamation of the Baptist (3:2), the new reality in virtue of which the call to "change of heart" is made is the onset of the kingdom—the reclamation of the world for God's rule, dispossessing that of Satan. The outward transformation of the world associated with the kingdom—peace, justice, the abolition of sickness, disease, and death—all these remain outstanding (though the miracles of Jesus anticipate them). But the *essence* of the kingdom, a new relationship with God, is already on offer. "Repentance" is the human disposition through which God freely draws human beings into this relationship. Human transformation *follows*—it does not condition—the new relationship with God.

Jesus Calls the First Disciples: 4:18-22

The mission of Jesus presupposes the founding of a community as the nucleus of a renewed people of God. It is not surprising, then, that the very first *action* recorded of him in the gospel should be that of calling disciples.

The lakeside scene in which Jesus calls two sets of brothers—Simon Peter and Andrew, then James and John, the sons of Zebedee—is loaded with symbolism. The four are all fishermen. Their job is to go out on the sea of Galilee and use their nets to harvest fish from the sea, loading them into their boats. What they hear from Jesus is a summons to leave this form of livelihood—and their father in the case of James and John—and to follow Jesus in a totally new mode of "fishing," one in which these present fishers

---

[2] Cf. the comment in 1 Macc 5:15: "All Galilee is filled with strangers."

of fish will become "fishers of people" (v. 19). Until now they have gone out upon the uncertain waters of the Sea of Galilee, using their nets and their boats to harvest fish from its depths. Now, with a new kind of "net"—the proclamation of the gospel—they will go out into a turbulent world and "catch" people, claiming them for the kingdom by bringing them into the "boat" that is the Church.

In these ways, then, their new calling is symbolically *continuous* with their old. It is quite *discontinuous* in terms of attachment. If they are going to be "fishers" in this new sense—with human beings as their "catch"—they must leave family ties and the security of their old livelihood. The speed and totality with which the four disciples do so here (v. 20; v. 22) shows the power and insistence of Jesus' call.[3]

The Setting for the Sermon: 4:23-25

After the call of the first disciples, the gospel gives us a summary of Jesus' activity (v. 23) and then a description of the response it receives across a remarkably wide area (vv. 24-25):

> Jesus went throughout Galilee, teaching in their synagogues and proclaiming the good news of the kingdom and curing every disease and every sickness among the people.
>
> So his fame spread throughout all Syria, and they brought to him all the sick, those who were afflicted with various diseases and pains, demoniacs, epileptics, and paralytics, and he cured them. And great crowds followed him from Galilee, the Decapolis, Jerusalem, Judea, and from beyond the Jordan.

These few lines are noteworthy on several grounds. First, they provide a programmatic description of the ministry Jesus is now undertaking. He is first and foremost a teacher and proclaimer of the kingdom. Alongside this and characteristic in Matthew's presentation stands his accompanying role as healer: he goes about "curing every disease and every sickness among the people."[4] If the Great Sermon (chs. 5–7) will particularly portray him as teacher-interpreter of the Torah, the following narrative section (chs. 8–9)

[3] The call seems to be modeled on that of Elisha by Elijah (1 Kings 19:19-21). But where Elijah allowed Elisha to go back and say "farewell" to his parents, here the urgency of the kingdom allows no turning back; cf. later 8:21-22.

[4] The summary in Mark 1:39, which seems to have provided the source for Matthew's summary here (4:22), simply refers to Jesus preaching and expelling demons.

will complement this by building a strong impression of him as healer. Not that the two functions are really separable: Jesus' teaching and interpretation of the Torah is as much a burden-lifting project as is his healing of the sick (11:28-30).[5]

Second, with these sentences the gospel begins to communicate to us its vision of humanity seen through the eyes of Jesus: that is, as burdened and afflicted in every way.

Finally, we learn of the remarkable response his ministry evokes (vv. 24-25). Rumor of his healing power spreads "through the whole of Syria,"[6] attracting to him, from near and far, people afflicted in all the ways described. Though they "follow" him and receive healing, the crowds are not disciples.[7] But they do constitute the burdened mass of humanity, the sight of which prompts and provides the setting for the instruction given to the disciples in the sermon that follows: "*Seeing the crowds,* Jesus went up the mountain . . ." (5:1a).

[5] The entire section placing side by side Jesus' teaching and healing activity is bound together by the "inclusion" formed by the summary here in 4:23-25 and the very similar one at the end of ch. 9 (9:35).

[6] "Syria" seems to be a kind of general geographical reference to designate Palestine and the surrounding regions, including those mentioned in v. 25, into which Jesus' reputation fanned out. Some scholars think that Matthew wrote "Syria" so as to include the region (Antioch) where the community behind his gospel lived.

[7] On "crowd(s)" in Matthew see the helpful discussion in W. D. Davies and Dale Allison, *A Critical and Exegetical Commentary on the Gospel According to Saint Matthew.* ICC. 3 vols. (Edinburgh: T&T Clark, 1988–97) 1:419–20.

Jesus, Teacher and Interpreter of the Torah I: 5:1-48

The Great Sermon making up chapters 5–7 of the gospel is central to Matthew's presentation of Jesus and outlines the way of life that should characterize the Church. It is, in effect, the Torah for the renewed people of God, not in the sense that it abolishes or supersedes the Mosaic Torah but as that Torah reinterpreted and "fulfilled" (5:17) by the Son in the light of God's will for the kingdom.

It is understandable that a chapter division (between 4:25 and 5:1) should mark the beginning of the sermon. The division does have the disadvantage of separating the sermon from the summary statement at the end of chapter 4 (vv. 23-25) describing Jesus' ministry to the burdened masses who throng around him for healing. As already indicated, the phrase that introduces the sermon makes very clear that it is this vision of afflicted humanity that prompts Jesus to begin the long instruction to the disciples that follows:

> 5:1 *Seeing the crowds,* Jesus went up the mountain; and after he sat down, his disciples came to him. 2. Then, opening his mouth, he began to teach them, saying . . .

By ascending the mountain, then, Jesus is not seeking to escape from the crowds. Nor should we try to identify a real mountain somewhere in Galilee. The gesture is symbolic: in the biblical tradition mountains are the place of revelation.

Jesus' ascent of the mountain evokes Moses' ascending Mount Sinai to receive the Torah. But Jesus is far more than a "new Moses." Moses simply *received* the Torah on Sinai and then promulgated to Israel what he had received. Jesus, with the unparalleled authority that belongs to him as God's Son, will *impart* in the sermon a new and definitive *interpretation* of the Torah. In addition, then, to the roles the gospel has already accorded to Jesus (Messiah, Son of David, Son of God, Emmanuel, Servant)—we now see him in the role of authoritative interpreter of the Torah.

Jesus sits down—the gesture of one who is to impart teaching—and his disciples "come to him" (v. 1b). This approach of the disciples tells us that it is *they*, rather than the mass of people, who are the audience of the sermon.[1] From the narrative so far we know of only four disciples whom Jesus has called (4:18-22). But the sermon is not really anchored to a specific occasion in the story. In addition to those called to be disciples in the course of Jesus' ministry, it is meant for all who are to be "made disciples" (28:19) through the mission of his Church.

The sermon is not, then, addressed to the world at large. But the "world at large," represented by that afflicted mass at the foot of the mountain, remains very much in view. These people are allowed to "overhear" (cf. 7:28) the instruction Jesus imparts to his disciples about how they are to live in order that they may be something for the afflicted mass huddled below. So the sermon involves three distinct "parties," which we can picture in this way:

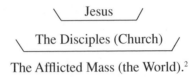

Jesus

The Disciples (Church)

The Afflicted Mass (the World).[2]

It is through living out the instructions given in the sermon that the disciples (Church) can be "salt of the earth" (5:13) and "light of the world" (5:14-16).

This means that, despite what is sometimes said, the sermon does not teach human values that are universally and perennially valid—at least in the sense of immediate application. It is indeed meant to have an impact on the world, to be part of a divine project to humanize/divinize the world. But this is to come about through a community that shares a distinctive vision and is prepared to pay the cost of living by that vision in a world that in large measure either opposes or remains indifferent to it. In this sense the sermon is an integral part of Jesus' campaign to break the grip of alienating, dehumanizing forces upon the world and reclaim human beings for the rule of God.

Everything Jesus commends or requires in the sermon rests upon a distinct *theological* vision overarching all from beginning to end. The instructions only make sense to those who share and have been grasped by

---

[1] *Pace* Daniel J. Harrington, *The Gospel of Matthew.* SP 1 (Collegeville: Liturgical Press, 1991) 76, 78; Ulrich Luz, *Matthew 1–7: A Commentary.* Translated by Wilhelm C. Linss (Minneapolis: Augsburg, 1989) 224.

[2] The scene is reminiscent of the charge given at an ordination or induction.

that vision—a perception of the character of God as revealed by Jesus, a God who is faithful and supremely caring toward creation, a God who is now intervening salvifically in the world to save it from destruction. The various ways of acting in regard to fellow human beings that the sermon will commend, some requiring generosity or risk-taking in a high degree, make sense only because, as Jesus points out, this is the way God acts in our regard. When Jesus says "Be perfect as your heavenly Father is perfect" (5:48)—that is, display faithfulness as your heavenly Father shows faithfulness—the key term is the little conjunction "as": the measure of perfection is the character and action of God. Such a view of God revolves above the sermon like a satellite receiving and transmitting data to and from the earth. Each and every statement is "bounced off" that image of God, even when, as in most cases, there is no explicit appeal to it.

It is also important to realize that the sermon does not aim to be exhaustive in its prescriptions for the community of disciples. The particular prescriptions given *illustrate* the kind of approach to living termed "surpassing righteousness" in the foundational passage, 5:17-20. The Jesus who speaks the sermon as authoritative interpreter of the Torah is also Emmanuel present to the Church as living Lord to the end of time (28:20). In view of his abiding presence in this sense, we shall later hear him on two occasions commit to the Church the power of binding and loosing that he here personally displays (16:19 [Peter]; 18:18-20 [local community]). He is equipping the Church to discern and decide how it is to live out the righteousness of the kingdom in the changing circumstances in which it will find itself as times goes by. The sermon is not, then, an inflexible, wooden code—something that would render it, in Pauline terms, "letter" (2 Cor 3:6). It enshrines a way of life open to reinterpretation and reapplication in the light of a living tradition, under the guidance of the risen Lord.

The long sermon is not all that easy to get a grip on as whole. An appreciation of its structure helps us see how the detailed requirements and the insistence on action that emerge toward the end flow out of and rest upon a sense of relationship with God built up at the start. The sermon also illustrates Matthew's predilection for arranging things in groups of three. Aside from the introduction (4:23–5:2) and conclusion (7:28-29), it falls into three major sections, and within these further triads can be discerned. We can set it out as follows:[3]

[3] My exposition of the structure is indebted to, though it does not exactly replicate, that of M. Eugene Boring, "The Gospel of Matthew," in Leander E. Keck, ed., *The New Interpreters Bible*. Vol. 8 (Nashville: Abingdon, 1995) 173.

4:23–5:2: Setting and introduction

I. 5:3-16: A community blessed and set before the world
    1. 5:3-12: A blessed community, now and hereafter
    2. 5:13: "Salt of the Earth"
    3. 5:14-16: "Light of the World"

II. 5:17–7:12: How the community should live out this role and identity
    1. 5:17-48: A Torah interpretation for "surpassing righteousness"
        5:17-19: The Law, not set aside but brought to completion
        5:20: "Surpassing righteousness": Introduction
        5:21-47: Six illustrations (antitheses) of "surpassing righteous-
            ness"
        5:48: Overriding principle: "Be perfect as your heavenly Father
            is perfect."
    2. 6:1-18: Righteousness in acts directed to God.
        6:1: Introduction
        6:2-4: (a) In almsgiving
        6:5-15: (b) In prayer [Lord's Prayer: 6:9-13]
        6:16-18: (c) In fasting
    3. 6:19-34: True "treasure" in respect to material goods
    4. 7:1-11: Righteousness in relations to others
    7:12: Conclusion: Golden Rule

III. 7:13-27: Eschatological warnings: Action required
    1. 7:13-14: The two gates (ways)
    2. 7:15-23: Two kinds of prophets (true and false)
    3. 7:24-27: Two kinds of house-builders (wise and foolish)
    7:28-29: Conclusion: Impact of the sermon (". . . not like the scribes").

The Beatitudes: 5:3-12

The Beatitudes with which Jesus begins the sermon are one of the most familiar texts in the gospels, a favorite reading for weddings and similar celebrations. But how many people who hear them in such circumstances grasp the radicality of what is being stated or realize that they are not simply an agreeable opening to the sermon but actually its foundation? Before setting out for his disciples the demanding way of life that the main part of the sermon will outline, Jesus communicates a very strong sense that those who do embrace such a way of life are "blessed," are "fortunate," are in the very best place to be. They are in such a "place" because God has sought them out and associated them with Jesus and the coming rule of God, which, though it suffers "violence" (11:12), will triumph in the end. If they can catch this vision, if they can have a sense that people who live in this way are indeed truly "blessed," then such a way of living will be something they *want*—rather than are required—to do.

The beatitudes are not, then, even in Matthew's formulation, *primarily* prescriptive in an ethical sense. They are not saying, "You must be poor in spirit, must be merciful, etc." Jesus is certainly *commending* the values and attitudes enshrined in them, but he is doing so not as a harsh moral demand but in the light of a vision of God that is the mainspring of his life and that he is at pains to share with those he is calling to be the community of the kingdom.

In addition, the beatitudes also presuppose a crucial distinction between the present state of affairs, which is one of suffering and trial, and that which will obtain when the kingdom is fully in place. In the biblical tradition the "beatitude" form, "blessed is the one who . . ." is a declaration or recognition that certain individuals or classes of people are in a happy circumstance. The basic idea is not too far away from what we do when congratulating a person on some achievement or good fortune: graduating, getting a job, getting married—even winning the lottery. In a more religious sense beatitudes are spoken in respect to those seen to be in a good situation because "blessed" by God. Usually that is because the good state of the person is already to be seen. What Jesus does in the beatitudes, however, is declare certain kinds of people "blessed," not because of their *present* situation, which is actually quite disadvantaged and vulnerable, but in view of a *future* situation that will come about for them through the power and fidelity of God.

Other things being equal, the attitudes and situations Jesus commends are not in themselves a recipe for getting on in the world. Some simply state a situation of disadvantage, some look more to attitude, some imply action. All cohere around the core idea of living in a non-competitive, non-grasping way. To be "poor in spirit" (v. 3a),[4] to experience sadness

---

[4] Matthew's "poor in spirit" does represent, it is true, a certain "spiritualizing" of Luke's (and likely Jesus') blunter formulation "Blessed are the poor" (Luke 6:20). While the sense of economic poverty is not excluded, Matthew's formula reflects a biblical tradition in which "the poor" is an honorific name for the faithful in Israel who, conscious of lack of resources on their own part, look to YHWH alone for salvation.

("mourn") because of the present state of affairs (v. 4a),[5] to be gentle and unselfish rather than on the make (v. 5a),[6] to have a passionate commitment to justice (v. 6a),[7] to exercise mercy instead of taking advantage (v. 7a),[8] to be "pure in heart" (v. 8a),[9] to be "peacemakers" (v. 9a),[10] to endure persecution and calumny for the sake of a right way of life ("righteousness") and allegiance to Christ (vv. 11-12): all these things make one vulnerable here and now, entailing much loss.

The second clause in each beatitude states the reason for the "blessedness" in every case. All those passives: "shall be comforted," "shall be filled," "shall have mercy shown to them," and so forth, indicate, in biblical parlance, the action of God.[11] To live according to these values makes supreme sense if God truly is as Jesus reveals God to be. In the present it may involve vulnerability and loss; in the light of the hope for the kingdom it is hard-headed commonsense. That is why those who adopt this way of life are to be "congratulated," why they are "blessed."

Salt of the Earth; Light of the World: 5:13-16

The two images of the disciples as "salt of the earth" and "light of the world" flow immediately from the beatitudes, and indeed from the vision

---

[5] Those who "mourn" (v. 4a) do not do so out of self-pity or a natural disposition to be sad; oppressed by the present state of the world, they long for its liberation from poverty, injustice, violence, and disease.

[6] The "meek" (v. 5a) are not people who go around with head hung low, passively accepting—and possibly seeking—the role of "victim." The Greek word *praous* denotes a gentleness flowing from inner strength, the opposite of grasping. The meek do not have to "have it all now" at the expense of others.

[7] In regard to "hunger and thirst for righteousness" (v. 6a), Boring catches all the nuances of "righteousness" in Matthew: "persons who long for the coming of God's kingdom and the vindication of right that will come with it, and who on the basis of this hope actively do God's will now" ("Matthew," 179).

[8] As Jesus later points out (9:13; 12:7), the "merciful" are doing "what God wants": "mercy, not sacrifice" (Hos 6:6).

[9] "The pure in heart" are those totally dedicated to God and God's cause, with no concealed loyalties to other allegiances on the side; the singlemindedness of their focus upon the Lord now will, appropriately, be rewarded with clarity of vision in the kingdom.

[10] The reference is not simply to the peaceful in a passive sense, but to those who actively work for peace.

[11] Basically, they are all variants on the idea of "possessing the kingdom," which, save for the expanded concluding beatitude, appears twice—at the beginning and end (v. 3b; v. 10b)—forming an inclusion. In biblical discourse all give expression to the blessings understood to be awaiting God's people in the messianic era.

of afflicted humanity (4:23-25) that provides the context for the sermon. The suggestion is that people who are prepared to live in the vulnerable, non-grasping way pronounced "blessed" in the beatitudes are the ones who can really help lift humanity's burdens, thereby becoming and remaining "salt of the earth" and "light of the world." The vulnerable "make the world safe for humanity." In this way the community that receives and puts into practice the Torah reinterpreted by Jesus reclaims the vocation of Israel to be "light to the nations" (Isa 42:6; 49:6; 51:4; 60:3; cf. 58:8, 10).

A few sentences of explanation and warning fill out the images of "salt" and "light." Salt can hardly "lose its taste," but it may be so mixed with other elements as to become impure and thus useless for either savor or (more importantly, in times before refrigeration) preservation. Then it is good only for salting the path outside the house, where people will trample it underfoot (v. 13). Disciples who fall away from their vocation may face a similar fate.

In Jewish tradition Jerusalem was the archetypal "city built on a hilltop" (v. 14). When the Temple was illuminated—as during the annual feast of Tabernacles (cf. John 7–9)—Jerusalem was indeed "the light of the world" (John 8:12; 9:5). The image then reverts to the more domestic scene: what one does with a lamp (v. 15). The disciples' good works must function as a lamp giving light to a darkened world—not to draw attention to themselves but to lead outsiders to the knowledge and praise of the God who has set them to be "salt" and "light" for the world (v. 16).

Fulfilling the Torah in True Righteousness: 5:17-20

The significance of this small section of the sermon would have bulked larger for the early readers of the gospel than it does for us. It contains the Matthean community's response to criticism from the Synagogue that it has abandoned the Torah, something that within the Jewish frame of discourse would undercut any claim to belong to the people of God. The opening words from Jesus, "Do not think . . ." (v. 17) reflect such a charge; some people *do* think this about the community. Jesus insists that he has come not to abolish the Law or the prophets but to fulfill them. Significant in this statement is both "fulfill" and the addition of the phrase "the prophets" alongside "the Law." In this gospel "fulfill" has to do with determining and carrying out "what God wants"—wants, that is, in this messianic time "before heaven and earth pass away" (v. 18). As God's Son, Jesus has unique authority to declare and implement an interpretation of the Torah that is according to God's will, made clear not only in the Torah strictly so called (the Pentateuch), but also in "the prophets," notably in the key text Hos 6:6: "What I want is mercy, not sacrifice" (cited 9:13; 12:7). All particular prescriptions of the Torah and, *a fortiori,* all that represents human tradition must be strained through this criterion and tested against the "greatest commandment of the Law," the one combining love of God and love of neighbor (22:36-40).[12] Jesus may, then, *appear* to sweep aside the Torah. In fact he is authoritatively declaring and fulfilling what he will later call its "weightier matters": justice, mercy, and faith (23:23).

To live out the Torah interpreted in this way is to practice "surpassing righteousness" (v. 20)—"surpassing" in the sense (again polemically) that it surpasses that of critics, here portrayed as "the scribes and Pharisees." From a legalist perspective such a fulfillment may seem a less exacting option. In fact, as the six cases Jesus is now going to cite (5:21-47) will show, it is very demanding. The crucial thing is that the demand comes from following the example of God (5:45), and giving priority always to love, compassion, generosity, and trust in dealing with one's fellow human beings. Such is the "perfection" (5:48) required in the community of the kingdom.

Jesus Interprets the Torah: Six Case Studies: 5:21-47

The six pronouncements Jesus makes as authoritative interpreter of the Torah are frequently called "antitheses" because that is the form they take. Jesus cites a ruling from the Torah, appealing to Scripture, and then modifies, radicalizes, or extends it in some direction. The form "But I say to you . . ." shows his complete authority *vis-à-vis* the Torah, Moses, and the Pharisaic oral tradition. A very high christology emerges.

As noted above, the six instances chosen are illustrative rather than exhaustive. In fact, all six bear upon relations between human beings to the exclusion of other areas. (Relationship with God is in view later in the sermon [6:1-18].) Common to most is the sense that righteous behavior has to do with the heart and with attitude rather than mere conformity with external prescription.[13] Some of the instructions Jesus gives come in the

---

[12] Cf. J. Andrew Overman, *Matthew's Gospel and Formative Judaism: The Social World of the Matthean Community* (Minneapolis: Fortress, 1990) 86-89; Klyne Snodgrass, "Matthew and the Law," in David R. Bauer and Mark Allan Powell, eds., *Treasures New and Old: Recent Contributions to Matthean Studies.* SBL Symposium Series 1 (Atlanta: Scholars, 1996) 106–11.

[13] "The inner springs of human conduct, which Law as such cannot regulate" (Boring, "Matthew," 189).

form of "focal instances": specific prescriptions of an exaggerated or totally impractical character (e.g., tearing out one's eye [5:29], cutting off one's hand [5:30]). Such commands are not meant to be followed literally. They are a prophetic stratagem designed to shock hearers into a whole new way of looking at human behavior by commending something totally at odds with what is normally thought reasonable.[14]

Concern for the heart is particularly clear in the first ruling (5:21-26) dealing with hostility between people. The old commandment simply stated, "You shall not murder" (Exod 20:13; Deut 5:17). Jesus radicalizes the matter by insisting on going to the heart and addressing at that level the anger that can lead to a whole scale of insult and injury to others, of which murder would simply be an extreme outcome.[15] The positive antidote is reconciliation with an alienated brother or sister, a duty so supremely important as to warrant postponing the offering of a gift to God in the Temple (mercy before sacrifice!). Particularly noteworthy here is the delicacy of what Jesus counsels: not "if you remember that *you* have something against your brother or sister . . ." but "if you remember (= suspect) that your brother or sister has something against *you*. . . ." It is not simply a matter of dealing with one's own feelings of anger, but of positively going out to recognize those of the aggrieved party and seeking to defuse them. The advice to "settle out of court" given in vv. 25-26 looks like a piece of worldly wisdom, but it reinforces the supreme importance of reconciliation, with overtones, never far from the surface in Matthew, of accountability before the end-time tribunal of God.

The same radical sense—going to the heart—is explicit in the next ruling, dealing with sexual behavior (5:27-30). The old commandment simply forbade adultery. In a way that sounds very contemporary Jesus insists that the problem really begins with perception: with a man's fundamental attitude to a woman. Is a woman simply an object for a man's sexual exploitation (lust)? Or is she a fellow human being with whom dealings in any area, including the sexual, must be based on equality of relationship, fidelity, and consent? The extreme advice about what to do with wandering eye and hand (vv. 29-30)—"focal instances" as explained above—reinforces the sense that sexuality has to do with the totality of a person (one's "whole body"), including relationships.

---

[14] Cf. Charles H. Talbert, *Reading Luke: A Literary and Theological Commentary on the Third Gospel* (New York: Crossroad, 1989) 73.

[15] The penalties mentioned in v. 22 are a parody of rabbinic casuistry, which Matthew here lampoons and rejects; they are not to be taken literally; cf. Boring, "Matthew," 190.

The next pronouncement (5:31-32) deals with the related area of fidelity in marriage. The old dispensation looked at the issue entirely from the male perspective and discussed grounds upon which a man could divorce his wife, simply giving her a bill of divorce stating that she was no longer bound to him. The Matthean Jesus excludes divorce absolutely, save in one particular situation, that of adultery.[16] This is not so much a legal ruling (though of all the six cases it has been most widely interpreted as such) as, again, a vision of marriage that is more radical and more human at the same time. Instead of marriage being a social institution having in view a man's exclusive sexual and domicilian rights to one woman, Jesus sees it to be a lifelong union bound not by law but by mutual fidelity and companionship.[17]

No doubt many people in second marriages hear this ruling of Jesus (and the parallel in 19:9) as an instance of burdens imposed rather than lifted. The Matthean formulations do lift the burden slightly in the shape of the exceptive clauses—not something, however, that will be of much comfort in cases where no question of adultery arises. Whatever development the ecclesiastical discipline, especially the very strict discipline of the Catholic tradition, may undergo in the future, it will be important to keep in mind that, while illustrating the "surpassing righteousness" required of disciples (5:20), Jesus' statements in this area (1) are not legal rulings that are absolutely clear; (2) envisage a life expectancy and social stability vastly different from that obtaining today; (3) are primarily concerned to reclaim marriage from something where all the power and decision-making rest one-sidedly with one partner (the man) to something corresponding

---

[16] The meaning of the Greek word *porneia* occurring here (and in 19:9 in a slightly different phrase) is disputed. Some consider that the reference is to incest, marriage within degrees of kinship forbidden by Levitical law (Lev 18:6-18). The exception would then bear upon the situation of Gentile converts who had contracted marriages within those degrees before becoming believers. Their marriages could—or perhaps should—be broken up. This seems to be the meaning *porneia* has in the rulings concerning Gentile converts set out in Acts 15:20, 29. In Matthew *porneia* more likely refers to "adultery" or sexual misconduct in general, in which case the Matthean Jesus does countenance divorce on one ground. Whether the ruling countenances remarriage after such a divorce is not clear. For a thorough discussion see W. D. Davies and Dale Allison, *A Critical and Exegetical Commentary on the Gospel According to Saint Matthew.* ICC. 3 vols. (Edinburgh: T&T Clark, 1988–97) 1:528–32.

[17] Strictly speaking, Jesus does not abrogate the Old Testament law here because that law said nothing about the propriety of divorce. It simply assumed divorce to be a fact of life and laid down a procedure for the man to follow so as to exclude misunderstanding and conflict.

to the original design of the Creator, a lifelong, equal companionship of permanence and fidelity (cf. Gen 2:18-25; Matt 19:3-6).

The same sense of fidelity motivates the following ruling (5:33-37) excluding the taking of oaths.[18] Whatever be the situation in the wider world, such trust and faithfulness should prevail in the community of the kingdom that its members should not have to have recourse to such procedures to have their word taken seriously.[19]

The interpretation of Jesus arrives at its most radical point in the final two rulings, on retaliation (5:38-42) and love of enemies (5:43-48). The old prescription about "an eye for an eye and a tooth for a tooth" (Exod 21:24; Deut 19:21; Lev 24:20) is commonly cited as an example of the harshness of the Old Testament dispensation. This is unfair. In the tribal situation of early Israel, where institutions of justice were barely established, the law of strict reciprocity was a realistic measure to contain and limit the spiral of violence—to bring "payback" to a closure that all parties recognize as fair. What Jesus commends is a readiness to disarm violence by being prepared to accept double what the perpetrator requires. Again, we have a series of "focal instances"[20]—specific renunciations feasible on an individual or small group level but hardly realistic on that of society as a whole, where evil and evildoers must be resisted and restrained. If disciples of Jesus adopt so generous a stance toward injury and unreasonable demand, it can only be on the basis of knowing themselves to be so enriched by the divine generosity that to act with such generosity in turn is not impossible.

Again, in the case of the ruling about enemies (5:43-48) interpretation should not drive a wedge between the old and the new. Leviticus 19:18 says "You shall love your neighbor as yourself," adding nothing about

---

[18] The references to not swearing by "heaven," "earth," or "Jerusalem" in vv. 34-35 reflect the Jewish practice of avoiding mention of the divine name. Jesus points out that this does not lessen the seriousness of the matter; God is still invoked as witness in each case.

[19] In the history of Christianity only radical groups have taken this injunction seriously. Indeed, in the Roman Church the imposition of oaths on those taking up office seems to be multiplying apace.

[20] The "shirt" ruling (*NSRV*'s "coat" is not accurate) reflects the prescription in Exod 22:26-27 requiring the restoration before nightfall of a garment taken in pledge. To take the outer garment ("coat/cloak") as well would leave a person, when "sued," naked in court. The Lukan parallel (6:29b), more reasonably, sees the situation the other way round: first the outer garment, then the inner one, resulting in nakedness. Being forced to go one mile refers to the legal right of soldiers of the occupying power (Rome) to force local civilians to perform tasks for them (cf. Matt 27:32 [Simon of Cyrene forced to carry the cross of Jesus]).

enemies. Hating one's enemy represents a more general human tendency. Jesus here resists it in the context, now made explicit, of the disposition and action of God, whose "children" the members of the community know themselves to be. "Like parent, like child," the adage runs. So the disciples will truly show themselves to be children of God if they reflect the divine action in this radical way. And this, finally (v. 48) is the true "definition" of "perfection": being perfect *as* one's heavenly Father is perfect, that is, acting toward others, including one's enemies, as the Creator acts toward all.

Jesus, Teacher and Interpreter
of the Torah II: 6:1–7:29

In this middle section of the sermon Jesus addresses three areas of behavior traditionally associated with religion in the strict sense: almsgiving, prayer, and fasting. The second area expands to include the "Lord's Prayer" (6:9-15), which many consider to be the heart of the entire sermon.

Righteousness in Acts Directed to God: 6:1-18

Once again everything hangs upon a particular vision of God that determines the appropriate way to act in matters of religion. The opening sentence gives the ruling principle: "Beware of practicing your righteousness before others in order to be seen by them; for then you have no reward from your Father in heaven" (6:1). The three acts of religion under consideration—almsgiving (6:1-4), prayer (6:5-15), and fasting (6:16-18)—involve a piety that must truly respect the nature of the God in whom the disciples believe ("your Father in heaven"). It deforms such piety to carry out these practices in a public and ostentatious way aimed at bolstering one's own religious standing by winning the approval of others.

The advice in each case is set over against the counterpractice of "the hypocrites." The latter are the religious leaders who are so often the target of severe critique in this gospel, reflecting retrojection back into the life of Jesus of the Matthean community's polemic against the Synagogue. Nonetheless, the countermeasures Jesus recommends—not letting your left hand know what the right is doing when giving alms, going into one's inner room and shutting the door when praying, putting oil on one's head when fasting—surely render the color and vigor of his own speech. The Father "sees all things done in secret," not in a "Big Brother is watching you" way, but in the sense that disciples live out their lives in conscious awareness of the presence of the God with whom they have an intimate filial relationship. The constant reference to "reward" may sound like earning "Brownie points" but really harks back to the "present-future" tension of the beatitudes. One performs these practices in the sight of a God presently unseen, known by faith alone. One performs them in the hope that the relationship presently hidden will one day be revealed in full glory and splendor. That is the essence of any future "reward."

The Lord's Prayer: 6:9-15

The instruction on prayer (6:5-17) particularly brings out the sense of God that Jesus wishes to communicate to his disciples. He prefaces the prayer that has become known as the "Lord's Prayer" (6:9-13) with an example, taken this time from the Gentile world, showing how *not* to pray. The pagans heap up empty phrases in their prayers because for them prayer is an attempt to move an ill-disposed or at best neutral deity to a more favorable frame of mind; the key thing is to hit upon the right phrase that will unlock the divine favor (v. 7). How different the situation in the case of the disciples! The Father knows what they need even before they ask (v. 8) and is only too willing to be generous. Believers' prayer—and specifically the prayer that Jesus now goes on to teach the disciples—is not about moving God. It is about creating in the human heart the kind of disposition that will enable the divine generosity to flow in full measure.

To promote such a disposition the petitions of the Lord's Prayer follow a distinct sequence. They move from a focus on God and God's "agenda" to petitions more specifically directed to human need. In other words, the prayer first attempts to lift the human mind and heart away for a moment from fixation on its own concerns to a broader program, which is that of the "Father in heaven."[1] This opening address, which in all likelihood echoes the distinctive address of Jesus himself to the Father,[2] establishes the context in which the prayer is made: a community of disciples whom Jesus is molding into the "family of God" (12:48-50) and seeking to draw into the relationship of intimacy and trust existing between himself and the Father.

---

[1] We recall the definition of prayer attributed to St. Augustine: "the lifting of the heart and mind to God."

[2] It is likely that beneath the simpler Lukan form, "Father," lies the Aramaic *Abba,* preserved in the Markan version of Jesus' plea in Gethsemane (14:36) and by Paul in Rom 8:15 and Gal 4:6.

The three opening petitions—that God's name be held holy, that God's kingdom come, that God's will be done on earth as in heaven (vv. 9a-10)—are not separate items on a list. The first and third are simply variations in biblical language of the essential prayer for the coming of God's rule or kingdom, which is of course the center of Jesus' proclamation (4:17). The presupposition is that the world has fallen out of the hand of God and is captive to hostile spiritual forces that manipulate human affairs, bringing bondage to sin and death, and the alienation of the world from its true source of life. The coming of the kingdom represents the reversal of all this: breaking the grip of hostile forces, reclaiming the world for the rule of the Creator, and the acknowledgment of that rule on the part of humanity (the "hallowing" of God's "Name").

The prayer that God's kingdom may "come" acknowledges that its full realization remains an object of hope. The community that prays the prayer—the disciples of Jesus—does so as a kind of "beachhead" of the kingdom, enjoying its essence in the shape of filial relationship with God, but still very conscious that, so far as the external context of the world is concerned, the arrival of God's liberating rule is far from complete.

The second set of petitions (vv. 11-13) looks more to human need but retains the focus on the future. The prayers reflect the situation of a people "on the move," a "pilgrim" people. "Give us today our bread for tomorrow"[3] (v. 11) has echoes of the feeding of Israel with the manna from heaven during the years of wandering in Sinai (Exodus 16). The manna fell on six days but not on the seventh (the Sabbath). The Israelites had to gather twice as much on the sixth day in order to have "bread for tomorrow," the day of rest. The petition is not just for bread in the literal sense but for "a double measure" of all that the community needs for survival on its journey through the "wilderness" of the present situation of the world. "Bread for tomorrow" may also point to the plenty of the final banquet of the kingdom, of which the Eucharist and indeed all earthly meals shared in faith are a foretaste.

Again, because the community has not arrived at the perfection of the kingdom it is a community standing in continual need of forgiveness—both from God and mutually among its members (v. 12). The sense is not that God waits to see whether the members forgive one another before bestowing forgiveness. Rather, the flow of divine forgiveness is blocked if

---

[3] The sense of "something for tomorrow" is one of the three possible meanings conveyed by the mysterious Greek adjective *epiousios* that qualifies "bread" in both the Matthean and Lukan forms of the petition. The other meanings are "bread required for survival" and "bread for today."

it is not passed on through them to transform human relationships as well (cf. Matt 18:21-35). The comment following the prayer proper (6:14-15) makes this explicit.

The final double petition (v. 13) could suggest that God actually "leads" people into a situation where they will be exposed to severe temptation. The idiom is biblical;[4] the perspective, once again, eschatological. The petition arises out of a sense that the final battle with the forces of evil will be climactic and that those forces may seem for a time to gain the upper hand.[5] The community prays that it will not be exposed at this moment (which the early generations believed was soon to come about) to extreme test.[6]

The Lord's Prayer, then, is very much the prayer of a people on a journey. For all the incompleteness of that journey, the community moves on, knowing that it enjoys already the familial relationship with God characteristic of the kingdom. The community prays for the full realization of that kingdom, aware that the contest with opposing forces not only occurs in the surrounding world but runs through its own life and the hearts of its individual members. We do not, perhaps, pray the Prayer today with the same sense of eschatological urgency as the early believers. But we can pray it with the same sense of creaturely dependence, familial intimacy, and hope as those to whom Jesus first taught it.

True "Treasure": 6:19-34

Running through the section of the sermon that makes up the remainder of chapter 6 and lending it a unity is Jesus' concern to inculcate a proper attitude to the good things of this world. Once again everything depends upon an understanding of God, which when truly in place should result in a liberating absence of worry. Presupposed is a sense that the human animal is a very insecure being, much preoccupied with the future and whether food, clothing, lodging, and so forth will be available in sufficient degree to guarantee security. The conventional way to ensure that this will be the

---

[4] Biblical idiom tends to attribute all occurrences ultimately to God, not distinguishing clearly between what God wanted and caused to happen from what God simply allowed. The sense of "lead," then, is "do not allow us to be brought into a situation of evil and be overcome by it."

[5] The best translation of the final clause seems to be "Deliver us from the evil one (= Satan)" rather than the more traditional "Deliver us from evil."

[6] The petition echoes the prayer Jesus will urge upon his sleep-prone disciples just prior to his arrest in Gethsemane: "Stay awake and pray that you may not enter into temptation" (26:41).

case is to amass wealth—not necessarily in vast quantities but at least in sufficient measure to ensure comfort.

For Jesus, the desire to amass wealth—to have "treasure on earth" (v. 19)—fed by insecurity, can become all-absorbing, in fact, an enslavement (v. 24). Reliance upon such "treasure" is also illusory since its own security cannot be guaranteed (v. 19). The true source of security is the amassing of "treasure in heaven" (v. 20)—the good favor of God—which alone transcends the barrier of death.

Once again it all comes back to a question of the heart (v. 21), the inner core of a person from which attitudes and behaviors proceed. If what one "treasures" above all is material wealth and the security it provides, that is a sure sign that one's "heart" is set in that direction and not upon God. Jesus' disciples must have their heart set on God. Then all other concerns will find their proper place (cf. v. 33).

The mysterious statement about the eye being the lamp of the body (vv. 22-23) seems to follow from this in the sense that it is all a matter of perception.[7] The direction of the heart flows from clear discernment (through a "healthy eye") of who God is—One to whom I can entrust my future absolutely. This perception fills one's whole being with "light," claiming one for the light of God's kingdom (4:15-17) rather than the opposing darkness.

In the matter of serving two masters (6:24) the crucial term is "serve," which in the Greek *(douleuein)* really means "be a slave to." Disciples may have a legitimate concern for material goods, but if that concern, fed by insecurity, amounts to an "enslavement" to wealth,[8] then they will be in the impossible position of someone bound in slavery to two separate masters.[9] God is the only being one can "serve" in the fullest sense and have freedom enhanced rather than restricted.

A poetic instruction follows (6:25-34) providing the grounds for such freedom by putting before the disciples an imaginative vision of God's

---

[7] The image rests on ancient optical theory, where the eye was not considered the organ *through* which light (from outside) entered the body (as in modern optics [intromission]) but rather the organ that gave light within, enabling vision (hence its function as "lamp" of the body [extramission]); see further W. D. Davies and Dale Allison, *A Critical and Exegetical Commentary on the Gospel According to Saint Matthew.* ICC. 3 vols. (Edinburgh: T&T Clark, 1988–97) 1:635–36.

[8] "Mammon" is simply a Semitic expression for wealth or property, which the Greek leaves untranslated, perhaps to lend the suggestion of a false deity.

[9] "Love" and "hate" do not refer to attitudes or emotions but are Semitic expressions denoting allegiance and non-allegiance respectively.

care. Running through it like a refrain is the phrase "do not worry" (v. 25, v. 27, v. 28, v. 31, v. 34 [twice]), which perhaps could be better translated "do not fret about," "do not be preoccupied with." The introduction (v. 25) indicates two areas of concern: that of the sustenance (food and drink) needed for staying alive ("life"), and clothing. Each of the two is then taken up in turn—food (vv. 26-27), clothing (vv. 28-30)—in an argument that rests upon a kind of *a fortiori* logic common in the New Testament. If God takes such care to see that the birds of the air are fed, and the lilies of the field so splendidly arrayed, how much more will the "heavenly Father" take pains to see that such things will not be lacking to the disciples, vastly more precious as they are in the divine sight than birds or flowers.

Hearers could protest that human beings have a lot more to be anxious about than birds or lilies. Jesus, however, is not making a moral point but an imaginative appeal. He employs poetic exaggeration to inculcate an attitude to God. The "Gentiles"—those who do not know God—worry about such things (v. 32). Those who do truly know God as the heavenly Father revealed by Jesus cannot be concerned about them in the same way. While they have, of course, to take reasonable care of themselves—and of those for whom they are responsible—such concerns take second place to dedication to the rule of God and the "righteousness" (v. 33) for which it calls.[10] Give *that* the priority it requires, and God will see that the other needs are met ("will be given to you")—not meaning that the disciples should be completely passive, but in the sense that those who give radical priority to the kingdom will experience so many ordinary things as gifts of a loving God.[11]

Righteousness in Relation to Others: 7:1-6, 12

How to treat other people has, of course, been central to the six illustratory rulings on the Torah (5:21-48) and also the Beatitudes (5:3-12). Here Jesus adds specific instructions regarding judgment. What is in view is not so much judicial condemnation or even church process (for which see ch. 18) but the fundamental attitude one should adopt toward another. If one's first and continuing tendency is to find fault and condemn, one exposes oneself to similar treatment at the final judgment (v. 2). As the

---

[10] "Righteousness" here is best taken in the Matthean sense of the behavior required by the Torah as interpreted by Jesus.

[11] The pessimistic tone of the concluding advice in v. 34 may stem from its origin in a folk wisdom saying. Its present sense seems to be: since God and only God has control over the future, leave the worries about the evil it might bring to God.

humorously exaggerated image about the log in vv. 3-5 seeks to show,[12] only a person who has come to genuine self-knowledge and appreciation of his or her own weakness is qualified to set about fraternal correction. The warning is notably pertinent in communities of faith where strong commitment to principle can have as a byproduct an equally strong inclination to fault-finding and severity of judgment.

The meaning and relevance of the following counsel (v. 6) about not giving what is holy to dogs and not throwing one's pearls before swine is not at all clear. Perhaps the best explanation is to see its inclusion here by way of balance to the nonjudgmental attitude just commended. Yes, we should not judge others. But if people are firm in their resistance to the Gospel and no change can be foreseen, then to persist with them on the basis of a nonjudgmental attitude is simply naïve. To do so may be destructive as well as futile.

Leaving aside for a moment the instruction on confidence in prayer that (somewhat intrusively) follows (vv. 7-11), we can see in the command to treat others as one would want them to treat oneself (v. 12) a fine rounding-off principle for this section. It may seem banal to reduce the "law and the prophets" to this simple maxim, especially as later (22:37-40) the same reduction is made in regard to *loving* one's neighbor as oneself. But what the maxim requires as a preliminary to action is an exercise of moral imagination in a high degree: to ask myself, "what do I really want from another person—understanding, tolerance, respect, loyalty, compassion?" —and then to ensure that all my actions in their regard enact rather than run counter to such qualities. The appeal to "the law and the prophets" in fact echoes Jesus' insistence, at the beginning of his interpretation (5:20), that he had not come to abolish but to fulfill them. The "inclusion" thus formed implies that treating others as one would have them treat oneself goes to the heart of the interpretation of the Torah in the light of "the prophets" (Hos 6:6) that Jesus has come to promote.

Confidence in Prayer: 7:7-11[13]

This instruction again flows entirely from the vision of God that Jesus is commending to his disciples. The three instructions, "ask," "search,"

---

[12] Another example of a "focal instance"; see above, p. 59.

[13] An instruction on confidence in prayer would follow much more logically after the Lord's Prayer (6:9-15), as in fact occurs in the Lukan parallel (11:1-13). Its placement

"knock" (v. 7) do not represent stages in prayer, moving from one degree of intensity to another. Rather, they illustrate various aspects of the one act of prayer, which at times will resemble one, at times another, but always with the confidence of gaining a hearing (v. 8). The two examples from human parental-child relations bolster this confidence on the same *a fortiori* logic featured in 6:25-34. If it is unthinkable that human parents would act in such a mean and nasty way, how much more unthinkable that the heavenly Parent would not give "good things" to those who in the community of disciples gathered by Jesus are sons and daughters.[14]

The overall teaching Jesus has been putting before his disciples in the sermon is demanding. This particular instruction placed here toward the end conveys the sense of God's willingness to communicate not simply the demand but also, to those who ask in confidence, the capacity to carry it out. The only thing that conditions the divine generosity is the quality of the human faith that is its instrument of reception.

Eschatological Warnings: Action Required: 7:13-27

The third and final part of the sermon presents not so much new teaching as exhortations and warnings designed to bolster the disciples' adherence to the demanding way of life Jesus' Torah interpretation calls for. It features Matthew's characteristic emphasis that belief must issue in action ("righteousness"), and also a particular concern that charismatic activity in the community ("prophecy") be assessed not simply by the fervor of its utterance but by its "fruits" (action).

The two gates (ways): 7:13-14

The exhortation begins with the "two gates" image (7:13-14), which in Matthew's version (contrast Luke 13:23-24) has been expanded, somewhat confusingly, to include "two roads."[15] The thought is not so much to

---

probably reflects a desire on Matthew's part to preserve the maxim in v. 12 as the summarizing conclusion of the entire central section of the sermon (5:17–7:12).

[14] The phrase "you who are evil" (v. 11) is a Semitic exaggeration and part of the *a fortiori* logic. In comparison with the divine goodness, human beings are "evil." There is no suggestion of total human depravity.

[15] The image presupposes the pattern of an ancient city surrounded for defensive purposes by a strong wall, with only a few gates as points of entry. The city gate had the kind of importance attaching to the immigration barrier at international airports today.

divide humanity, let alone members of the community, into two groups inevitably set upon divergent paths, one to (eternal) life, one to (eternal) loss. Nor is Jesus giving "information" in a doctrinal kind of way about the number likely to be saved. The whole point of the image is exhortatory: the way of life that Jesus has set before the disciples (and the community of the Church they will become) is a difficult and challenging way, one that will run counter to that taken by the great majority. But it is the way that leads to life, to entrance into the great City where the banquet of the kingdom will take place.

True and false prophets: 7:15-23

Charismatic activity of various kinds (prophecy, exorcism, miracle working) was a feature of the early communities—as indeed it has resurfaced in mainstream Christian churches in recent decades. The warnings couched in various images (sheep/wolves; fruit-bearing trees) show that for Matthew's community, as indeed for the Corinthian community addressed by Paul (1 Corinthians 12–14), it was a prized gift, but one open to abuse. Despite fervent protestations ("Lord, Lord . . .") and impressive religious effects, it can be deceptive and an opportunity for those simply hungry for power ("wolves in sheep's clothing"). The supreme test is what sort of "fruit" this "tree" produces. The good fruit to be looked for is clearly "righteousness" in the Matthean sense: doing the will of the Father in heaven (v. 21), summed up in the twin commandment of love (22:37-40; cf. 7:12), what Jesus will later refer to as the Torah's "weightier" commandments: justice, mercy, and faith (23:23). At the Great Judgment (25:31-46) only these will count.

Two kinds of house-builders (wise and foolish): 7:24-27

A parable rounds off the sermon, reinforcing the need not merely to hear the words of Jesus but also to put them into practice. In perfectly balanced symmetry Jesus tells the story of two builders, one wise and one foolish, and the totally different outcomes they each experience. People building houses in Palestine during the dry season, when not a drop of rain falls, can easily neglect to take into account wilder weather to come; wise builders plant their houses on a firm foundation of rock.[16] To take to heart

---

[16] Cf. M. Eugene Boring, "The Gospel of Matthew," in Leander E. Keck, ed., *The New Interpreter's Bible*. Vol. 8 (Nashville: Abingdon, 1995) 218.

and put into practice the way of life Jesus has commended in the sermon is
to embark upon a way of life that may appear vulnerable in the extreme
(cf. the Beatitudes). But those who do so are building the "house" of their
existence on a foundation of rock. The paradox makes sense in light of the
vision of God that has hovered over the sermon from the start and the
prospect of the crisis to come, when the "winds and rain" of the final conflict will "beat" upon all human lives. In this light, to heed the words of
Jesus and adopt the way of life he commends is to build upon the "rock" of
the power and faithfulness of God.

Concluding Comment: 7:28-29

The sermon finished, the Evangelist records the impression Jesus'
words had made upon the crowd. He has taught them "as one having authority, and not as their scribes" (v. 29b). An important christology lurks in
this impression. Unlike the scribes who had to rely upon their own tradition, appealing to Moses, Jesus has spoken as the authoritative interpreter
of the Torah, able to challenge that tradition in the name of an interpretation valid for the time of the kingdom. The report also suggests that, while
the sermon may have been directed at the disciples, the wider crowd has
"overheard" it. They can look to the disciples to be the "salt" and the
"light" (5:13-16) of which they, as representatives of the wider, burdened
world, stand so sorely in need. M. Eugene Boring sums it up superbly:

> The community of discipleship speaks its own language, makes its own con-
> fession, addresses its ethical demands to those who are committed to Jesus
> as the Christ and exalted Lord. Yet the church knows that it is not an esoteric
> group, but that it has a responsibility to the world (28:18-20), so that even its
> "internal talk" is carried on with an awareness that the world is listening in.[17]

[17] Ibid. 219.

Jesus as Healer and Reconciler: 8:1–9:34

The Sermon on the Mount (Matthew 5–7) portrayed Jesus as teacher and interpreter of the Torah. Now, alongside this portrait of him as teacher the gospel sets a complementary impression of him as healer and reconciler. It does so chiefly through a series of miracle stories, interspersed with some other material and concluding with a summary that very much echoes the vision of humanity that had prompted the Great Sermon (cf. 4:23-25):

> Then Jesus went about all the cities and villages, teaching in their synagogues, and proclaiming the good news of the kingdom, and curing every disease and every sickness. When he saw the crowds he had compassion on them, because they were harassed and helpless, like sheep without a shepherd. (9:35-36)

The two summaries, at the beginning and the end, hold together the dual portrait of Jesus contained in chapters 5–9. Together with a quotation in 8:17 pointing out his fulfillment of the role of the Servant (Isa 53:4: "He took our infirmities and bore our diseases"), they reinforce the impression that his teaching, on the one hand, and his healing/reconciling activity, on the other, are complementary aspects of the one saving mission to burdened, afflicted humankind.

The presentation comes in a series of nine miracle stories, which subdivide into three clusters of three stories. Attached to the clusters are blocks of material describing interactions on Jesus' part with other individuals and groups:

Healing of the Leper: 8:1-4
Centurion's Servant: 8:5-13
Peter's Mother-in-law: 8:14-15

Summary: Healings: 8:16-17

Would-be disciples: 8:18-22

Storm at Sea: 8:23-27
Possessed Persons at Gadara: 8:28-34
Paralytic: 9:1-8

Call of Matthew: 9:9
Celebration with Sinners: 9:10-13
Fasting, New Cloth, New Wine: 9:14-17

Raising of the Official's Daughter / Woman with Hemorrhage: 9:18-26
Two Blind Men: 9:27-31
Mute Demoniac: 9:32-34

The blocks of intermediate material attach to the clusters in various ways, forming links and narrative bridges. The theme of discipleship (8:18-22) continues into the boat scene (8:23-27). Jesus' authority to forgive sin (9:1-8) transmutes into celebration with sinners (9:9-13). The vision of the crowds prompts him to go across the lake (8:18). The official comes along with his plea (9:18-26) while Jesus is speaking about new wine (9:14-17). Matthew has put a lot of care into constructing a unified running narrative.

We call the three clusters "miracle stories" because, with the world-view that has prevailed since the rise of modern science in the sixteenth century, it is normal for us to distinguish sharply between ordinary events of the natural world and phenomena that cannot be explained "naturally," that seem to require a special "intervention" from God. It is, however, anachronistic to project this distinction back into the world of the gospels. For that world God—or other spiritual forces—was/were constantly at work in nature and human affairs. There was no distinction of kind between ordinary events and those that seemed extraordinary. It was just that God's power was seen to be operative in these last in a more striking way.

Our first question when confronted with the gospel miracles tends to be: Did it really happen? And usually waiting in the wings is a followup sentiment: if it didn't, then the story loses all value. This is a pity because, though the tradition that Jesus was a miracleworker seems as rock-solid, historically speaking, as anything else recorded of him, it is very difficult in regard to any particular miracle to be sure about "what (if anything) actually happened." And pursuing the enquiry in this direction points us down a *cul-de-sac* that misses the main thing the gospels want to communicate in describing the miracles of Jesus.

This is that in his person and his activity he is fulfilling the promises sketched out in Scripture—especially (Second) Isaiah—for the messianic age. The miracles are tangible effects of the onset of God's rule: the wresting of human lives from the alienating grip of Satan and the outward expression in human bodily life of renewed relationship with the Creator.

We might well object: "Well, that's all very well for the comparatively few people fortunate enough to have had access to Jesus' healing power during his lifetime. What about all those who missed out then—not to mention the wholesale continuance of sickness and disability in the world ever since?" The notion of "sacrament" may be of help here. The miracles are signs pointing to a more complete wholeness that is God's ultimate intent for humanity. They disclose God's purpose here and now, even if the full realization of that purpose must await the final arrival of the kingdom. Moreover, they are not simply acts of great kindness Jesus performed for certain individuals "back there" (during his historical life). As told in the gospels they are "our story" as well, invitations to us to enter into the narrative, identify with the characters, and see whether the transforming power of the risen Lord cannot also be at work within our own bodies, including our wounded, alienated, and indeed "leprous" parts.

In all of this the role of faith is paramount. The miracles of Jesus do not create faith. They presuppose it as the essential channel of God's power. Its presence or absence is a theme that surfaces again and again in the miracle stories, inviting the modern reader to enter them imaginatively in faith-filled participation.

Along with healings described in this section, Jesus continues to call and gather disciples (8:18-22; 9:9). They become his apprentices in preaching and healing, soon (ch. 10) to be instructed and sent out on mission. Eventually, of course, they will become the Church and carry his mission to the nations of the world (28:19-20).

For the time being the mission is to Israel (10:5). But the seeds of detachment from Israel are already being sown as Jesus' healing and reconciling ministry attracts resistance and challenge. Overt acts of exorcism do not bulk large in Matthew (in contrast to Mark). But it is clear that everything Jesus does—be it healing, teaching, or reconciling—represents the onset of God's rule within the world and a loosening of that of Satan. It is not possible to reclaim human beings for life and renewed relationship with God without threatening those who see their interests best served by the social and religious setup presently in place.

All this said by way of introduction, I do not propose to linger on the individual episodes, but simply to draw attention to the main features that illustrate the approach I am taking. Not that Matthew has narrated the episodes in any great detail: readers familiar with the parallel accounts in Mark may be disappointed by the extent to which Matthew has scaled down and rounded off Mark's wealth of detail. Matthew's approach is different and, in its own way, effective. He gathers the healing episodes together and unfolds them swiftly one after the other to create a strong, cumulative impression of Jesus as healer and reconciler. Here is a Messiah of great power and authority—not in the political sense characteristic of conventional messianic expectation but as One who employs his powers in a ministry of service: the healing and reconciling of humankind.

The first cluster: The healing of the leper, the centurion's servant, Peter's mother-in-law: 8:1-15; summary: 8:16-17

In the New Testament the description "leper" covers a variety of skin diseases rather than being restricted to the affliction known clinically today as Hansen's disease. Besides physical distress, all such conditions involved ritual uncleanness and the stigma of social exclusion prescribed by biblical law (Leviticus 13–14), not to mention the belief that disfiguring diseases of this kind were a divine punishment for sin (cf. Num 12:10-15; 2 Kings 5:25-27). One sufferer dares to break through the barrier and approach Jesus directly (8:1-4). He reveals his faith in the power of Jesus by saying not "If you can . . ." but "If you will. . . ." In response (v. 3), Jesus breaks through the barrier majestically in his turn, stretching out his hand, touching the man and authoritatively declaring: "I do will. Be made clean!"[1]

---

[1] This episode is unforgettably portrayed in Pietro Pasolini's film *The Gospel according to St. Matthew.*

The gesture and declaration symbolize in miniature what his entire mission is about: a divine outreach in compassion and healing to afflicted, alienated humanity. The Torah, taken literally (Leviticus 13–14), ruled that such contact rendered the toucher unclean and excluded from worship. For Jesus the "clean/unclean" process works the opposite way around: "uncleanness" does not flow from the man to Jesus; *"cleanness"* flows from Jesus to the man. Uncleanness is not something human beings "catch" from physical objects or conditions, in the manner of a contagious disease. Uncleanness, or rather unholiness, is a moral condition and has to do with the heart (as made clear later in 15:18). True cleanness (holiness) is something human beings "catch" by coming close to God, which is precisely what this man has achieved by having the faith, despite his condition, to approach Jesus. Nonetheless, the Torah is not swept away. By instructing the man to show himself to the priest and offer the gift commanded by Moses (v. 4) Jesus ensures his social restoration and "fulfills" the Torah in the way "God wants": mercy before sacrifice (9:13; 12:7).

Equally symbolic is the cure—at a distance—of the servant[2] of a Roman centurion (8:5-13). Jesus is prepared to go to the house of this Gentile (again breaking through a barrier), but the centurion forestalls him. Just as he himself can get things done at a distance by ordering his soldiers to see to them, so he believes the power of Jesus to be similarly effective without physical presence. In both his situation and his faith he foreshadows all those for whom, through the preaching of the Church, Jesus will be the Messiah in whose "name (= power) the Gentiles will place their hope" (12:21, quoting Isa 42:4). Unlike the present disciples of Jesus, they will never have seen and heard and touched him in the flesh. But through their faith, his presence and power as risen Lord (28:19-20) will be just as accessible to them for healing and reconciliation. This Roman centurion is the forerunner of the "many who will come from east and west" (v. 11) to enjoy the banquet of the kingdom.[3]

By contrast, the healing of Peter's mother-in-law (8:14-15) is strictly "domestic." In the parallel accounts (Mark 1:29-31; Luke 4:38-39) the

[2] The Greek word *pais* can mean "child," but "servant" is more likely in the present context; cf. W. D. Davies and Dale Allison, *A Critical and Exegetical Commentary on the Gospel According to Saint Matthew.* ICC. 3 vols. (Edinburgh: T&T Clark, 1988–97) 2:20–21.

[3] In the negative reflection in v. 12 we begin to meet Matthew's vigorous depiction of exclusion from the kingdom ("outer darkness," "weeping and gnashing of teeth"). Matthew does not minimize the loss that final exclusion will entail and employs the full resources of Jewish apocalyptic imagery to reinforce the point.

disciples call Jesus' attention to her condition. Matthew tells us that Jesus "saw" her lying in bed with fever. She and her condition are part of the vision of afflicted humanity that in this gospel continually calls forth his ministry of healing. Her strength restored, she prefigures all those within the community who will "rise up" at his touch and begin to serve him (cf. 27:55-56).

A wider ministry of exorcism and healing that same evening (8:16) prompts another of Matthew's "fulfillment" quotations (v. 17). In all this activity Jesus fulfills the burden-bearing role of the Isaian Servant: "He took our infirmities and bore our diseases" (Isa 53:4).

The second cluster: Would-be disciples, the storm at sea, the possessed persons at Gadara; the paralytic; celebration with sinners; question about fasting: 8:18–9:17

Before the next cycle of miracle stories the theme of discipleship returns in the shape of two requests, one from a scribe who wants to follow Jesus wherever he will go (8:19), one from a disciple who first wants to bury his father (8:21).[4] Jesus' responses to both express the urgency of the kingdom and the priority it demands: the abandonment of the comfort and security of a settled lifestyle on the one hand (v. 20), and the surrender of even the most sacred family duties on the other (v. 22).

The episode of the storm at sea (8:23-27) continues the theme in that the disciples "follow" Jesus into the boat—an image of the Church on its stormy voyage across time. Discipleship involves entering this "boat" with Jesus, exposing oneself to the onslaught of persecution and trial symbolized by the windstorm that suddenly arises.[5] Like the disciples in the boat, members of the Church may well feel that their Lord is "asleep," unheeding of their peril. When they echo the cry, "Lord, save us! We are perishing" (v. 25),[6] they can take comfort from the majestic authority with which he instantly brings about calm by rebuking—like God in Pss 65:7; 89:9;

---

[4] The request does not necessarily mean that the father has just died. More likely the man is asking to delay his departure from home until he has discharged his duty of caring for his aged parent until death.

[5] Water out of control is a standard biblical image for forces of chaos and destruction. "Windstorm" translates the Greek word *seismos,* a term that more usually has the sense "earthquake," lending a sense of cosmic upheaval that will recur at the time of Jesus' death and resurrection (27:51; 28:2).

[6] The appeal has a liturgical ring about it.

106:9—the winds and the sea. For the disciples there is a more gentle rebuke: their panic and forgetfulness of Jesus' continuing presence ("God with us" [1:17; 28:20]) shows up their "little faith" (v. 26). But they do ask the right question: "What sort of man is this, that even the winds and sea obey him?" (v. 27). The real significance of the episode lies not in the miracle of nature but in the revelation of Jesus as Lord and Savior of the buffeted Church.

As soon as Jesus arrives on the opposite shore ("the country of the Gadarenes")[7] two demon-possessed individuals confront him (8:28-34). Matthew's rather scaled-down account highlights the authority of Jesus, whom the demoniacs acknowledge as the Son of God come to overthrow them (v. 29). The destructiveness of the demons is apparent in their inducing those they possess to live in the abode of the dead (the tombs) and in driving the pigs they later infest headlong into the sea. Their protest that Jesus is "tormenting" them "before the time" reflects a sense that in his presence the rule of God is already beginning to break their destructive hold upon human lives. The episode ends, however, on a sad note. The people of the locality, more comfortable, it would appear, with the ferocity of the demoniacs than with a display of divine power, beg Jesus to leave their neighborhood. His liberating ministry—and that of the Church that will carry it on—does not always meet with welcome and faith.

The healing of the paralytic man (9:1-8) is another case in which Matthew has scaled down the Markan description (2:1-12). Clearly what the man and those who bring him to Jesus are seeking is release from paralysis. But Jesus, responding to their faith, goes straight to a deeper problem: he assures the man that his sins are forgiven (v. 2b). It is easy—but wrong—to conclude from this that a sinful life lies behind the man's affliction, that it is a divine punishment for sin. This is a conclusion that several strands in the Bible challenge and overthrow (cf. especially John 9:1-3 and the entire book of Job). That Jesus first assures the man that his sins are forgiven reflects the general proclamation of the gospel: "Repent, for the kingdom of heaven is at hand" (4:17). The paralyzed man represents a human need for forgiveness that is not exceptional but universal.[8]

---

[7] The textual witness across the synoptic tradition is extremely confused regarding this location, "Gerasenes" and "Gergesenes" also featuring. The region of Gergesa, though weakly attested, has probably the best claim to originality since at least it was on the lakeshore, whereas the other two localities, though better known, were well inland.

[8] Cf. M. Eugene Boring, "The Gospel of Matthew" in Leander E. Keck, ed., *The New Interpreter's Bible*. Vol. 8 (Nashville: Abingdon, 1995) 234.

Some scribes who are present see in the declaration nothing but blasphemy: a human being making a declaration that pertains to God alone (v. 3). Knowing their thoughts, Jesus dramatically demonstrates his authority to forgive sins by making the man's release from physical paralysis the outward sign of a release from sin, itself something interior and hidden. For *him,* "God with us" (1:23), who has come to "save the people from their sins" (1:21), it just as "easy" to say to a paralytic "Stand up and walk" as to say "Your sins are forgiven" (v. 5). As the concluding remark (v. 8b) stresses, the main point of the scene is not the miracle but what the miracle attests: that in the presence of Jesus (the Son of Man) the divine power of forgiveness is personally present "on earth" (v. 6).[9]

Forgiveness is not only something to receive. It is also a gift to celebrate, which is exactly what Jesus does—again controversially—in the next scene (9:9-13). Preceding the celebration is the call of the tax collector, Matthew, sitting at his tax booth (9:9). Matthew will later feature among the inner circle of Twelve who are to be sent out on mission (10:1-4). The Evangelist is signaling that the foundation pillars of the Church included those who, by reason of their profession, were reckoned outcasts and "sinners."[10] The dinner that follows (v. 10), where Jesus and his disciples sit at table with many tax collectors and sinners, becomes a celebration of forgiveness received. The Pharisees, who complain about it to the disciples (v. 11), think that the only way for the righteous to deal with sinners is to shun them. For Jesus that would be to act like a doctor who avoided sick people rather than tending them to cure them (v. 12).

Jesus follows up the proverbial statement about the physician with the first of his two appeals in the Gospel of Matthew to Hos 6:6: "Go and learn what this means, 'I want mercy, not sacrifice.' For I have come to call not the righteous but sinners" (v. 13; cf. 12:7). The querulous Pharisees are not simply put right. They are given an interpretive task: "Go and learn. . . ." Let them reflect upon the clear indication of divine will contained in the quotation and ponder its implications for applying the Torah to everyday life, including the social situation presently in view. They might then be less inclined to criticize Jesus and his disciples for celebrating with tax collectors and sinners the mercy and forgiveness of God. Jesus is "fulfill-

---

[9] Whereas in the Markan (2:3-12) and Lukan (5:18-26) parallels the amazement of the crowd is focused on the miracle, in Matthew they glorify God "who has given such authority to human beings."

[10] This is why, presumably, the Evangelist makes the tax collector "Matthew," instead of "Levi," as in Mark (2:14) and Luke (5:27).

ing" the Torah in the way Hos 6:6 indicates to be what God wants, placing mercy before all other considerations.[11]

The fact that the disciples, including the former tax collector Matthew, join Jesus in the celebration makes the scene a paradigm of the life of the Church, with strong overtones of the Eucharist, its central celebration. The Church is not primarily a community of the righteous but a community of forgiven sinners whose need for forgiveness and healing continues. Far from distancing its members from God, sinfulness is actually a guarantee of the presence of "Emmanuel," the embodiment of mercy. The Church must, of course, have legal structures and procedures. But those who administer them and all who exercise authority in Christ's name are surely enjoined never to lose sight of the command, "Go and learn what this means, 'What I want is mercy, not sacrifice.'" By the same token, members of the Church, in union with their living Lord, are themselves called to be instruments of the mercy God wishes to see prevail in a wounded world (cf. 5:7).

The disciples of John the Baptist also have some criticism to make (9:14-17).[12] They want to know why Jesus' disciples do not fast, when they and the Pharisees do. Jesus' response rests on a clear difference between his own ministry and that of John. Like John (3:1-2), Jesus calls for repentance in view of the kingdom (4:17). But beyond this he can actually declare forgiveness and celebrate with forgiven sinners the mercy of God received. For his disciples to fast would be like fasting at a wedding—something inconceivable in the rural Galilean culture of the time where weddings were one of the rare occasions when ordinary people could enjoy a really good feast.

The disciples may not now be fasting but, extending the image allegorically with reference to himself (v. 15b), Jesus points to a time when they will indeed fast: the time of his being "taken away" in suffering and death.[13] The comment reflects the later community's sense of living "between the times": between the past of Jesus' earthly ministry and the future when he will return as Son of Man to gather and vindicate his faithful

[11] The phrase, "mercy, not sacrifice," does not imply the complete exclusion of sacrifice. Operative in the text, both in its original location in Hosea and as quoted by Jesus, is a Hebrew idiom lending the sense "mercy *before* sacrifice"; cf. 5:23.

[12] They are far less hostile, of course, but represent still another Jewish group from which Jesus and his disciples are beginning to draw away as the definitive community of the kingdom takes shape.

[13] There could be an echo here of the "taking away" of the "Servant" figure in Isa 53:8.

(Matthew 24–25). During this time, which of course is our time too, the community recalls and continues his celebration of God's mercy. It also prays and fasts, keeping watch for his return. The changing seasons of the liturgical year (Advent, Lent, Eastertide) make allowance for both responses.

The criticisms leveled at Jesus and his disciples stem from people who have failed to grasp that with his appearance and ministry a new era has dawned, rendering current categories of judgment outdated and indeed destructive. This is what two appended sayings—the one about the cloth (9:16) and the one about the wineskins (9:17)—seek to establish. In every age believers have to live out a similar tension between the claims of tradition and those of a Gospel ever new.

The third cluster: Raising of the official's daughter/ woman with hemorrhage: 9:18-26; two blind men: 9:27-31; mute demoniac: 9:32-34

In Matthew's account of the raising of the official's daughter (9:18-26) the child is already dead before her father makes his request.[14] He has faith that Jesus' touch can raise the dead. By contrast, the woman suffering from a hemorrhage who interrupts the progress to the official's house (vv. 20-22) does not presume to ask Jesus to touch her—something that in conventional understanding would render him ritually unclean. But she has faith to believe that if only she can touch *him* quietly and secretly she may find healing. In fact, she touches only the fringe of his cloak, the garment with tassels that Jesus, as an observant Jew, is wearing.[15] Aware that he has been touched, Jesus turns and sees her.[16] His declaration that her faith has made her well (literally "has saved" her) works the healing[17] and makes public her fitness to be restored to the community. As in the case of the leper (8:1-4), *he* has not contracted uncleanness from her; on the contrary, she through her faith has *received* healing and salvation from contact with him.

---

[14] Matthew does not name him or mention specifically that he is the ruler of a *synagogue*. Matthew's community was not experiencing good relations with such people. So he is simply "a ruler"—an official.

[15] Cf. Num 15:39: "You have the fringe so that, when you see it, you will remember all the commandments of the LORD and do them"; cf. Ulrich Luz, *Matthew 8–20: A Commentary.* Translated by James E. Crouch. Hermeneia (Minneapolis: Fortress, 2001) 42.

[16] Only Matthew records Jesus' seeing her—another instance of Jesus' vision of afflicted humanity.

[17] In Mark (5:29) and Luke (8:44b) it has already taken place. For Matthew it is Jesus' word that works healing.

Arrived at the ruler's house, Jesus finds nothing but the rituals of death and disbelief that the child is anything but dead (vv. 23-24). For him the death is real, but it is akin to "sleep" because, granted his lifegiving presence, it is not the final situation. This he demonstrates by taking the girl by the hand so that "she was raised" (v. 25).

How many parents down the ages, grieving for lost children, have heard or read this account and felt acutely the absence of Jesus and his power when *their* child died? There is no simple answer, and pastoral sensitivity requires great caution. One may simply observe that by so echoing the language of resurrection Matthew has made the story of this particular raising symbolic of a wider hope. Jesus' own experience of death has not abolished death, but his resurrection means death does not have the last word. Relationship with God—and within that, all other relationships—transcends the barrier of physical death and lives on in eternal life. At every funeral liturgy the Church repeats the prayer in faith of this grieving parent: "My daughter (son, sister, brother . . .) has just died; but come and lay your hand on her and she (they) will live."

We need not delay over the two miracles that complete this third cluster: the healing of two blind men (9:27-31) and the expulsion of a demon rendering a person incapable of speech (9:32-34). Both are peculiar to Matthew[18] and reinforce themes that have been building up in the narrative. The two blind men display strong faith in calling upon the healing powers of the Messiah, Son of David (vv. 27-28).[19] The expulsion of the speech-inhibiting demon (vv. 32-33a) reminds us that all Jesus' healing activity is a blow struck against Satan's grip on human life,[20] an instance of the rule of God bringing bodily as well as spiritual liberation. While the crowds applaud his achievement (v. 33b), the Pharisees, by contrast, make a negative assessment. They do not deny that Jesus works wonders, but they attribute his capacity to do so to the "ruler of demons" (v. 34). It is at

---

[18] The first foreshadows a very similar healing of two blind men as Jesus leaves Jericho, just prior to his final visit to Jerusalem: Matt 25:29-34.

[19] However, like those criticized toward the end of the Great Sermon (7:21), their "Lord, Lord . . ." is not matched by obedience in that they disobey Jesus' command to keep the matter quiet (vv. 30-31); cf. Boring, "Matthew," 239.

[20] This depends, of course, on the ancient view that demonic possession lay behind sickness and disability of various kinds. While modern medicine and psychology have eroded such explanations, the increasing recognition of a spiritual dimension to almost all forms of sickness calls for fresh reflection upon the meaning of the biblical miracle stories, including the exorcisms.

the cost of growing conflict and opposition that Jesus brings life, healing, and social inclusion to afflicted humanity.

The Twelve Instructed for Mission:
9:35–10:42

As we have seen, the instruction Jesus gave to his disciples in the Great Sermon (Matthew 5–7) had as its context a vision of the afflicted multitudes who had come to Jesus from near and far (4:23-25). A similar summary (9:35-36) rounds off the description of his healing activity in chapters 8–9, creating a unified sense of his teaching and healing ministry on behalf of burdened humanity. The summary also provides a context for the next section of the gospel, featuring the second of Jesus' discourses, the instruction of the Twelve for mission (10:1-42). The second sentence of the summary tells us once more how Jesus "saw" the crowds:

> When he saw the crowds, he had compassion for them, because they were harassed and helpless, like sheep without a shepherd. (9:36)

Matthew does not usually report on Jesus' emotions, but here he uses a very strong term, *splangchnistheis,* to describe the compassion that over-whelms him at the sight of the crowds. Their appearance as "sheep without a shepherd" recalls the prayer of Moses at the end of his life for a succes-sor (Joshua) "so that the congregation of the LORD may not be like sheep without a shepherd" (Num 27:17; cf. 1 Kings 22:17). Subsequent rulers of Israel, in succession to the former shepherd-boy David, were expected to be "shepherds" of their people (cf. Ezekiel 34). What Jesus sees, then, in the crowds is an Israel devoid of true leadership. The selection of twelve disciples to be the nucleus of a new leadership will signal a reconstitution of Israel, a fresh start for the people originally founded upon the twelve sons of Jacob. The people may now be harassed and helpless, but they are potentially a "rich harvest" (9:37-38) that awaits gathering in for the kingdom.

The Choice of the Twelve: 10:1-4

This context makes Jesus' choice and mission of the Twelve "an expression of the divine compassion for the needy people of God"[1] and a first
stage in the reconstitution of that people preparatory to the full arrival of
the kingdom. Having been associated with Jesus for some time, his twelve
leading "apprentices" are now to have an active share in his preaching and
healing mission.

It is at first sight rather curious that we are not told the names of the
twelve disciples before being informed as to the powers conferred upon
them. We learn that they are to have "authority over unclean spirits, to cast
them out, and to cure every disease and every sickness" (v. 1).[2] Only then,
almost as an afterthought, comes the list of names—two pairs of six, headed
as in all the lists by "Simon, also known as Peter" (vv. 2-4). Matthew's
order makes an important point. The Twelve may symbolically represent
the reconstitution of the people of God but they are not to be static "pillars":
they, and the Church to be built upon them, are there for the liberating
mission just outlined.

The Missionary Discourse: 10:5-42

The Discourse given to the Twelve in view of their mission (10:5b-42)
is one of the most difficult parts of Matthew's gospel. The opening instructions fit well within the stage the narrative has reached so far—the early
Galilean ministry of Jesus. Before long (from v. 17 onward), however, we
are confronted by warnings about persecutions and trials that are not realistically located in that setting but reflect experiences of the early generations of believers after Jesus' death and resurrection. In short, this is one of
the parts of the gospel that reminds us most forcefully that the narrative,
though ostensibly telling a story set in the lifetime of Jesus, is constantly
oscillating between that setting and the later time and conditions of the
Church. In particular it reflects the failure of the later community's mission
to Israel, which at the time of the gospel's writing appears to be complete.

This leaves the problem that some of the instruction, especially the
early part (vv. 5b-15), does seem to apply quite strictly to the original

---

[1] M. Eugene Boring, "The Gospel of Matthew," in Leander E. Keck, ed., *The New Interpreter's Bible.* Vol. 8 (Nashville: Abingdon, 1995) 252.

[2] Typically, Matthew expands on the "healing" aspect; the Lukan parallel (10:1) simply
has "to cure diseases."

Galilean setting, with little possibility of transference to a later, let alone a modern situation. On the other hand, the later warnings about persecutions and, most poignantly, the foretelling of inner-family conflict and division, confront us with a description of early Christian life that seems to have arrived a bit too "early" for this stage of the narrative. What are we to make of it all?

First of all, it helps to see that the discourse appears to be very carefully crafted. Its content seems to unfold according to the following structure:[3]

A. vv. 5-15: Mission of the Disciples: how they are to travel and find lodging; their response to the acceptance/non-acceptance they receive.

B. vv. 16-23: Encouragement and advice in the face of the persecution to come: arraignment before tribunals and inner-family betrayal.

C. vv. 24-25: The reason for all this: they are sharing the fate of the Master. If he has been maligned, it is to be expected that they will be too.

D. vv. 26-31: Exhortation: "Have no fear." The disciples are completely in the hands of the Father in whose sight they have surpassing value.

C'. vv. 32-33: If they loyally confess Jesus on earth, he will confess *them* at the great reckoning before his Father in heaven.

B'. vv. 34-39: Division in families is to be expected; family loyalties must take second place to the following of Jesus.

A'. vv. 40-42: Those who welcome them will be richly rewarded because they are actually welcoming the risen Lord who is sending them, and ultimately the One—the Father—who sent *him*.

Set out in this way, the various parts of the discourse appear in a chiastic order: that is, an arrangement in which there is a correspondence between the first and the last member, the second and the second-last, the third and the third-last, with the fourth constituting the center where the order reverses—the point of "crossing" (Greek *chiasmos*). Thus the first element (vv. 5b-15) and the last (vv. 40-42) cohere around the idea of

---

[3] This structure basically follows the careful analysis of W. D. Davies and Dale Allison, *A Critical and Exegetical Commentary on the Gospel According to Saint Matthew.* ICC. 3 vols. (Edinburgh: T&T Clark, 1988–97) 2:162.

"welcome/acceptance"; the second (vv. 16-23) and the second-last (vv. 34-39) refer to persecution in which inner-family conflict and betrayal is prominent; the third (vv. 24-25) and the third-last (vv. 32-33) explicitly relate Christian suffering and loyalty to the suffering and loyalty of Christ. This leaves the central element (vv. 26-31) in the place of prominence where, amid all this warning about trials to come, it can give the grounds for confidence and standing firm: the truth that the Father, who cares even for sparrows, puts the highest premium on believers and their fate. The whole discourse revolves around this central exhortation. No other element should be considered apart from it.

That said by way of introduction, I shall not go through the discourse point by point, but simply comment on leading themes and considerations appearing within it.

First of all, it is remarkable how closely the instructions given to the disciples about what they are to do (vv. 5b-8a) parallel the activity already attributed to Jesus. These apprentices are to proclaim the good news of the kingdom (cf. 4:17); then, like Jesus, they are actually to testify to its dawning by curing the sick, raising the dead, cleansing lepers, and casting out demons—all activities associated with the messianic age in the biblical prophecies. Only Jesus' teaching role is, for the time being (cf. 28:20), omitted.

The missionaries are not to go among the Gentiles but only to "the lost sheep of the house of Israel" (vv. 5-6). For the time being the privilege of hearing the good news is for Israel alone. The restriction will, of course, be lifted when the risen Lord commissions the Church to "make disciples of all the nations" (28:19-20).

Since the kingdom is the pure gift of God, the missionaries are to pass on the good news of its onset and work its first effects (healing and exorcizing) without recompense (v. 8a). They are to travel lightly, taking the risk of hospitality. The gift they have to offer (the "peace" [Hebrew *shalōm*] associated with the kingdom [vv. 12-13]) is so precious that those who genuinely receive it can be counted upon to supply food and all other necessities. Where they do not receive a welcome they should simply pass on, with a prophetic gesture as a warning of the judgment to come (vv. 14-15).

The gap between the lightness of mission commended here and the structures of endowment and remuneration in the present life of the Church, especially in Western countries, is immense. Can a text like this realistically speak to the Church today? Just as it would be misguided to draw a straight line across the ages and attempt in the conditions of our time a literal fulfillment of Jesus' instruction to the Galilean missionaries, so it would be equally wrong to dismiss it as totally irrelevant. We are back, in any case, with the sense of vulnerability that rang through the Beatitudes (5:3-12), and for the same reason. Only disciples overwhelmed by a sense of the riches contained in the message they bring (the good news of the kingdom) could be ready to sit so lightly to concerns about food, clothing, and lodging, to take the risk of hospitality in such a high degree. By the same token, only those prepared to appear before others in so vulnerable and non-grasping a way will be effective and credible ministers to the harassed and dejected "sheep" (9:36) to whom they are sent (v. 16).

Again, the instructions about persecutions and trials, the exhortations to fearless confession when hauled before magistrates and tribunals (vv. 16-25; 34-39), are remote from the experience of First World Christians today —though not a distant memory for those who have survived decades of persecution under totalitarian regimes. Believers who have to live out their commitment and struggle for justice as a minority group in a surrounding sea of fundamentalism and intolerance will hear Jesus' words with far greater immediacy. Those of us not in such situations may have to ask ourselves whether we are assuming a far too easy symbiosis between Christian discipleship and surrounding cultural mores. If we never experience discomfort and embarrassment in professing and living the faith, if we never have to "confess Jesus" in a way that means standing apart from the crowd, have we truly heard the good news for which at our baptism we were claimed? If, as seems to be the case, practicing believers are becoming a minority even in countries once known as "Catholic" or "Christian," we may find before long that the gap between our situation and that presupposed in this discourse has appreciably narrowed.

Perhaps the most troubling statements in the discourse are those that bear upon intra-family betrayal and conflict (vv. 21-22; 34-37). Again these reflect in the first instance the experience of the early Christian communities where believers often had to choose between the demands of their new faith and the claims of family members who were not at the time believers (cf. 8:21-22). Faced with situations of conflict and betrayal, believers could draw comfort from the fact that all this had been foreseen by Jesus and placed within a wider perspective. That wider perspective emerges explicitly in the section that the arrangement suggested above shows to be the heart of the entire discourse (vv. 26-31). As members of a reconstituted people of God, believers enjoy a familial relationship and intimacy with their "Father in heaven." The privilege of belonging to this "family," the sense of being valued and watched over by God that goes with it, place in a wider context and go some way to relativizing the lesions and wounds to natural family life that discipleship exacts. We go astray if we read any part of the discourse in isolation and forgetfulness of this central consideration.

Believers, like all human beings, are not immune from fear. There is a fear that is salutary and well-grounded; there is fear that is based on illusion and ignorance of the total picture. A large part of all pastoral care and spiritual direction consists in helping people to discern the difference between these two kinds of fear. This is basically what Jesus is doing in this central instruction, in which "fear not/fear" is a constant refrain (v. 26; v. 28a; v. 28b; v. 31). In the context of the vision of God that Jesus proclaims, the only thing ultimately to fear is final separation from the source of life (v. 28; v. 33). All else, even the destruction of the body in death, rests in the hands of the Father.

2. LATER GALILEAN MINISTRY: "NOT THE MESSIAH WE WERE EXPECTING!": 11:1–16:12

Misunderstanding and Opposition: 11:1–12:50

At this point the gospel has made us thoroughly familiar with all aspects of Jesus' ministry: his preaching, teaching, and works of compassion (healing) on behalf of the burdened and afflicted crowds. We have just (ch. 10) heard the disciples enlisted, instructed, and sent out for a similar ministry in extension of his own.

Jesus' healing and reconciling ministry has already met with opposition, especially from the religious authorities, whose attitude stands in contrast to the enthusiasm of the crowds. Now we shall see that hostility become more widespread as the ministry in Galilee enters its later stages. The issue that is emerging with ever-growing intensity concerns the kind of Messiah Jesus is proving—or not proving—to be. A series of episodes, starting with a question from John the Baptist (11:2-3), clarifies and justifies his distinctive messianic identity, and begins to address the failure of the bulk of his contemporaries ("this generation") to accept him.

Jesus and John the Baptist: Different Roles/Similar Response: 11:1-24

A typically Matthean link sentence (11:1) closes off the instruction to the Twelve and points again to the wider preaching activity of Jesus. The question from John (vv. 2-3) is at first sight surprising. We know from earlier in the gospel that John had recognized Jesus and pointed him out to the crowds as the "Coming One" (3:12). Why now this hesitation? The explanation seems to be that John, having heard in prison about "the deeds of the Messiah,"[1] is puzzled by the gap between the role of the Messiah as he had described it to the crowds and what he is now hearing about Jesus' actual behavior. John had pointed to a severe proclaimer of impending judgment (3:12). What he has heard about subsequently does not fit the picture. True, Jesus summons people to repentance in view of the kingdom (4:17). But he is as much engaged in healing the afflicted crowds (Matthew 8–9) as instructing them, and his interpretation of the Torah (Matthew 5–7) and his behavior in its regard make mercy and compassion the supreme criterion. This is not the Messiah John had been expecting or announcing.

Jesus does not give a direct answer, but simply points to his activity (v. 4): "Go and tell John what you hear [that is, his teaching] and what you see [his works of healing]." The list (v. 5) covers all the works of compassion reported in chapters 8–9.[2] It draws together a number of statements in the prophet Isaiah traditionally related to the blessings of the messianic age (Isa 29:18-19; 35:5-6; 61:1). Jesus' response, then, amounts to this: I may not be fulfilling the Messiah's role exactly as you conceived it. But is my activity really at odds with what the prophets foretold? Those who do not find in it a stumbling block (literally, "are not scandalized") are "blessed" in that they show that God's grace is already at work in their hearts preparing them for life in the kingdom (v. 6).

The messengers gone, Jesus speaks about John to the crowds (vv. 7-15). His praise, overall, is somewhat ambiguous. On the one hand John is held up as a true prophet: ascetic, fearless, wholly dedicated to his message. On the other hand he is respectfully but firmly put in the place assigned for him in the scheme of salvation. He may have proclaimed the onset of the kingdom (3:2), but he is not strictly part of it. His "greatness" becomes a foil for asserting the surpassing "greatness" of those who belong to the

---

[1] It is important to translate the Greek phrase *ta erga tou Christou* fairly literally (not as in the *NRSV:* "what the Messiah was doing") in order to pick up the inclusion with the "deeds" *(erga)* of Wisdom in v. 19.

[2] A recently published fragment from the Dead Sea Scrolls found at Qumran ("Messianic Apocalypse" [4Q521]) provides a remarkable contemporary parallel to these words of Jesus (stemming from "Q" [cf. Luke 7:22]); it too mentions raising of the dead among other miraculous activities listed in connection with the Lord's "Messiah." Text in F. Garcia Martinez, *The Dead Sea Scrolls Translated: The Qumran Texts in English* (2nd ed. Grand Rapids: Eerdmans, 1996) 394–95.

kingdom (11:11).[3] His role is that sketched out for returning Elijah (v. 13): the "messenger" the prophet Malachi (Mal 3:1) spoke of as destined to be sent ahead of the "Lord" (understood as the Messiah) to prepare the way before him (11:10).[4]

Nonetheless, neither John nor Jesus has met with a widely positive response in his ministry. Jesus goes on (11:16-19) to reflect upon the failure of "this generation" in this regard, using an image wonderfully illustrative of his capacity to seize a picture from life around him. We have to think of two separate groups of children sitting in the marketplace. One group, looking for diversion, tries to engage the other group in their games, but without success. So the first group complains: "We tried playing weddings (flute) and you wouldn't dance; we tried playing funerals (wailing) and you wouldn't mourn. You're not much use!" Just so, "this generation" has responded negatively both to the "mournful" (= funereal) ministry of John and the festive ("nuptial" [cf. 9:15]) ministry of Jesus. They rejected John as too severe, Jesus as too lax: "a glutton and a drunkard, a friend of tax collectors and sinners!" (v. 19a). The accusation, despite itself, aptly testifies to Jesus' ministry: the celebration of the compassionate mercy of God (9:10-13). The behavior of Jesus (his "deeds": cf. v. 2) simply shows him to be the personal presence of God's saving Wisdom on earth (v. 19b).

The severity of the "woes" upon the unrepentant cities of Galilee (11:20-24) comes like a shock of cold water thrown upon the narrative. Here the Messiah *does* seem to speak in the tones the Baptist announced! We are being prepared for a rejection that will be more widespread yet. The response of the Galilean cities—Chorazain, Bethsaida, Capernaum— foreshadows the "No" of the bulk of Israel to the message of its Messiah and explains the need for a reconstituted Israel inclusive of believers from

---

[3] Cf. W. D. Davies and Dale Allison, *A Critical and Exegetical Commentary on the Gospel According to Saint Matthew.* ICC. 3 vols. (Edinburgh: T&T Clark, 1988–97) 2:251.

[4] The original meaning of the statement in v. 12 about "violence" in regard to the "kingdom of heaven" (along with its quasi-parallel in Luke 16:16) seems to be irretrievably lost; for a review see Davies and Allison, *Matthew* 2:254–56. I think the Greek verb *biazetai* is best interpreted as a middle ("advances forcefully" [cf. *NIV*]) rather than as a passive ("suffers violence" [cf. *NRSV*]). The kingdom "advances forcefully" in the sense that it requires self-denial and discipline (the kind of virtues exemplified by John) to enter it (cf. Matt 7:13-14). The "violent take it by force" (v. 12b) in the sense that they are prepared to do violence to such things as family feeling in order to gain it. The passive interpretation falls down in regard to v. 12b because the verb *harpazein* means getting possession of something by force, not simply acting forcefully.

the nations.[5] Besides the threat of judgment, we should hear the anguish that rings through the prophetic tones of Jesus. It is the anguish of love frustrated, effort wasted on these cities and this people closest to his heart—the knowledge that "many will come from east and west and will eat with Abraham and Isaac and Jacob in the kingdom of heaven, while the heirs of the kingdom will be thrown out . . ." (Matt 8:11-12a).[6] The fact, too, that Jesus' ministry in Galilee will continue—notably in Capernaum (17:24)—suggests that, in line with prophetic tradition (cf. above all Jonah), Jesus is not so much pronouncing an unalterable eschatological fate as intensifying the call to repentance.[7]

A Moment of Intimacy and Invitation: the "Light Burden": 11:25-30

In stark contrast to the woes just pronounced, the gospel now gives us access to a moment of intimacy between Jesus and the Father where *successful* reception of his message is in view. He thanks the Father for having hidden "these things" from the wise and intelligent while revealing them to "little ones" (vv. 25-26), insists upon his own unique role as instrument of revelation and knowledge of God (v. 27), and finally invites "the burdened" to come to him for "rest" (vv. 29-30). For what it implies concerning the relationship between Father and Son the passage is exceptional in the synoptic tradition (cf. also Luke 10:21-22).[8] As in the scenes of the baptism and transfiguration, we glimpse for a moment the unique status of Jesus.

For all its attractiveness, the appearance of such a passage at this point in the gospel is polemical. The woes have illustrated a widespread incapacity or unwillingness on the part of the Galilean cities to see the "works" Jesus has performed among them as pointing to his messianic status and

---

[5] In the biblical tradition the cities of Tyre and Sidon were a byword for nearby examples of *pagan* arrogance. Jesus' oracle devastingly reverses the tradition by insisting that, had his miracles been worked in them, *they* would have repented, whereas the Jewish cities that did see them remained unmoved.

[6] The oracle here in Matthew corresponds to Jesus' weeping over Jerusalem in Luke 19:41.

[7] Cf. M. Eugene Boring, "The Gospel of Matthew" in Leander E. Keck, ed., *The New Interpreter's Bible*. Vol. 8 (Nashville: Abingdon, 1995) 273.

[8] The sequence was famously described by the late-19th-century German scholar Karl von Hase as a "bolt from the Johannine heaven"; see Davies and Allison, *Matthew* 2:282, n. 218.

the credibility of his summons to repentance. Now, in the face of this rejection (cf. the introductory "At that time . . ." [v. 25]), Jesus thanks the Father for the fact that what has been "hidden" from the wise and intelligent *has* been revealed to "little ones." Rejection has been more than matched by acceptance and understanding on the part of others not normally thought capable of it. The fact that *they* have responded implies revelation from God—because, lacking wit or opportunity for study, they have no other means of knowing.

Moreover, Jesus adds (v. 26), this was how things were meant to go. It was God's "good pleasure" that the crucial revelation for the messianic age, the "good news" of the kingdom, should be proclaimed, not to the powerful and clever, but to the poor and simple (cf. v. 5; 1 Cor 1:26-27). The misunderstanding and rejection Jesus is encountering are not simply an unfortunate outcome. This is part of a divine plan concerning the giving of revelation in connection with the kingdom.

In support of this, Jesus goes on (v. 27) to speak of the mutual "knowledge" existing between himself and the Father. Father and Son are locked in a mutual exchange of knowledge that, in the full Semitic sense of "knowing" another person, includes deep intimacy and approval (3:17; 12:18; 17:5). No other person—including those who rely upon research and skill in religious matters—can know God in the way Jesus does. The only way to attain such knowledge is through Jesus' imparting of it as he wills (v. 27d). All the teaching and healing activity in which Jesus has been engaged ("these things" [v. 25]) is ultimately a revelation on his part of God and God's compassionate saving will for humankind.[9] As Jesus will later explain to Peter (16:17), this is not knowledge attainable by human resources ("flesh and blood"), but only through revelation.

What Jesus claims here reinforces the privileged position of the "little ones" as regards capacity to know God. Who are the "little ones"? And who are the "wise and intelligent" that Jesus puts so very much in second place? "Little ones" seems to have been a cherished self-description of the Matthean community, while "wise and intelligent" would refer, in the first instance, to the scribes and Pharisees, who laid claim to superior wisdom based upon knowledge of Scripture and their own tradition. Over against them, the members of the Matthean community are the "little ones" who, though despised, have access through Jesus to true knowledge of God.

---

[9] Cf. C. Deutsch, "Wisdom in Matthew: Transformation of a Symbol," *NovT* 32 (1990) 13–47; see especially 37.

But we can hardly leave the statement simply in that distant past. Jesus' words are a timeless challenge to all pretension to theological and religious expertise that does not begin from awareness that, at best, it is only reflection upon what "little ones" have come to know about God. Theology, if it is to speak of God as Jesus reveals God to be, must stoop down and go through that narrow door.

Having presented himself in this way as the One who truly knows the Father and the Father's saving will, Jesus then issues an invitation (11:28-30). The authority of his appeal comes from his status as unique divine Son and is, again, polemical. "Come to me . . ." implies "and not to them"—"they" in this context being the religious authorities who through the rigorous interpretation of the Torah in accordance with their tradition impose heavy burdens upon people, burdens that (as Jesus later complains [23:4]) they are unwilling to lift. "All who are weary and burdened" would then be ordinary people, unlettered as regards interpretation of the Torah, who labor under such burdensome rulings. Clad with the high authority in regard to the Torah that pertains to him as God's Son and with his unique access to God's salvific will, Jesus invites them to come, instead, to *him:* to take *his* yoke upon them and learn from his instruction.[10] In this way they will find "rest."

The "rest" Jesus promises to the burdened is not simply respite in a general kind of way. The Greek word *anapausis* conjures up the refreshing break that travelers across a desert find in some oasis along the way. In the biblical tradition God's "resting" on the seventh day following the work of creation (Gen 2:2-3) and the idea of the Sabbath as a day for rest and union with God led to descriptions of the messianic age as a time of "rest."[11] The sense is not that of idleness and absence of activity but of arrival at the fullness of life in the kingdom, the enjoyment of an eternal Sabbath with God. Jesus is presenting himself, then, as the one who can safely lead burdened humanity to "rest" in this final sense.

But the relief is not something just for the future. Those who come to Jesus will experience him as "gentle and humble in heart" (v. 29) and will find his yoke "easy" and his burden "light" (v. 30). The reference seems to be to life as presently lived within the Torah-interpretation of Jesus. The

---

[10] "Yoke" refers literally to a wooden frame placed over the necks of two animals (usually oxen) drawing a cart or plough. It was traditional to speak metaphorically of the "yoke" of the Torah and this is certainly the reference here; cf. Davies and Allison, *Matthew* 2:289.

[11] "Rest" *(anapausis)* in this sense is prominent in the eschatology of the letter to the Hebrews: see especially 4:1-13.

gospel presents him as personally gentle and humble of heart, a Messiah who, far from lording it over others, has in every way sought to lift the burdens of those who flocked to him from near and far. But, having heard his Torah interpretation in the Great Sermon, can we really describe his yoke as "easy" and his burden as "light"? Is not the "surpassing" righteousness for which he calls (5:20) more demanding, and in this sense more "burdensome," than anything taught by the scribes and Pharisees?

There is no easy way around the apparent inconsistency between Jesus' Torah interpretation in the Sermon and the claim of "ease" and "lightness" he makes here.[12] It may be an area where resolution is not possible in theory but only in the personal life of individual believers. What must be insisted upon is the strong sense of Jesus' personal presence that radiates from the text: "Come to *me* . . ."; "*I* will give you rest"; "*my* yoke . . ."; "*my* burden. . . ." The quality of "ease" and the "lightness" cannot consist in a lesser level of virtue or ethical demand. It must have something to do with the sense that all fulfillment in practice is preceded and facilitated by an intense relationship with Jesus and a sense of being grasped by his love. His claim to be "gentle and humble of heart" is ultimately a claim to personal attractiveness and an invitation to enter into an exchange of love. Such love, which is ultimately an extension of the love of the Father (v. 27), is what can make even the most difficult requirements "easy" and "light." As we noted in regard to the Great Sermon, there is also the sense—though secondary to the consideration just made—that all Jesus' Torah rulings give priority to engagement of the heart and to the promotion of human relationships over purely ritual and external prescriptions. When the heart is engaged, when values are lived out within a sense of community that shares and seeks to promote them, then too perhaps an "ease" and a "lightness" become palpable.[13]

Once again, we cannot simply leave the invitation of Jesus back in the era of polemic between the Matthean community and the rival interpretation of the Synagogue scribal tradition. We are painfully aware of instances in which life in the Church has become "weary and burdensome" for many,

---

[12] For a survey of how interpreters have dealt with the problem in the Christian tradition see Ulrich Luz, *Matthew 8–20: A Commentary.* Translated by James E. Crouch. Hermeneia (Minneapolis: Fortress, 2001) 172–76.

[13] To be avoided is a contrast—frequent in the past—between a "heavy," burdensome and ritualistic Jewish law and the new (Christian) law brought by Jesus. In Judaism no less than Christianity a sense of union with God in the covenant relationship precedes all legal obligation. Christians should be aware of how Jews traditionally speak of "the joy of the Torah" (*simchat hattorah*).

when instead of lifting the burdens that are part of all human lives, religious allegiance and practice have actually increased them—which is why, in today's climate of freedom, so many have cast them off, and with them the belief and belonging that seemed to impose them. The Church cannot, of course, water down the ideals of Jesus or cease to place before people the "narrow path" to life (Matt 7:13-14; cf. 16:24-28). But the invitation we have been considering surely requires authorities constantly to review the edicts and structures in which those ideals find concrete historical expression, to see whether they are not—in the name of Christ, though in fact contrary to his will—imposing rather than lifting burdens.

Interpreting the Sabbath law according to mercy: plucking grain: 12:1-8; healing a man with a withered arm: 12:9-14.

Two controversy stories, both involving the Sabbath, illustrate the claim and invitation Jesus has just made to the burdened (11:28-30).[14] Once again they define the kind of Messiah Jesus is revealing himself to be by setting his interpretation of "the law and the prophets" over against the tradition of the Pharisees, which is exposed as inhumane. Jesus does not set aside the Sabbath, one of the defining institutions of Judaism. Enshrined in the commandments associated with the Covenant (Exod 20:8-11; 34:21) and modeled upon the "rest" of God on the seventh day of creation (Gen 2:2-3), the Sabbath was a day of rest from labor,[15] of enjoying the fruits of the earth with gratitude to God. Strict as the rule against working on the Sabbath was, Judaism did then, as it does now, allow for exceptions: in time of war, to save life, and so forth. As in all systems of religious law, there was debate concerning the range of exceptions. In both the controversies now before us we see Jesus entering that debate—challenging from his prophetic sense of "what God wants . . ." a too-constricting view derived from the Pharisaic tradition.

The Torah allowed people, especially the poor, to glean from the corners and edges of fields, provided they did not use implements or containers (Lev 18:9-10; Deut 23:24-25). The disciples, as Matthew makes clear (12:1), are not just casually helping themselves to some grain as they go along; they eat to assuage genuine hunger—possibly connected with the itinerant nature of their following of Jesus (8:19-20). When the Pharisees

---

[14] The introductory phrase, "At that time . . ." (12:1), ties the coming episode tightly to what has gone before.

[15] The Sabbath had a significant social dimension in that the rest extended to slaves and poor bonded laborers, as also beasts of burden.

accuse them of breaking the Sabbath (v. 2), Jesus defends them, appealing to two precedents in which a legal prohibition yields to a higher necessity and implying—not without high christological import—that such necessity applies here.

The first precedent concerns an incident recorded in 2 Sam 21:1-7. When David and his young companions, under pressure from Saul, were hungry they asked for and received the loaves of the bread of the Presence, which the Law reserved strictly for the priests (Lev 24:5-9).[16] Strictly speaking the incident did not involve breaking the Sabbath. But it does provide scriptural precedent in that it represents a case of human need (hunger) overriding a significant item of law. At a deeper level Jesus' appeal to the example of David implies a high messianic claim: If David could provide for his companions in this way, how much more entitled is the Messiah, Son of David, to allow *his* disciples so to act. Beyond mere human need, it is the presence of the Messiah and their association with him that gives the disciples the right to override the Sabbath ban.

The christological claim emerges with greater force in Jesus' second appeal to precedent (vv. 5-6). This does not concern an incident in biblical history but actual Temple practice as prescribed by the Torah. To fulfill the requirement for Sabbath offerings laid down in Num 28:9-10 the priests in the Temple had to infringe the Sabbath prohibition of labor. They are "guiltless" (that is, free from the guilt of breaking the Sabbath) because the Sabbath yields to something greater: God's presence in the Temple and the priestly duty of worship. The reason that the practice of the Temple clergy constitutes a precedent for the present situation is that "something greater than the Temple is here" (v. 6). If Sabbath requirements give way in the Temple, how much more must they give way in the presence of "something greater"! We should not fail to notice the christological claim being made here. The Temple was the dwelling place of God, the focus of God's reconciling action on behalf of Israel. Yet to be in the presence of Jesus is to be in the presence of "something greater than the Temple" in the sense that in him God is "with us" ("Emmanuel" [1:23]), working reconciliation more intensely and personally than God is or ever was in the Temple.[17] The

---

[16] The "bread of the Presence" refers to twelve loaves, baked on Fridays and set before the Holy of Holies on the Sabbath as a thank offering (Exod 25:23-30; 40:22-23; Num 4:1-8).

[17] The fact that "greater" is neuter in Greek leads Ulrich Luz (*Matthew 8–20,* 181–82) to reject the christological interpretation in favor of seeing *mercy* as that which is "greater." This does lead well into the Hos 6:6 quotation. However, a difficulty for Luz is that "mercy" is precisely what is *not* "here"—because the Pharisees have withdrawn from it. The only "thing" that "is" here and that could be greater than the Temple is Jesus.

community of disciples—and ultimately the community of the Church—live, like the priests, continually in the presence of "God with us." Their freedom in regard to the Sabbath flows from the fact that their Lord is also, as messianic Son of Man, "Lord of the Sabbath" (v. 8).

Before clinching the issue with this remark, Jesus (only in the Matthean account) makes the second of his appeals to Hos 6:6, saying to the Pharisees, "If you had known what this (text) means, 'What I want is mercy, not sacrifice' . . . you would not have condemned the guiltless" (v. 7; cf. Matt 9:13). They have gone astray because they have not interpreted the Torah according to the expressed will of God, an interpretation giving mercy priority over sacrifice—in this case understanding that the Sabbath ruling ought to yield in the face of human need, specifically hunger. Apart from its high christological import, the episode perfectly illustrates how the Matthean Jesus both interprets and practices the Torah by giving priority to human need. God did not institute the Sabbath to add burdens to an already overburdened humanity. The Sabbath is a moment for God's people to pause and take time out to come to know better the God whose delight is to be with them.

The second Sabbath controversy (12:9-14) occurs on the same (Sabbath) day (v. 1). Jesus enters a synagogue and is immediately confronted by what appears to be a setup. There is a man there with a withered hand and "they"—presumably still the Pharisees (cf. v. 14)—exploit the situation by asking whether it is lawful to cure on the Sabbath (v. 2).[18]

As we have noted, Sabbath law made provision for exceptions to deal with emergencies. Jesus points (v. 11) to the common practice ("Which of you . . . ?") in regard to an animal fallen into a pit, then (v. 12a) draws a conclusion based on the *a fortiori* logic so frequent in the gospel: if for a single sheep, how much more for a human being who is so much more valuable than a sheep! "Much more valuable" has the overtone "much more valuable in the sight of God" (cf. 6:30; 10:31). God, who wants "mercy" to be the criterion of interpretation of the Torah (9:13; 12:7; 23:23), because of the supreme value of human beings will surely want to see "good," rather than nothing, done to an afflicted human being on the Sabbath (v. 12b).

The healing itself (v. 13)—the restoration of the man's arm simply at a word from Jesus—is not the main point of the episode. It serves to con-

---

[18] There was no law against healing as such on the Sabbath. But if the healing involved some kind of physical activity, then that could come under the Sabbath restriction; cf. John 9:6-7, 14-16.

firm that Jesus' pronouncement about the Sabbath and his exercise of mercy are in conformity with the divine will. Since the man's condition was hardly life-threatening, Jesus could have avoided the problem by putting off dealing with it till the following day. But, presented with the situation, Jesus confronts the issue head on: for him the Sabbath is not primarily about avoiding things one should not do but for doing more intensely what God wants: the enhancement of human life through the exercise of mercy.

The Healing Messiah Is Fulfilling the Scriptures: 12:15-21

Jesus' challenge to the Pharisees in regard to the Sabbath leads them to conspire to "destroy him" (12:14)—a first indication that the interpretation of the Torah according to mercy that he promotes may entail the cost of his own life. In accordance with his established pattern Jesus does not further confront this hostility but "withdraws" *(anachōrein)* in the face of it to continue his healing ministry among the crowds (v. 15) in a less public way (v. 16). The "withdrawal" provokes from the Evangelist another "fulfillment prophecy" (vv. 17-21) in the shape of a lengthy quotation from the First Song of the Servant (Isa 42:1-4):

> 18 Here is my servant, whom I have chosen,
> my beloved, with whom my soul is well pleased.
> I will put my Spirit upon him,
> and he will proclaim justice to the Gentiles.
> 19 He will not wrangle or cry aloud,
> nor will anyone hear his voice in the streets.
> 20 He will not break a bruised reed
> or quench a smoldering wick
> until he brings justice to victory.
> 21 And in his name the Gentiles will hope.

The text brings together several features of Jesus' messianic ministry that have emerged so far. The opening lines (v. 18) echo the declaration of the Father's love and choice of him following his baptism and reception of the Spirit (3:17).[19] The central part (vv. 19-20) provides scriptural ratification, not just for the present "withdrawal" of the Son, but for the way in

---

[19] This suggests that "servant" (Greek *pais*) here could well have the meaning of "child/ son."

which he has been fulfilling his messianic role from the start: not through force and violence but as one who, personally "gentle and humble of heart" (11:29), has made the afflicted crowds ("the bruised reeds"; "the smoldering wicks") his principal object of concern. He "brings justice to victory" in the sense of restoring them to the fullness of life in the kingdom that is their right and destiny in the saving plan of God (11:5-6).[20]

The double reference in the text to "the Gentiles" (v. 18d; v. 21) is at first sight surprising, granted the restriction of the Messiah's ministry to Israel (10:5). But the references foreshadow a "withdrawal" on a much larger scale to come. Just as Jesus withdraws here in the face of hostility from the local Jewish authorities in Galilee, so later in Jerusalem he will "withdraw" in the sense of submitting to, rather than confronting, the authorities who will arrest him, condemn him, and hand him over for execution. That "withdrawal" will not mean defeat, but rather the enactment of a divinely scripted messianic role to the end. As risen Lord and through the ministry of the Church (28:19-20) Jesus will become not simply Messiah of Israel but the Messiah in whose "name" (= saving power) the Gentiles too "will hope" (12:21). In all these ways the quotation from Isaiah contributes to the definition of Jesus' messianic identity now taking shape.

The Two "Kingdoms":
Defense, Attack, and a Call for Decision: 12:22-50

At this point we enter upon a long polemical section of the gospel in which Jesus first defends his activity against accusations that it is the work of Satan ("Beelzebul"), then goes over to the offensive against his adversaries (12:22-37), rejects their request for a sign of his messianic status (12:38-45) and finally, on a positive note, indicates the "true family" that is coming to be in the shape of his band of disciples. Behind the personal conflict between Jesus and his adversaries stands the conflict of "kingdoms": the struggle between the rule of Satan that holds the world in a state of alienation from God and the rule of God, which is breaking that grip through the presence and power of Jesus. This conflict has been running through the narrative from the start. Now it is much more out in the open, confronting Jesus' hearers with a choice: which side are you on?

---

[20] The Greek word *krisis* is more normally translated "judgment." But this does not seem appropriate here—especially in view of the later appearance of *krisis,* along with "mercy" and "faith," in the triad Jesus dubs the "weightier matters of the Torah" (23:23).

(v. 30). Jesus does not explicitly identify his adversaries as instruments of Satan, but the clear implication is that by putting the worse possible construction on his activity (attributing it to the "ruler of demons") they are siding with Satan and exposing themselves to condemnation at the great judgment when his rule will end once and for all.

The tirades uttered by Jesus here bear the imprint of the Matthean community's struggle with the leaders of the Synagogue following the fall of Jerusalem, when Israel's "No" to the crucified Messiah became definitive. It is hard to know how much to attribute to controversies of Jesus' own lifetime and how much to see as reflecting hostilities of this later period. Even if such discernment could be made, the interpretive problem is hardly solved since conflict at either stage is for the modern reader a historical relic, lamentable in its consequences for Jewish-Christian relations.

First of all, we do have to take the conflict of "kingdoms" seriously. In particular we should ask what might correspond in our day to the grip of Satan (the demonic) in human affairs, which the presence of Jesus continues to challenge and unmask. It is all too easy—and ethically reprehensible— simply to leave it there in the past and say, "These were problems Jesus and the later Matthean community had with representatives of Judaism." The conflict of the kingdoms is a timeless reality calling for discernment. Jesus' adversaries see what the crowds see—his healing activity—but attribute it not to its true source (the Spirit and the onset of the kingdom [v. 28]) but to Satan. The reason they commit this blasphemy[21] is a problem in their "heart" (v. 34b); their hearts are like bad trees that can only produce "rotten fruit" (v. 33). The struggle for allegiance to one or other of the "kingdoms" begins and ends in the heart (cf. the rulings in 5:21-47). If the heart—the essential moral disposition of a person—is not right, no amount of observation and rational analysis can prevent one from aiding the opposing kingdom (vv. 34-37).

Second, the adversaries want to see a sign (vv. 38-42). Unlike the crowds, who rightly appreciate Jesus' activity (v. 23), they have their own ideas about messianic credentials and want Jesus to meet them. In line with a tendency seen across the New Testament (Matt 16:1-2a; Mark 8:11-13;

---

[21] The thought of an "unforgivable sin" has long burdened Christian consciences. We should not think of a particularly heinous *kind* of sin but of a pervasive disposition blocking salvation. "Since the Holy Spirit is the source of repentance and forgiveness, to blaspheme against the Holy Spirit and to reject his clear operations within one's range of experience is to close oneself off from all hope of salvation" (John P. Meier, *Matthew.* New Testament Message 5 [Wilmington: Michael Glazier, 1980] 135).

Luke 11:29; 12:54-56; John 6:30; cf. 4:48; 1 Cor 1:22a), he categorically refuses to do so. It is not for human beings to lay down conditions for God and God's appointed agents to fulfill. God *gives* signs that those who are well disposed will recognize, even if this "evil and adulterous generation" (v. 39) does not. The "only sign" that will be given to "this generation" is the "sign of Jonah" (v. 39): that is, Jesus' resurrection from the dead as the definitive "sign" given to Israel. His added remarks (vv. 41-42) about the people of Nineveh and the "Queen of the South" (Queen of Sheba) develop this in the sense that both refer to non-Israelites who responded positively to prophetic preaching (Jonah) and wisdom (Solomon). They foreshadow later developments when the bulk of Israel will not accept God's raising the crucified Messiah from the dead and instead give credence to other explanations (cf. 28:11-15), whereas numerous Gentiles will respond to the Gospel (28:19-20; cf. 8:11-12).[22] Instead of applying texts such as this to Jewish people today, responsible Christian interpreters will do well to ask themselves to what extent they themselves subtly require signs from God and fail to allow faith in the resurrection to cast its light over what can be so often the darkness and despondency of human life.

The sequence ends on a positive note (12:46-50). Made aware that members of his family ("his mother and brothers") are outside and wish to speak with him, Jesus takes the opportunity to point to his disciples as the new "family" he has acquired.[23] The indication is inclusive, an invitation like the "Come to me . . ." in 11:28-30. Old Israel may be fragmenting and dividing, but anyone prepared to do the will of the Father in heaven, practicing righteousness in the sense of "what God wants" (Hos 6:6; Matt 9:13; 12:7), belongs to a renewed Israel that here and now enjoys a familial relationship with God.[24]

---

[22] The mysterious pericope about the return of the evil spirit (12:43-45) likewise seems to be, at the Matthean level, a reflection upon the experience of Israel: Jesus attempted to "clean out" the rule of Satan from its house but, following the rejection of the Gospel, the last state has become worse than the first.

[23] In the lists of family members appearing here only "father" is missing: Jesus—and believers in union with him—have only "one Father," God; cf. 23:8-9.

[24] Daniel J. Harrington, *The Gospel of Matthew.* SP 1 (Collegeville: Liturgical Press, 1991) 193, shrewdly observes that the fact that the disciples—and ultimately the Church—are described in terms of "family" does not promise that all will be sweetness and light: even the best of families have their quarrels.

Jesus Speaks in Parables: 13:1-52

We come now to the third discourse in Matthew's gospel. It is known as the "Parables Discourse" because it chiefly consists of seven parables, accompanied in three cases by allegorical interpretations.[1] Along with the parables there are two intermediate blocks (vv. 10-17; vv. 34-35), plus a concluding reflection (vv. 51-52). At first sight this non-parabolic material seems to intrude upon and interrupt the parables. In fact, it provides the clue to the appearance of a discourse consisting mainly of parables at this stage in the gospel. It sets the parables within the wider context of the narrative, which, as we have seen, is dealing with the hostility and rejection Jesus' distinctive messianic ministry has provoked. Increasingly the mission to Israel as a whole is failing and the band of disciples is emerging as the nucleus of a reconstituted people of God. The chief burden of the discourse is to explain this situation in respect to human response and to locate it within the wider design of God, indicated—as always—in Scripture.

Introduction: Parable, Allegory, and Structure

Matthew follows Mark (4:2-34) in exploiting the wide sense that "parable" has in the biblical tradition. This stems from its origins in the Hebrew word *mashal,* which can refer not only to an illustrative story or image but also to a puzzle, riddle, or enigma. Because of this background, "parable" has a variety of uses and effects. As an illustrative story or image it is a vehicle of communication and learning, as a puzzle or riddle it can just as well tease, mystify, and alienate. That Jesus' preaching was replete with

---

[1] Though it is easily missed, the final parable, the Dragnet (13:47-48), has its interpretation, not separated, as in the case of the Sower and the Weeds, but tacked on to its end (vv. 49-50).

images and parables is certain. And that he used parables chiefly as instruments of communication is also likely. This does not mean, however, that he did not exploit the capacity of parabolic language to shock and disarm, to open up new worlds of meaning, especially in connection with the kingdom of God, the unforeseen nature of which was so central to his message. While many found his use of parables illuminating, there were doubtless others whom they mystified and disturbed.

The early believers who received Jesus' parables in the tradition seem to have adapted them in two ways. On the one hand they exploited the "riddle" aspect, relating it in particular to the great trauma of Israel's rejection of Jesus as Messiah. The fact that Jesus spoke in ‘parables to his contemporaries and that many experienced them as riddles and turned away foreshadowed their own experience of rejection, allowing it to be seen as part of a mysterious divine plan. Second, they took the simple stories and images of Jesus, many of them tied too closely to Palestinian agricultural society to be intelligible in the urban milieu of early Christianity, and turned them into allegories, rendering them more directly applicable in that new context.

The distinction between parable and allegory that Adolf Jülicher introduced in the late nineteenth century remains clarifying—even if recent interpretation tends to see it as too sharply drawn.[2] A parable is an extended image in narrative form making a single point. Determining that precise point is rarely a matter of agreement, since it is of the very nature of parables to be open to multiple interpretations. However, in a parable proper one is chiefly looking for a single sharp impact—like the devastating blow delivered to David in the prophet Nathan's accusatory parable in 2 Sam 12:1-7. An allegory, on the contrary, seeking to warn, exhort, or explain, relates a whole range of details in a story or extended image to different aspects of a particular situation.

While it is not impossible that Jesus used allegory, the allegories attached to his parables in the gospel tradition reflect the situation of the early Church and seem to stem from that period. Sometimes, as twice in this chapter, they stand apart from the parables which they purport to explain; sometimes, as is especially the case with parables appearing later in Matthew's gospel (the Murderous Tenants [21:33-34]; the Spurned Invitation to the Wedding [22:1-14]; the Ten Bridesmaids [25:1-13]), the parables appear only in a heavily allegorized form, with the result that it becomes difficult to discern and recover the parable as originally told by Jesus. (A sure sign of allegory is the appearance of details difficult to relate

---

[2] Cf. M. Eugene Boring, "The Gospel of Matthew," in Leander E. Keck, ed., *The New Interpreter's Bible*. Vol. 8 (Nashville: Abingdon, 1995) 298–300.

to the situation presupposed in the main story, rendering it unrealistic [e.g., the coda about the guest without a wedding garment in Matt 22:1-14].) However, the fact that, in this discourse at least, the interpretations added to the two main parables (the Sower and the Weeds) do not follow immediately upon the stories they interpret allows us to hear each of the stories in the first instance on its own terms. The original story takes us close to the "voice" of Jesus. It is good to let its own meaning stand for a while before the interpretation takes over.

Many of Jesus' parables create their effect by telling a story that ends in a surprising or shocking way. The shock at the end overthrows conventional expectation, making space for fresh insight and revelation. The parables in Matthew 13 are no exception. All play upon a difference or disparity between what is the case in the present and what will be the case later on. The shock or surprise comes in the size of the disparity. Jesus takes situations familiar to his audience from everyday life—from agriculture, from fishing, and so forth—but the outcome at the end of the story is often fantastic, way beyond expectation. In this way the parable communicates a sense of the overwhelming power of the kingdom despite its present humble beginnings and widespread rebuff from the crowds, especially the religious authorities.

For all the interest of the individual parables, we do have to keep in mind the wider purpose to which they are subordinate in this discourse. This is not so much exhortation—though that element is present to some extent—as *explanation*: to account theologically for the phenomenon of unbelief and to set it within two parameters. The first parameter is that of Scripture, which indicates that all has been foreseen and included within the plan of God. The second is the final judgment, when the coexistence of good and evil will be definitively sorted out and God's rule established once and for all.

For many readers the stress on judgment in some of the allegorical interpretations and, in particular, the language (taken from apocalyptic Judaism) in which it is described will cast a shadow over what is otherwise attractive material. As I hope to show, judgment is there not so much to warn and menace believers as to assure them that evil will not go undealt with forever. It is part, then, of the "explanation."

With Mark 4 as template, Matthew's discourse unfolds in three main sections, each displaying a triple pattern of parable, reflection, and interpretation:[3]

---

[3] Cf. W. D. Davies and Dale Allison, *A Critical and Exegetical Commentary on the Gospel According to Saint Matthew.* ICC. 3 vols. (Edinburgh: T&T Clark, 1988–97) 2:371;

	Parable (Sower): vv. 1-9
13:1-23:	Reflection on parable usage (Scripture): vv. 10-17
	Interpretation of the parable of the Sower: vv. 18-23

	Three Parables (Weeds; Mustard Seed; Yeast): vv. 24-33
13:24-43	Reflection on parable usage (Scripture): vv. 34-35
	Interpretation of the parable of the Weeds: vv. 36-43

	Three Parables (Hidden Treasure; Pearl; Dragnet): vv. 44-48
13:44-52	Interpretation of the parable of the Dragnet: vv. 49-50
	Reflection: vv. 51-52.

The formal arrangement (varied only by a reversal of order in the third section) makes clear that the *fact* that Jesus speaks in parables and his reason for so doing is more important for Matthew than the content of the parables themselves.

The Parable of the Sower and Its Interpretation: 13:1-9, 18-23

Preceding the first parable is a long introduction (vv. 1-3a) setting the scene for the discourse. The press of the crowd gathered by the sea compels Jesus to get into a boat, from which, having sat down, he begins to teach.[4] While at one level a practical move, the position a little offshore in a boat foreshadows the movement away from the mass of Israel to the community of disciples, who are now becoming the primary focus of attention.[5]

As is typical in the parables told by Jesus, the Sower parable moves directly from ordinary, everyday life. In the Palestine of his day the sower scattered the seed around in fairly casual fashion. By no means all the seed landed in good soil. Quite a bit could land in the three situations—on a path, on rocky ground, among thorns—where it suffered the fate described. Nonetheless, the hearers are no doubt arrested and struck by the waste of the three losses entailed. The surprise comes in the three outcomes for

---

Boring, "Matthew," 301. Many interpreters find a clear point of division in v. 36, where Jesus moves away from the crowds to concentrate solely upon his disciples. Yet, as the story goes on, we find him still teaching (13:54) and healing (14:14, 35-36; 15:29-31) the crowds. The turning away here may not be tied too closely to the present context, but be more widely symbolic of his and the later community's response to Israel's rejection of him as Messiah.

[4] Sitting down is the posture of a teacher; cf. 5:1.

[5] Cf. Boring, "Matthew," 301.

the seed that falls upon good soil: hundredfold is a fantastic yield; even thirtyfold seems way over the top.

Jesus "sows" the word of the kingdom in a way that is similarly casual and "wild." In a great many hearts the word suffers the fate of the seed in the three losses. But when it finds a receptive heart and truly strikes home, the way is set for the arrival of the kingdom in the extraordinary fullness described. The parable clearly implies that for Jesus the primary address of the kingdom is to the human heart; that is where the struggle to obtain ascendancy over the opposing rule of Satan begins, even if it must go out from there to transform communities and social situations. The onset of the kingdom is conditioned, then, by the readiness of human beings to receive it; it presupposes the repentance (change of heart) called for as part of its proclamation (4:17). The parable addresses and accounts for the mixed response Jesus' preaching of the kingdom is receiving. It meets head on the discouragement the disciples could feel in view of the fact that in so many cases his effort seems wasted or without lasting effect. Like the sower, Jesus continues to throw the word about widely because of his confidence that when and where the "seed" does strike home, the "harvest" for the kingdom is so overwhelmingly great as to more than compensate for all the earlier losses.

The parable can stand, then, by itself as a statement of hope, of confidence in the liberality and power of God. What the allegorical interpretation (vv. 18-23) offers (it is most convenient to consider it now) is a deeper exploration of the reasons for the lack of response in each of the three losses. Its case by case commentary reflects the situation of the post-Easter Church when it was not simply *initial* response to the word that was at stake but appropriating it into one's pattern of life and, above all, persevering in the face of the challenges outlined. The parable is now being placed at the service of a spirituality for the long haul, where—typically for Matthew—hearing must be accompanied by "understanding" (v. 19; v. 23) and "bearing fruit," that is, action (v. 23; cf. 7:21-27).[6]

As will be clear, the focus of the interpretation is more on the three failures than on the successes. It does not communicate the sense of hope that radiates from the parable as Jesus told it. But its exploration of the three losses usefully unmasks principal threats to Christian maturity: lack of understanding of the faith, rendering it vulnerable to being swept away by early challenge; pressures that arise when adherence to it becomes

---

[6] The "doing" (Greek *poiei*) that Matthew, typically, adds to "bearing fruit" is obscured in most translations.

costly; rival calls upon the heart (cares of the world; lure of wealth) that choke original commitment. In such ways the interpretation complements and expands the riches of the original parable.

Why Jesus Speaks in Parables: 13:10-17

At this point the principal focus of the discourse—the issue of un-belief—breaks into the sequence of parables in the shape of a reflection on Jesus' reason for speaking in parables. Presupposed from here on is a clear distinction between the disciples and the crowds at large. To the disciples "it has been given"—the passive signals the action of God—"to know the mysteries of the kingdom of heaven" (v. 11), that is, the mysterious way, not anticipated in conventional expectation, in which God's rule is coming to effect in the world. Discipleship and understanding go hand in hand.[7] Without the commitment that responding to Jesus' call involves, under-standing will be lacking, and hence ability to grasp the "mysteries of the kingdom."[8] Jesus speaks in parables *in response* to unbelief (v. 13).[9] As ex-plained above, the sequence is exploiting here the enigmatic aspect of "parable" (going back to the Hebrew *mashal*). The sense is, "The reason that what I say to them *comes across* to them as 'parables' (= 'riddles') is because of their lack of understanding"—a lack Matthew finds foreseen by Scripture in a prophecy from Isaiah, which he quotes in full (Isa 6:9-10).[10]

Typically, Matthew continues the quotation right down to its wistful ending: "(so that they might) . . . turn and I would heal them" (v. 15). "Turn" here has its biblical sense of "conversion." The crowds are not so much condemned as pitied. In refusing to hear the good news with repen-tant hearts they isolate themselves from what above all Jesus longs to bring them: namely, healing. The reflection concludes on a positive note that recalls, as at the beginning (v. 11), the contrasting "blessedness" of the dis-ciples. Because they can really see with their eyes and hear with their ears (cf. v. 13), they "see" the messianic fulfillment for which many prophets and righteous ones could only hope and long.

---

[7] Cf. Boring, "Matthew," 304–305.

[8] The mysterious statement in v. 12 reinforces this point: without the true gift of under-standing, any insight one may gain is ultimately rendered futile.

[9] Matthew uses the Greek causal conjunction *hoti* rather than *hina,* as in Mark, to avoid the sense that the parables were spoken to *create* unbelief.

[10] The widespread appearance of this text across the New Testament (besides the synoptic parallels in Mark 4:12; Luke 8:10, cf. John 12:39-40; Acts 28:26-27) shows how helpful early believers found it in coming to terms with Israel's failure in regard to the Gospel.

The Parable of the Weeds and Its Interpretation:
13:24-30, 36-43

The next "agricultural" parable, the Weeds among the wheat, has received a great variety of applications in Christian history.[11] Taken by itself it can plausibly be set within the context of Jesus' preaching as an explanation, once again, of what is happening in regard to the kingdom. Like the Sower, but from a different perspective, it explains why, though the kingdom is being preached and "sown" in many hearts, evil and rejection remain. Why is the kingdom, if it really is dawning as Jesus proclaims, not making more progress? Why is its growth accompanied by continuing, indeed intensifying evil? Why—and this would seem to be the central point—does God not go in once and for all, root out the evil and so make final the triumph of the kingdom? The parable telling of weeds sown among good seed,[12] though somewhat unreal in several respects,[13] deals with both aspects effectively. The kingdom is not free simply to establish itself on receptive or even neutral ground; a powerful opposition is at work, holding human hearts against it, which explains the slowness of its growth. The reason God does not immediately intervene is that the struggle within the human heart is so subtle, so delicate, that the attempt to root out the evil may also destroy the good. Like the farmer in the parable, God is patient, prepared to tolerate evil along with the good, until the time for the harvest has come. But that time will come and the good (the kingdom) will prevail.

As in the case of the Sower, the parable retains its own independent meaning. Unlike religious zealots down the ages,[14] God is not inclined to root out evil so ruthlessly that good is also suppressed and much greater evil caused. God knows that good and evil in human hearts often stem from the same prior disposition;[15] go in and root out the one and the capacity for the other may also be ruined. Better to give grace time to work its victory

---

[11] Full survey in Ulrich Luz, *Matthew 8–20: A Commentary.* Translated by James E. Crouch. Hermeneia (Minneapolis: Fortress, 2001) 270–74.

[12] The weed would seem to be darnel, a poisonous plant that affects crops in Palestine. In the early stages of growth the darnel shoots look very like the young shoots of wheat. By the time both plants have grown sufficiently to be distinguished, the roots are so entwined as to make tearing out the darnel destructive of the wheat; cf. John P. Meier, *Matthew.* New Testament Message 5 (Wilmington: Michael Glazier, 1980) 147.

[13] Boring, "Matthew," 308 n. 295, lists eight aspects of "unreality"—some a little overdrawn.

[14] One thinks above all of the Inquisition.

[15] An irascible person may have a passion for justice; a lazy person can be a good listener.

subtly. Then what has been wounded and hindered by evil will not be crushed, but rescued and transformed for life.

The allegorical interpretation that follows later (vv. 36-43) in the shape of a seven-point identification of details in the parable rather nails down its application. It also pushes the focus strongly in the direction of judgment. Understood in this way the parable has often been applied to the prevalence of both good and evil in the Church, and seen as giving a divine sanction for tolerance—or at least for leaving dealing with evil and evildoers to the end-time judgment of God. This is legitimate and it is, of course, true that Matthew elsewhere does portray the Church as a mixed body, containing evil as well as good. But we should note that the primary identification of the "field" in the parable is "the world" rather than the Church (v. 38a). Moreover, the good seed is identified with "the children of the kingdom" and the bad with "the children of the evil one" (v. 38b), a pattern of identification more readily applicable to the world as a whole, of which the Church is part, rather than to the Church taken by itself. In the first instance, then, the interpretation, in rather close continuity with the original parable, seems to want to address and account for the situation whereby "the children of the kingdom" (= "the community of the kingdom," "the Church") continue to suffer at the hands of evildoers. The judgment represented by the "the harvest at the end of the age" and described in such vivid terms is more a consolation for the community than a warning or threat. Persecution and oppression will not last forever; evildoers will eventually suffer the fate their behavior deserves.

This interpretation, while at one level consoling, is also dangerous in the sense that it could suggest a rigid dualism in which evil is confined solely to outsiders while "within"—within the community of the Church— all is light and virtue. We are, of course, only too conscious that such is not the case, and so the inference must be restrained. At the same time it may be equally wrong to go to the other extreme and insist that the parable thus allegorized chiefly targets a situation in the Matthean community where early fervor had given way to laxity and serious deviance—in which case the stress on judgment would fall upon members of the community, a severe warning to repent before it is too late.

It seems to me best to see a continuity between the original parable and the allegory in the sense that both are primarily *explaining* and dealing with the mixture of good and evil, in both world and Church, and relating this to a particular vision of God and what may be hoped for in view of that vision. At a time when the Church has been made so painfully conscious of evil in its midst, the parable in this sense attains a fresh relevance. Yes, the evil must be addressed and, yes, we must all strive to become "wheat" rather than "weeds," but the existence of evil, even in the holiest places, is not a cause for disillusionment and the abandoning of hope. The kingdom is not here yet—human evil delays its coming. But dealing with that evil requires patience and hope—and close adherence to the patience of God.

The Parables of the Mustard Seed (13:30-32) and the Yeast (13:33)

These two parables illustrate Jesus' capacity to communicate much in brief, telling images. Both have to do with the kingdom and both operate on a distinction between the present state of affairs and the future. The point in each case lies in the contrast between the tiny beginnings and the large scale of the end result. The mustard seed is the smallest of seeds but, when sown, within a year (it is an annual) it grows into a shrub so large that in some cases it could almost be considered a tree. The picture seems to become somewhat exaggerated with the final detail about the birds making nests in its branches. They could perch there for a time, but the branches are hardly strong enough to sustain secure nests.[16] This is where the outcome becomes somewhat unreal and hence arresting. The parable, again, *explains* the present situation. The kingdom may have these tiny—and to many unimpressive—beginnings. But this does not mean that before long it will not have sprouted up into something very much greater.[17]

The same contrast between humble beginnings and extraordinary outcome is central to the parable of the Yeast (v. 33). It has been calculated that the "three measures," when leavened and baked, would feed a hundred people.[18] So once again, to capture the imagination, the parable recounts a fantastic outcome. But the point lies not simply in the contrast between beginning and end but in the yeast's power. Going about its work silently and unobtrusively,[19] it produces a result quite out of proportion to its size. The image addresses the way Jesus has been going about his messianic ministry: not as the warrior Messiah sweeping all before him, but as "meek

[16] Matthew and Luke (13:19) draw here upon the "Q" tradition. The Markan parallel (4:32) avoids the unreality by having the birds making nests "in its shade."

[17] Matthew may in fact understand the "birds of the air" as the nations of the world who will in due course hear and respond to the proclamation of the Gospel (28:19-20).

[18] Cf. Davies and Allison, *Matthew* 2:423, citing Joachim Jeremias.

[19] The Greek word *enkryptein,* usually translated here as "mix" (cf. *NRSV*) has the basic sense of "hide in," "conceal."

and humble of heart" (11:29) and fulfilling the role of the Servant, who does not "wrangle or cry aloud," and does not "break a bruised reed or quench a smoldering wick" (Matt 12:19-20).[20] Jesus' "withdrawn" ministry (12:15; cf. 14:13) may not impress those cherishing more dramatic messianic hopes, but, like the yeast, it is quietly bringing about the triumph of the kingdom.

Reflection (13:34-35) and Three More Parables: the Discovered Treasure (13:44); the Pearl (13:45-46); the Dragnet (13:47-50)

The note of "hiddenness" continues into the reflection (vv. 34-35) that follows, featuring the eighth of Matthew's "fulfillment" quotations. The fact that Jesus speaks to the crowds in parables—in the puzzling rather than clarificatory sense explained above—has been foreseen in Scripture, where the "prophet" (David) proclaimed: "I will open my mouth to speak in parables; I will proclaim what has been hidden from the foundation of the world" (Ps 78:2).[21]

The sequence of parables then resumes with two of the shortest and, in many ways, most attractive examples of the form. The close parallel between the two means that we can view them side by side and detect the pattern common to both. Each depicts a situation in which a person finds something he or she would dearly love to possess. In the case of the man— probably a poor day-laborer—who comes across a long-forgotten treasure in a field (13:44), here is a windfall beyond wildest imagining.[22] The merchant (13:44-46), on the other hand, has perhaps been looking all his professional life for "the perfect pearl"; now he recognizes that this is the one! The common point, however, is that neither the laborer nor the merchant can gain immediate possession of what each so eagerly desires. There is a "gap" between finding/seeing and possessing. But the mere sight of what each so dearly longs to possess relativizes the value of all else, giving each one the freedom to "sell all" (v. 44, v. 46). Having sold all, they at last have

---

[20] Cf. Boring, "Matthew," 309.

[21] The book of Psalms is included among the "prophets" on the basis of its attribution to David, himself traditionally regarded as a prophet.

[22] In a world before financial institutions such as banks, the only way to keep large sums of money or valuables secure was to conceal them. Unforeseen death or the ravages of war could result in such "treasures" remaining undisturbed for ages.

the wherewithal to gain possession of the one thing they really desire. We can set out the common pattern thus:

finds (joy, but not possession) — (freedom) sells all — buys (possession)

Both parables operate on the "present/future" tension running through so many parables of the kingdom. The kingdom is essentially future, not something one can "possess" right now. But people who have really caught a glimpse of it from the preaching of Jesus know the "treasure" upon which they have lighted. At present he cannot deliver it to them or place them fully within it. But the glimpse of it they already have gives them the freedom to "sell all," in order—one day—to gain it.

The two parables are, then, descriptive rather than prescriptive. They describe the freedom and joy of people who have caught a glimpse of the kingdom.[23] The two brief stories capture the essence of Christian spirituality. Christian life involves detachment: freedom from absorption in the attractions, pleasures, and concerns of this world—not because these are bad in themselves but because believers have been caught by a vision of God's love and God's future that simply relativizes all these things and puts them in their place. They may not yet possess the treasure, but its hope and prospect is already working transformation.

The parable of the Dragnet (13:47-50)[24] in itself —that is, as it was probably told by Jesus (vv. 47-48), less the interpretation about the "end of time" (vv. 49-50)—aptly holds together, within the same "present/future" tension, two further truths about the kingdom. (1) God's grace is a great "net" thrown over all, good and bad alike; you don't have to be good to be grasped by the kingdom and come within its scope. (2) Once one is within, however, conversion is required: those who do not over time respond positively to God's generosity will find themselves cast out, as fishermen throw away bad fish. Like the parable of the Weeds, the Dragnet *explains* the presence of both good and bad in the kingdom, but goes on to assert that this situation will not stand forever.

The attached interpretation concerning "the end of time" (vv. 49-50), like that given to the Weeds parable (vv. 36-43) and echoing much of its

---

[23] One thinks here particularly of St. Francis of Assisi. His commitment to radical poverty was not a hard moral imposition, but something that flowed naturally from a personal "glimpse," in the highest degree, of the "treasure" of God's love.

[24] The Greek word denotes a large net that was either dragged through the water between two boats or drawn to land after being dropped in the sea; cf. Davies and Allison, *Matthew* 2:440-41.

language, focuses on the negative and plays up the aspect of judgment. Once again it would be a pity to allow this note of menace, heavily imbued with Jewish apocalyptic eschatology, to entirely "swamp" the original parable. While a warning against laxity *within* the community may be included, Matthew's primary intent is probably explanation and reassurance: evil will not always prevail, but will be dealt with definitively in God's good time—when (a final positive note) "the righteous will shine like the sun in the kingdom of their Father" (v. 43a).

Concluding Reflection: 13:51-52

The discourse concludes with Jesus asking the disciples whether they have "understood all this" (v. 51). Their positive response further sets them apart from the crowds, who have heard the parables but without understanding (13:13, 19; cf. v. 23). The ideal is to become "scribe(s) discipled for the kingdom of heaven," an intriguing description, further elaborated (v. 52) with an image—almost an eighth parable—concerning a wise master of a household. Such a master has his "treasure" store well stocked and knows when to bring out what is new and what is old. The mention of "new" before "old" is striking, but not unexpected. The "discipled scribe" knows how to remint the scriptural tradition and the expectations flowing from it with images adapted to the surprising nature of the kingdom. This is what Jesus has been doing; this is the teaching task the disciple-scribes will take up in his name (28:20a).

Jesus' Ministry under Challenge:
13:53–16:12

Prophets Rejected:
Jesus, 13:53-58; John the Baptist, 14:1-12

Following the long Parables Discourse Jesus continues to preach to the crowds and heal them, but the note of conflict and rejection intensifies. Particularly poignant is a visit to his home town (Nazareth).[1] The towns-folk are amazed at the "wisdom" displayed by this one of their own and by his "works of power" (v. 54). They twice ask the right question: "From what source does he get all this . . ." (v. 54; v. 56). But hometown famili-arity with himself and his family hijacks any chance of following the ques-tion through to the right answer: that he is the Messiah, Son of God. For them he is simply "the carpenter's son," whose family members they can list (v. 55).[2] Prejudice vitiates their coming to the level of faith required for a full experience of his healing power. Nazareth fulfills the adage about prophets lacking honor in their own town (v. 57).

Jesus does not feature directly in the story of Herod's execution of John the Baptist (14:1-12). But Herod's opening speculation about him (vv. 1-2) is full of menace. A number of malign and weak characters bring about John's death, but behind all is his prophetic testimony against Herod for marrying in contravention of the Torah.[3] Herod not only broke the letter of the Torah but also, because of the injury caused to his brother, infringed its concern for justice and mercy. In his own way, then, John upholds the Torah as interpreted by Jesus. The price he pays for his prophetic witness foreshadows another death to come. We note that the disciples who bury John ensure that Jesus learns all about it (v. 12).

---

[1]The town is not named, but the conclusion of the infancy story (2:23) ensures that Nazareth is in view.

[2]On the question of Jesus' "brothers and sisters" see on 1:25 above (p. 25 n. 14).

[3]The problem is marriage within forbidden degrees of relationship (cf. Lev 18:16; 20:21).

Jesus Heals and Feeds the Multitudes: 14:13-21

As so often in Matthew's gospel, Jesus "withdraws" *(anachōrein)* in the face of threat from hostile authorities. After a moment of respite by himself (v. 13), compassion at the sight of the crowds compels him to resume his ministry of healing.[4] As evening comes on, his disciples (the Twelve) sensibly advise him to send the crowds away from the deserted place to buy themselves food for the evening (v. 15).

Jesus reacts to the word "buy." He will not send people away to "buy" anything—nor should his disciples: "There is no need for them to go; give them something to eat yourselves" (v. 16). When the astonished disciples point out that they barely have enough for themselves (five loaves and two fish), Jesus *freely* provides more than enough food for the whole multitude through the miracle of the multiplication. The incident looks back to biblical traditions telling of miraculous provision of food: the manna on which Israel fed in the wilderness (Exodus 16; Numbers 11); the prophet Elisha's feeding of a hundred (2 Kings 4:42-44).[5] It looks forward to the Eucharist and, ultimately, to the final banquet in the kingdom of God, of which the Eucharist is both foretaste and prefigurement (cf. 26:29).

The multiplication of the loaves is one of the more difficult miracles of Jesus to account for in terms of what might have "really happened." The quest to find out is ultimately fruitless since we simply have not got sufficient information to determine with any confidence what might lie behind the tradition in all the forms in which it appears across the gospels (Matt 14:13-21; 15:32-39; Mark 6:30-44; 8:1-10; Luke 9:10-17; John 6:1-13).[6] The multiple accounts point to the high theological significance of the tradition in early Christianity. It is on this that we should focus.

Central to that significance is the way in which Jesus anticipates the eucharistic gestures (Matt 26:26-29): "taking (the loaves)," "blessing," "breaking," "giving" (cf. 26:26).[7] The Evangelist expects that readers familiar with the eucharistic celebration will understand that when they

---

[4]Typically, Matthew has Jesus healing, whereas in the Markan parallel (6:34) he teaches.

[5]Features in common with the Elisha story include: a disproportion between the numbers to be fed and the food available; a servant's puzzled response when told to provide; the multiplication as the food is distributed; some food remaining afterwards; cf. Daniel J. Harrington, *The Gospel of Matthew.* SP 1 (Collegeville: Liturgical Press, 1991) 220.

[6]On the issue see the thorough discussion by John P. Meier, *A Marginal Jew.* Vol. 2. *Mentor, Message, and Miracles* (New York: Doubleday, 1994) 959–67.

[7]Matthew highlights the eucharistic aspect—for example, by allowing the fish to fade from view so that all focus lies on the bread.

participate in that rite they are enjoying the same divine hospitality the Galilean crowds experienced in this "lonely place" from Jesus, and experiencing it in the same extravagant degree. Far from having to go off and "buy" anything, they not only ate but "were filled" (v. 20).[8] The fact that leftover fragments were sufficient to fill twelve baskets highlights the divine abundance.[9]

The miraculous feeding makes clear that the essence of what God wants to do for humanity is simply to be a most generous host at the banquet of the kingdom. At the same time, since it depicts people being fed with real food it is also sacramental in the sense of bearing directly upon the problem of hunger still affecting so large a proportion of the world. The Lord who looked upon the large crowd and took pity on them is now the Lord of the Church. When the Church celebrates the Eucharist the same Lord is there present in the community, instructing its leaders as he instructed his disciples, "Give them something to eat yourselves." The Eucharist will never be complete so long as people still go hungry in our world.[10]

Jesus and Peter Walk on the Sea: 14:22-33; Healing at Gennesaret: 15:34-36

After the feeding Jesus sends his disciples off to cross the lake by boat while he disperses the crowd and goes up the mountain by himself to pray (vv. 22-23). As in the earlier boat scene (8:23-27), the image of the disciples struggling to make headway in a boat battered by the sea is symbolic of the later Church.[11] Like them, the Church struggles against forces that threaten to engulf it, keenly sensing the physical absence of its Lord.

Just before dawn[12] Jesus joins them, walking on the sea—in biblical imagery a prerogative of God (Ps 77:19; Job 9:8; Isa 43:16). Hence the

---

[8]"Were filled" echoes the fourth beatitude (5:6), foreshadowing the satisfaction of the hungry at the banquet of the kingdom.

[9]The final comment about women and children not being included in the reckoning (v. 21b) grates harshly today. For Matthew it simply serves to reinforce the sense of divine generosity by enhancing the number of those fed.

[10]Cf. Pedro Arrupe (former Jesuit General), "The Eucharist and Hunger" (Address at Philadelphia, August 2, 1976) in *Justice with Faith Today* Vol. 2 (St. Louis: Institute of Jesuit Sources, 1980) 171–81; Monica. K. Hellwig, *The Eucharist and the Hunger of the World* (New York: Paulist, 1976).

[11]The Greek word translated "battered" *(basanizesthai)* literally means "to be tortured."

[12]Literally, "at the fourth watch" (3 A.M. to 6 A.M.). The implication is that the disciples had been struggling almost the entire night.

terror evoked in the disciples (v. 26). Jesus' reassurance, "Take courage; It is I; fear not" (v. 27), is at one level a simple self-identification: they are not seeing a ghost but the Master they know and follow. At another level, "It is I" (Greek *egō eimi*) evokes the self-identification of God to Moses at the Burning Bush (Exod 3:13-15) and similar divine assurances in Isaiah (43:13, 25; 46:4; 48:12; 58:9). The presence of Jesus ("Emmanuel" [1:23; cf. 28:20]) is at one and the same time the saving presence of God. The Church, symbolized by the disciples in the boat, may go through long periods on its voyage through history seemingly abandoned by its Lord. This scene[13] assures the faithful that divine concern is never truly absent but is ever ready, even in the darkest moments, to save.

It is not entirely clear what prompts Peter's desire to come to Jesus across the sea (vv. 27-31).[14] Love, boldness, bravado? Perhaps all three— but also a measure of faith: "Lord, if it is you, command me . . ." (v. 28).[15] Faith enables Peter to participate in Jesus' divine power: to tread underfoot, for a few moments at least, the forces of destruction. Then doubt arrives. Peter takes his eyes off Jesus and "sees" instead only the force of the wind.[16] His plea for rescue, "Lord, save me!" (v. 30) has about it the ring of liturgical prayer. Likewise, Jesus' gentle rebuke—after he has stretched out his hand and rescued Peter—"O you of little faith, why did you doubt?" speaks to all members of the Church.[17] By "detaching" Peter from the other disciples at this point and allowing him to make his individual journey across the waves Matthew personalizes the ecclesial experience. Peter models the mixture of boldness and fear, strength and weakness, character-istic of all. Believers can make their own his cry for rescue and feel, as he felt, the Lord's strong hand reaching out to draw them up from the deep.[18]

---

[13]The intense overlay of biblical allusion and theology renders the recovery of any his-torical kernel all but impossible. See again Meier, *A Marginal Jew* 2:919–24.

[14]The episode with Peter is, of course, peculiar to Matthew's version.

[15]M. Eugene Boring ("The Gospel of Matthew," in Leander E. Keck, ed., *The New Inter-preter's Bible.* Vol. 8 [Nashville: Abingdon, 1995] 328–29) evaluates Peter's desire to leave the boat and come to Jesus negatively, seeing it as seeking proof of the presence of the Lord. But Peter *requests* Jesus to "command" him and so acts in obedience; cf. Ulrich Luz, *Matthew 8–20: A Commentary.* Translated by James E. Crouch. Hermeneia (Minneapolis: Fortress, 2001) 320.

[16]"See" here must have the sense "notice." One hardly "sees" wind.

[17]The Greek word expressing "doubt" *(distazein)* means "to waver"; it will reappear to express the response of "some" (disciples) on seeing the risen Lord (28:17).

[18]While Peter begins here to be singled out from the remaining disciples, his unique ecclesial role—to emerge in 16:13-19—is not yet directly in view; cf. Luz, *Matthew 8–20,* 321.

It is only as Jesus and Peter get into the boat that the rage of the wind subsides. When the disciples "worship" him, saying "truly, you are the Son of God" (v. 33), they show that the whole traumatic experience has led to a new awareness of God's saving presence among them in the person of Jesus.[19]

When the boat comes to land at Gennesaret, Jesus resumes his ministry of healing (15:34-36), the sick begging to touch "the fringe of his cloak" (cf. 9:20). Coming straight after the theophany on the lake, this moment of healing depicts the accessibility of divine presence. In the person of Jesus the afflicted can "touch" God and find healing.

True and False Defilement: 15:1-20

Conflict returns in the shape of a controversy between Jesus and the Pharisees over what defiles a person. Modern Christians should not read this section as an attack on Judaism as such or even as a rejection on Jesus' part of the Torah's prescriptions on ritual purity. As in the Great Sermon, this is a place in the gospel where Jesus' attitude to the Torah is made clear. He does not abolish the Torah (5:17) but, as unique Son of God, he gives it an authoritative interpretation that makes what God wants now (the era of the kingdom) the absolute criterion. And what God wants is that the love commandment (22:34-40), expressed in values such as justice, mercy, and faith (23:23; also 9:13; 12:7), take priority over all other considerations. What Jesus disarms here, in the name of such priority, is the Pharisaic *tradition* (v. 2; v. 6), the bundle of rulings and interpretations ("tradition of the elders") handed down orally alongside the written Torah. At its best this oral tradition usefully served to adapt the ancient Torah to the changed conditions of later times. But, as Jesus points out here, it could extend and develop legal prescriptions in ways that frustrated God's present will.

The "presenting" issue here is the tradition of washing hands before eating (v. 2; v. 20), a clear example of the tradition's extension of the Torah.[20] Jesus, however, goes over to the offensive by raising a far more

---

[19]Confessing Jesus as "Son of God" here anticipates Peter's confession at Caesarea Philippi in 16:16 and to some extent undercuts the narrative impact of that climactic moment. Matthew is more prepared than Mark to sacrifice that impact in the interest of creating scenes that reflect and express the experience of the later Church.

[20]The Torah prescribed certain washings for the priests (Exod 30:17-21). The Pharisees, a lay group, extended priestly purity to themselves and, in aspiration at least, to all Jews on the basis that Israel was "a nation of priests" (Exod 19:6); cf. Boring, "Matthew," 332.

serious case (vv. 4-6). The grave commandment to honor parents[21] can be frustrated by a vow dedicating one's property to the Temple.[22] For Jesus this illustrates the complaint Isaiah made in God's name:

> This people honors me with their lips,
> but their hearts are far from me;
> in vain do they worship me,
> teaching human precepts as doctrines (29:13).

Not only does this text distinguish merely human precepts from true worship of God. It also introduces the sense of "the heart" as the true focus and source of what God wants from human beings, something already prominent in the Great Sermon (5:28).

Rightness of "heart" then becomes the crucial factor in the instruction on defilement Jesus gives to the crowds (vv. 10-11), as also in the later explanation to the disciples (vv. 15-20). It is not what goes into a person from outside that determines (ritual) defilement; it is what comes from inside.[23] What goes in (food laws are principally in view), being material, is simply transformed into either nourishment or waste; it does not touch a person's moral core. What comes out, however, *proceeds* from that moral core, that is, from the "heart." The list of vices Jesus offers as examples (v. 19) all illustrate injustice to one's neighbor of a particularly premeditated kind. It is "these things" (v. 20a) that defile a person, not external things such as eating with unwashed hands (v. 20b).

The last observation takes the discussion back to where it began: why Jesus' disciples do not wash their hands before eating (v. 2). In the meantime Jesus has totally redefined the notion of "clean/unclean" in the direction of moral rather than ritual purity, with Scripture (Isa 29:13, quoted in v. 8) once again taken as indicating "what God wants." Jesus is not sweeping away the purity legislation of the Torah.[24] Nor is he saying that rightness of heart is all, as if right action, in conformity with the heart, were not

---

[21]Jesus highlights the seriousness of the matter by quoting not only the fourth commandment (Exod 20:12; Deut 5:16) but also the sanction for infringing it (Exod 21:17; Lev 20:9). "Honoring" one's parents included making financial provision for them.

[22]The vow, declaring one's property a gift to God ("Qorban"; cf. Mark 7:11) seems to have allowed one to continue to make use of the property while preventing its liquidation or alienation—much as declaring bankruptcy can function today.

[23]This is actually the Markan formula (7:15). Matthew 15:11 narrows it down to "into the mouth" / "out of the mouth," but the sense is the same.

[24]Matthew, reflecting the Jewish context, omits Mark's sweeping: "Thus he declared all foods clean" (7:19b).

also required (cf. 7:21-27). But the struggle to live as God wants begins in the heart—in a right perception at the core of a person that the Torah's "weightier" precepts (justice, mercy, and faith ([23:23]) have priority over ritual commandments.[25]

While doubtless true to much of Jesus' own prophetic preaching, the sequence reflects the preoccupation of the Matthean community with the heirs of the Pharisees toward the end of the first century C.E. Even so, it is no mere historical relic. Every religious community develops and cherishes a tradition. The Catholic Church in particular holds tradition, alongside Scripture, in high veneration. Aspects of tradition, in particular legal provisions developed for one age, can become oppressive in another, especially when they retain high authority precisely because bound up with sacred tradition. Gospel texts like this one constantly summon the Church to re-examine such things and the impact they have, so that "what God wants"— justice, mercy, faith—remains supreme.

Jesus and the Canaanite Woman: 15:21-28

Yet again Jesus "withdraws" (Greek *anachōrein*) in the face of hostility from Jewish authorities. He moves in the direction of Tyre and Sidon, an area of Gentile majority.[26] The destination is significant. Having just challenged the "clean/unclean" barrier in his dispute with the Pharisees, Jesus now *enacts* such boundary-crossing "geographically" by moving to the Gentile region. There the faith of a local woman breaks through the barrier in a still more significant way.

Contrary to what is usually the case, it is Matthew's rather than Mark's (7:24-30) version of the incident that is the more elaborate. The evangelist is at pains to stress that the woman is a Gentile ("a Canaanite from that region" [v. 22]).[27] But she addresses Jesus as the Jewish Messiah ("Lord, Son of David" [v. 22]), to whose healing powers she boldly lays claim. Despite the persistence and force of her plea (v. 23), Jesus ignores her completely. When the disciples urge him to do something about her ("Send her away" seems to imply "Get rid of her by granting her what she wants"), he coldly insists that his mission is only to "the lost sheep of the house of

---

[25]Cf. Boring, "Matthew," 333; Luz, *Matthew 8–20,* 333.

[26]Matthew seems to emphasize the Gentile aspect of the location by adding "and Sidon" to Mark's simple "Tyre" (7:24).

[27]"Canaanite" (contrast "Syro-Phoenician" in Mark 7:26) suggests Israel's ancestral enemies.

Israel" (v. 24). When, in one of the most moving gestures in all the gospels, she approaches, kneels before him, and simply begs, "Lord, help me" (v. 25), all she receives is a third rebuff in the form of the heartless image about not throwing the children's food to dogs (v. 26).

But here at last is her chance (v. 27). Wit combines with faith to wrest the image to her advantage. Certainly, food prepared for the children of the house is not intended for domestic animals. But children eat untidily and pet dogs under the table seize scraps that fall.[28] Outwitted, Jesus gives in, agreeing to her request and praising the greatness of her faith (v. 28).

The coldness Jesus displays to this woman, almost to the very end, understandably troubles many. At the level of the narrative itself the repeated pattern of rebuff brings out the absolute priority of Jesus' mission to Israel, a restriction also imposed earlier upon the disciples (cf. 10:5-6). The intensification of barriers between Jews and Gentiles serves, then, to highlight the significance of what takes place when the woman's wit and faith finally bring it crashing down. This unnamed woman, surely one of the great heroes of the gospel tradition, drags the Jewish Messiah from an understanding that his powers were solely for the benefit of his own people to one in which he uses them for a representative of the Gentile world. As earlier in the case of the centurion who pleaded with him for his servant (8:5-13), and in anticipation of the mission charge at the end of the gospel (28:18-20), a person of outstanding faith has led him to be also the Messiah in whose "name the Gentiles will hope" (12:21).

It is not easy for modern readers to grasp the immensity of the barrier being broken through here, one that preoccupied the Church for at least two generations. Our problem is the other way round: to appreciate sufficiently the particular place of Israel and the Jewish people in the covenant fidelity of God. The woman stands in for all of us Gentiles. We can learn from her faith. But we can also learn from her humble and honest acceptance of Israel's priority in the divine scheme of salvation (cf. Rom 11:13-32).

Jesus Heals and Feeds Four Thousand People: 15:29-39

For a last time the gospel offers a summary of Jesus' healing activity in Galilee (vv. 29-31). The report serves to consolidate the picture of Jesus

---

[28]In the Markan account the stress is on priority: the children are fed *first;* the dogs get the *same* food later. In Matthew *different* food is prepared for the children from that which the dogs might receive, but the dogs, opportunistically, get access to the children's food by eating the scraps that fall from the table.

as the compassionate Messiah, tending again and again to the lost sheep of Israel. The fact that the crowd repeats the description of the healing word for word (v. 31a) reinforces the picture of Jesus fulfilling the scriptural promises concerning the messianic age.[29]

The Messiah completes his care for the people by once more feeding them lest they faint from hunger as they go on their way (vv. 32-39). Again the disciples are intimately involved—though this time it is Jesus himself who takes the initiative and draws them into his own compassionate view of the crowd.[30] Resonant once more are eucharistic echoes in the actions of Jesus and the distribution performed by the disciples (v. 36), while the sense of "all being filled" (v. 37) foreshadows the hospitality of the kingdom.

From now on the attention of Jesus will no longer be on the Galilean crowds but on the formation of his disciples. From the leadership of Israel he will face increasing hostility and threat. But the abiding impression conveyed by scenes such as these is that the Messiah has faithfully fulfilled the divine promises to Israel.

Warning Against the Pharisees and Sadducees: 16:1-12

Hostility returns when a combined group of Pharisees and Sadducees approach Jesus, demanding a "sign from heaven" (v. 1).[31] They do not see these healings worked for the benefit of afflicted people on *earth* as "signs" that the messianic era is dawning—even though such healing is fulfilling the scriptural prophecies concerning the messianic age. They seem to want something more spectacular—a bolt from heaven or cosmic upheaval—that would unequivocally attest Jesus' status. As on a previous occasion (12:38-39), Jesus categorically rejects the call to supply a sign (v. 4). Signs presuppose faith; they do not genuinely create it. The only sign to be given to "this generation" will be the "sign of Jonah" (his resurrection).

[29]Especially in view would seem to be Isa 35:5-6:
> Then the eyes of the blind shall be opened,
> and the ears of the deaf unstopped;
> then the lame shall leap like a deer,
> and the tongue of the speechless sing for joy.

[30]The feeding has strong overtones of the gift of manna to Israel in Sinai, since it occurs in a "desert" place (v. 33).

[31]The combination of these two rival groups is historically unlikely. Matthew associates them (contrast Mark 8:11 [Pharisees only]) in order to convey the sense of the Jewish religious leadership making combined cause against Jesus; cf. Harrington, *Matthew,* 245.

Faced with this unbelief, Jesus abandons the conversation and rejoins his disciples (v. 4b). After a voyage to the other side (of the lake), he warns them to "beware of the yeast of the Pharisees and Sadducees" (v. 6). The disciples hear what he is saying as a comment on the fact that they have failed to bring with them any bread (v. 7; cf. v. 5b), a misperception that earns them a rebuke for "little faith" (cf. 14:31). Later (v. 12) they realize that by "yeast" it was (false) teaching that he had in mind—probably the corrosive and destructive conviction that he could not possibly be the Messiah because he was not treading the expected path. Jesus, at any rate, has finished his messianic ministry in Galilee and broken off the fruitless conversation with the leaders. The challenge now will be to educate his disciples, the nucleus of a reconstituted Israel, concerning the difficult direction that from this point on his messianic path must take.

3. THE NEW DIRECTION: THE MESSIAH'S JOURNEY TO JERUSALEM: 16:13–20:34

The Identity of Jesus and the Foundation of the Church: 16:13–17:27

We have now reached the turning point in Matthew's gospel. Faced with the hostility of the religious leadership, Jesus turns away from them and the Galilean crowds to concentrate upon the formation of his disciples into the nucleus of a reconstituted people of God, soon to be called "the Church." Central to that formation is the task of conveying to the disciples the new direction his messianic career is about to take: that it will involve going up to Jerusalem, there to suffer and die, before rising on the third day. Correspondingly, discipleship itself will involve a readiness to follow and share with him this costly journey. Matthew sets instructions on life in the community of the Church within this overall framework of the journey of the Son of Man to Jerusalem, where he will complete his messianic ministry by giving his life as a "ransom for many" (20:28).

The Confession of Peter and Foundation of the Church: 16:13-20

Signaling this new direction is a small bridge passage that has attracted more attention than any other part of Matthew's gospel. In the region of

Caesarea Philippi[1] Jesus formally and explicitly raises the question of his identity with his disciples. He questions them first on the views of the people at large and receives in response a variety of inadequate labels, all placing him in the category of one of the prophets (including John the Baptist) making an end-time reappearance (v. 14). When he turns the question directly upon the disciples (v. 15) he is giving them the chance to distinguish themselves radically from the crowds by the accuracy and perceptiveness of their response. Peter does not disappoint when, speaking in the name of all, he responds: "You are the Messiah, the Son of the Living God" (v. 16).

We have, of course, already heard the disciples confess Jesus as "Son of God" when he joined them in the boat after walking on the water (14:33). And Jesus has spoken of himself as "Son" in a unique sense (11:27). Thus Peter is not voicing something he and the remaining disciples have not believed for some time. But by drawing from him this explicit confession, in the context of inadequate responses from people at large, Jesus prepares the ground for the foundation of the Church now to follow. To put it more technically, he is ensuring that ecclesiology flows from and rests upon distinctive christological insight.

What is new in Peter's confession is the juxtaposition of two titles, "Messiah" and "Son of the Living God."[2] The joining of the two implies that Peter, unlike the wondering crowds, has been able to hold together both a conventional understanding of "Messiah" and the unique filial relationship Jesus has revealed himself to have with God. What will threaten to rend this understanding apart, however, is fresh information that Jesus is about to impart: that precisely as Messiah and Son he is destined to suffer and die.

In Matthew that painful moment is postponed for a time as Jesus, responding to Peter's correct confession, singles him out as specially "blessed" and bestows on him a series of roles in the Church now coming to be. Peter is "blessed" because the insight to which he has just given utterance is not something gained through human reasoning or perception, but through God-given revelation (v. 17). When God began to reveal to Peter the knowledge of Jesus' identity displayed in the double confession, God began the work of founding the Church. This knowledge of Jesus and

---

[1] A Gentile town on the southern slope of Mount Hermon about twenty miles north of the northern tip of the Sea of Galilee.

[2] Contrast Mark 8:29: "You are the Christ"; Luke 9:20: "the Messiah of God."

the knowledge of God that goes with it is what the Church uniquely "knows," the primary gift it has to impart to the world.

Having singled Peter out as specially "blessed" in this way,[3] Jesus now confers upon him three roles: "rock foundation" of the Church; holder of the keys of the kingdom of heaven; one who binds and looses.

Jesus does not necessarily give Simon his nickname "Rock" for the first time here (v. 18; cf. John 1:42).[4] But he makes a wordplay on the name to indicate Simon's foundational role in regard to the "Church," which the community of disciples is now to become.[5] "Church" (Greek *ekklēsia*), which was to become the distinctive name by which the Christian community identified itself as both local congregations and the entire body of believers,[6] recalls the description of the congregation of Israel in its post-Exodus wandering.[7] The Church is not to be a replacement for Israel but a community within—and eventually alongside—the wider mass of Israel, the base for the end-time reconstitution of the people of God.[8] "Simon Rock" is to be the firm foundation upon which Jesus will "construct" this Church, conceived of as a structure made up of human beings. As the beatitude just spoken over him shows, Simon personally—not just his faith—provides this foundation.

As a building founded upon this "rock," the Church will endure the onslaughts the underworld powers will hurl against it (v. 18c).[9] The guarantee implies, on the one hand, that the Church will be at the center of the struggle to wrest the human world from the grip of Satan and reclaim it for

---

[3] Jesus' question was addressed to all the disciples "Who do *you* [second person plural] say that I am?") and it seems we are to understand that Peter speaks as spokesperson for all. But this Matthean version, in which Jesus goes on to single Peter out for special blessing, conveys the impression of his being somewhat ahead of the others in God-given understanding.

[4] "Rock" ("Cephas" in Aramaic) is not known as a Jewish proper name before its bestowal on Simon.

[5] The wordplay is lost in English ("Peter"/ "Rock"), is close in Greek *(petros/petra)*, perfect in Aramaic *(kepha,* serving for both the nickname and "rock").

[6] The latter is the sense here, the local body in 18:17; cf. Ulrich Luz, *Matthew 8–20: A Commentary.* Translated by James E. Crouch. Hermeneia (Minneapolis: Fortress, 2001) 362.

[7] *Ekklēsia* regularly translates the Hebrew term *qahal* ("assembly") in Deuteronomy (Deut 5:22; 9:10; 10:4; 18:16; 23:2, 3, 4, 9; 31:30) and the historical books of the Old Testament.

[8] Cf. M. Eugene Boring, "The Gospel of Matthew," in Leander E. Keck, ed., *The New Interpreter's Bible.* Vol. 8 (Nashville: Abingdon, 1995) 346.

[9] "Gates of Hades" refers in the first instance to the abode of the dead. The more negative extended sense of the realm of Satan is likely intended here.

the rule of God.[10] On the other hand, the Church can rest assured that, no matter how grievous the onslaught of the powers of death, the building so founded will stand. This will be so not simply because of the firmness of its foundation, but because the Church will have the living Lord present with it until the end of the age (28:20).

Now (v. 19) the image changes. Peter is to hold the "keys of the kingdom of heaven." This is not exactly the "gatekeeper" role assigned to Peter in popular imagination. The explanation lies in Isa 22:20-25, where "the key of the house of David" is placed upon the shoulder of Eliakim as a sign that he is to be the major domo of the royal house.[11] Peter's possession of the keys, then, has to do with the exercise of delegated authority in the household of God, an authority further specified in the following comment telling Peter that whatever he "binds" on earth will be "bound in heaven" and whatever he "looses" on earth will be "loosed in heaven" (v. 19c). In 23:13 Jesus bitterly castigates the Pharisees because through their teaching—specifically their rulings on the application of the Torah—they "lock people out of the kingdom of heaven." This negative parallel suggests that the "binding/loosing" authority given to Peter has primarily to do with authoritative interpretations of the Torah. Entrance to or exclusion from the kingdom will depend upon observance of the prescriptions of the Torah rightly interpreted in this way (cf. 28:20a). Jesus assures Peter, then, that the rulings he gives on earth will have divine ratification—just as Eliakim could be confident that *his* rulings and directives would have the backing of the earthly Davidic king. The powers, then, are indeed very considerable. The Church is being provided with a teaching authority for the time when Jesus will not be physically present to interpret the Torah authoritatively as in the Great Sermon (Matthew 5–7).[12]

---

[10] This is to understand the Greek verb translated "prevail" in an active, aggressive sense: "overcome." The alternative, passive sense "withstand" (where Church becomes the "aggressor," compelling the realm of death to surrender up its captives for eternal life) goes well with a literal understanding of "gates," but it is not easy to picture a "building" battering down gates.

[11] The words are addressed to the previous officeholder Shebna, whom Eliakim is to replace: "On that day I will call my servant Eliakim son of Hilkiah . . . I will commit your authority to his hand . . . I will place on his shoulder the key of the house of David; he shall open, and no one shall shut; he shall shut, and no one shall open."

[12] Later in the narrative (18:18) the "binding/loosing" authority bestowed here personally upon Peter is communicated to members of the Church more generally. There it has to do with the power of excommunicating or not excommunicating members of the *local* community of the Church. Here the "Church" in view is the universal community, of which Peter has been designated (v. 18) the "rock" foundation.

The assurance given to Peter here has, of course, been a most controversial item in the Gospel of Matthew. Particularly since the Reformation the claims of the Roman primacy have been asserted and denied in its regard with equal vigor. The more ecumenical climate of recent decades has allowed discussion of the text to proceed in more dispassionate fashion. Protestant exegetes now concede that the "rock" upon which the Church is founded is the person of Peter himself, and not just his faith.[13] Most will also acknowledge that Peter is more than just a representative figure here—that he is genuinely singled out and given a unique role. What remains strongly at issue is whether that role is uniquely and *unrepeatably* his or whether he is the original holder of a "Petrine office" to which others also might succeed. (This is itself a prior and separate issue from the question as to whether such an office, granted that it does exist, is to be located, as the Catholic tradition holds, in the line of bishops of Rome.) When the Gospel of Matthew was composed Peter had presumably been dead for two decades or more. It can be argued that the existence of Matt 16:17-19 in the gospel is testimony to his unrepeatable foundational role in regard to the tradition cherished by the Matthean church, as well as the guarantee of the authenticity and authority of that tradition.[14]

The problem with this is that it "freezes" the powers given to Peter in one historical moment, albeit a foundational one. If the Petrine office does not somehow continue in the life of the Church, then the Church lacks the capacity flexibly, creatively, and also *authoritatively* to adapt Jesus' interpretations of the Torah to the ever-changing conditions of human life. It could be claimed that such authority rests now with the entire community as indicated in 18:18. But to this two things may be said. (1) The "binding/loosing" capacity envisaged in 18:18 concerns the local community only and has to do with disciplinary action rather than teaching. (2) Why, if the capacity envisaged in 18:18 be considered ongoing in nature, should a similar sense of continuity or succession be denied to what is conferred upon Peter in 16:17-19? In both cases something vital for the *continuing* vitality of the Church would seem to be in view.

That said, and with all due ecumenical respect, I cannot see how a sense of a continuing Petrine ministry can be excluded from the interpretation of Matt 16:17-19. At the very least it can lay strong claim to being a

---

[13] Cf. W. D. Davies and Dale Allison, *A Critical and Exegetical Commentary on the Gospel According to Saint Matthew.* ICC. 3 vols. (Edinburgh: T&T Clark, 1988–97) 2:627.

[14] So especially Luz, *Matthew 8–20,* 367, who draws strong parallels with the figure of the Beloved Disciple in the Fourth Gospel.

legitimate interpretation among others or at most a convenient (in the literal sense) *extension* of the meaning.[15] It was (as noted above) a fresh and separate step when such a continuing Petrine ministry was located in the line of bishops of Rome, that is, in the Roman papacy. However, the papacy is the only body that has historically laid claim to the Petrine office and many Christians outside the Roman communion feel the need, especially in an increasingly globalized world, for a visible, personal focus of Christian unity and guarantor of the tradition. The shadows of history hang heavily over such a vision, and the mode in which the Roman curia has exercised and continues to exercise authority in disciplinary and doctrinal matters dismays many otherwise sympathetic observers. Such controversial matters, however, should not distract us from the central positive affirmation of the text: the sense of the Church as founded upon God-given knowledge of Christ, a knowledge it is the Church's supreme privilege to treasure and communicate to the world in every age.

Following the address to Simon Peter, Jesus instructs his disciples sternly not to tell anyone that he is the Messiah (v. 20). The instruction reinforces the sense of distance between them and the populace at large. They are privileged recipients of divine revelation, which is not yet to be shared more widely. The reason is that it remains to be completed by another mystery, which Jesus now (v. 21) begins to put before them.

The Messiah Destined to Suffer and Die: 16:21-28

In order to nip in the bud any false expectations concerning his messiahship just affirmed (v. 16), Jesus "from that time on" (v. 21)[16] begins the long process of educating his disciples concerning his destiny to suffer and die. His spelling this out very plainly provokes a remonstrance from Peter: "Gracious God! This (destiny) is not for you" (v. 22).[17] The counter-

---

[15] Luz, *Matthew 8–20,* 372, recognizes such a hermeneutic of the "trajectory of a text," while ultimately remaining very hesitant about the Roman interpretation. Cf. a final comment: ". . . Matthew says nothing about the unique Peter that is not also valid for all the other disciples" (376). This seems to me an impossible attempt to harmonize the portrayal of Peter as both "unique" and "typical" in the First Gospel.

[16] The phrase "From that time on he began . . ." repeats exactly the phrase that introduced the beginning of Jesus' public ministry (4:17), signaling a major division of the gospel.

[17] "Gracious God" is an attempt to render the Greek exclamation *hileōs.* The sense is almost: "A gracious God could never allow such a thing to befall his Son!"; cf. John P. Meier, *Matthew.* New Testament Message 5 (Wilmington: Michael Glazier, 1980) 185.

response ("Get behind me, Satan! . . ." [v. 23]) stands in starkest contrast to the "beatitude" so recently pronounced (v. 17). The sharpness suggests that Jesus experiences in Peter's remonstrance something of the earlier suggestion made by the devil at the temptation (4:1-11): that he be the messiah of conventional expectation, far removed from the fate just outlined. Peter has now become a "rock" of stumbling rather than of insight, tripping up Jesus' fulfillment of the role marked out for him by God. The exchange shows how incomplete Peter's grasp of Jesus' mission remains, despite his being the privileged recipient of revelation. He and the remaining disciples have a long and painful journey to travel before they can hold together two seemingly incompatible truths: that Jesus is unique Son of God and that he "must" enter into the pain and suffering of this world to heal it from within.

Peter's unsatisfactory response leads Jesus (vv. 24-26) to lay openly upon the table not merely his own fate but that of all those who would "follow after" him.[18] Discipleship will mean "following after him" in the sense of treading in his tracks as he goes on the journey he has just outlined, even to death on the cross. Centuries of Christian talk of "the cross" have dulled us to the radicality of such a suggestion in the world of the gospel, where the horrors of crucifixion would have been familiar to many readers. It is not so much that believers would themselves suffer crucifixion as that each will have to confront a measure of suffering, possibly even loss of life, as the price of being followers of this kind of Messiah. Each will have his or her own "cross" to bear. What is common to all is a "denial of self"—not an attempt to extinguish all joy and fulfillment in life, but a refusal to acquiesce in the self-centered and ultimately futile attempts of the false self to grasp at the gratifications and ambitions a purely competitive view of life makes obligatory. A denial of "self" (the false self) promotes the interests of the true self because it refuses to be turned aside until it has located and sought to fulfill the deepest human aspiration. This is to live in communion with divine love, and the invitation to life in the fullest sense that such love holds out.[19]

[18] The Greek phrase "after me" *(hopisō mou)* occurs both in the rebuke ("Get behind me, Satan!") in v. 23 and the description of discipleship in v. 24, serving as a link between the two pericopes. The rebuke is in effect a command to adopt the correct position of discipleship; cf. Boring, "Matthew," 349.

[19] To promote such a discovery is the essential aim of the program of prayer and discernment contained in the *Spiritual Exercises* of St. Ignatius Loyola. For a classic contemporary introduction to Ignatian spirituality see Gerard J. Hughes, *The God of Surprises* (London: Darton, Longman and Todd, 1996).

The rest of the instruction (vv. 26-28) justifies the radical path just outlined with a reflection on the true value of "life." Within the eschatological perspective of the gospel, "life" (Greek *psyché*) can be understood in two ways: (1) as referring simply to one's present span of life, which death will terminate; or (2) as referring to a personal existence that includes present life but also extends, through God's gift, to life "in the kingdom," transcending physical death. Even with respect to life in the former sense no other good is comparable, since all benefits are useless unless a person is alive to enjoy them. But the same principle is even more true for life in the transcendent sense—true to such an extent that, paradoxically, one ought be prepared to "lose" life in the former sense in order to preserve it (literally, "find it again" [v. 25]) for eternity. The radical, transcendent sense of "life" relativizes the value of the otherwise supreme good of being alive in this world.

The eschatological perspective becomes explicit in the final sentences (vv. 27-28). A chief task of the Son of Man when he comes as judge will be to "repay everyone according to their deeds." Though this may include punishment upon wrongdoers, the context, where encouragement is chiefly in view, places the accent upon the positive: those who have faithfully given up their "lives" (either literally or ascetically) in the earthly sense will receive from the Son of Man the gift of eternal life that their following his self-emptying way has merited.[20] A final comment (v. 28) suggests that such recompense will not be long delayed.[21]

The Transfiguration and the Issue Concerning Elijah: 17:1-13

The mysterious episode of the Transfiguration (17:1-8), together with the discussion about Elijah (vv. 9-13), continues the dialogue concerning Jesus' identity and destiny that began in 16:13. The disciples have been left for "six days" (v. 1) to mull over the extraordinary juxtaposition of Jesus'

[20] It seems appropriate to use the word "merit" here even though that may cause anxiety about "justification by works." Matthew (like Paul in Rom 2:6-11; 2 Cor 5:10) does envisage a judgment according to works but, as 25:31-46 makes clear, the "works" in question are those of mercy.

[21] The comment is difficult to interpret since at the time of the composition of the gospel very few, if any, of the original disciples would have been still alive. Matthew may have related the saying to the disciples' vision of Christ's risen glory (28:16-20), an anticipation of his final coming as Son of Man.

uniquely privileged status ("Son of the living God") and his destiny to suffer and die, which Peter had found so impossible to accept. What three chosen disciples will experience on the mountain will stamp a divine guarantee upon that juxtaposition.[22]

The Transfiguration is often interpreted as an anticipatory glimpse of Jesus' future glory, either that of his resurrection[23] or else that of his end-time coming as Son of Man. I think interpretations of this kind referring the vision to the future are misleading.[24] The vision, confirmed by the Father's voice, is about who Jesus is here and now, a further instance of his ability to move between the divine and human worlds, as shown already by his command of the winds and waves (8:26-27) and his walking on the sea (14:22-33). All the details—the location on a high mountain,[25] the trans-figuring of his appearance (particularly the illumination of his face),[26] the appearance of the figures of Moses and Elijah, now in heaven, and Jesus' conversation with them—point to this union with the heavenly world.[27] What the three disciples see is Jesus in the glory that belongs to him as "Son of the living God"; he is as much "at home" here as he is walking the roads and lakeshore of Galilee with them.

Peter's exclamation, "Lord, it is good for us to be here," and particu-larly his offer to construct "three tents," one for Jesus, one for Moses, and one for Elijah (v. 4), have long puzzled interpreters, and none of the expla-nations offered seems assured.[28] The exclamation suggests both delight in

[22] The same three will witness Jesus' agony in Gethsemane on the night of his arrest (26:37).

[23] Cf. Daniel J. Harrington, *The Gospel of Matthew.* SP 1 (Collegeville: Liturgical Press, 1991) 256

[24] The transfiguration has little in common with the resurrection appearances, and the aspect of judgment associated with the end-time return of Jesus as Son of Man is entirely absent.

[25] The ascent of a mountain symbolizes approach to the divine realm.

[26] The detail about Jesus' face is a Matthean addition to the Markan description (9:2-3; cf., however, Luke 9:29).

[27] Echoes of Moses' ascent of Mount Sinai (Exodus 24 [ascent of Sinai with three com-panions]; Exod 34:29-35 [shining face after meeting with God]) are particularly prominent. According to biblical and post-biblical tradition both Elijah and Moses experienced mysteri-ous conclusions to their lives involving some kind of "ascent" (Elijah: 2 Kings 2:9-11) or "assumption" (Moses: Deut 34:5-6) to heaven, and both were the subject of eschatological speculation: that Elijah would return (Mal 3:1; 4:5-6) and that a prophet "like (Moses)" would arise (Deut 18:15-18).

[28] For instance, that "tents" ("booths") is an allusion to the Feast of Tabernacles, which Jewish tradition (e.g., Zech 14:9, 16) associated with the joys of the messianic era; cf. Harrington, *Matthew,* 254; or that the allusion is to the "Tent of Meeting" of the Exodus tradition (Exodus 29–34); cf. Boring, "Matthew," 364.

the experience and a desire to prolong it by providing structures in which the heavenly figures can dwell.[29] That the suggestion is inappropriate is shown by the terrifying theophany that occurs "while he was speaking" (v. 5a).[30] The (Father's) voice from heaven not only identifies Jesus as "Beloved Son, in whom I am well pleased" (exactly as after the baptism [3:17]) but adds: "Listen to him!" This is no generalized command, but a specific instruction to attend carefully to what he has been saying and will continue to insist upon in the days ahead: namely, that he is destined to suffer and die in Jerusalem and that those who would be his disciples must be prepared to go along with him on that journey. In other words, the two truths Peter had found so difficult to hold together—Jesus' being "Messiah, Son of the living God" and his being destined to suffer and die—are here joined in direct revelation from God. It is precisely *as* God's beloved Son that Jesus will suffer and die—something to which both Paul (Rom 8:32; cf. 5:6-10) and the Fourth Gospel (3:16) give very similar expression.

There is something wonderfully human about the final act of the episode. Overwhelmed by the experience, the disciples remain prostrate, frozen in fear (v. 6), until Jesus comes, touches them, and bids them rise and not be afraid (v. 7). We look up with the chastened disciples and, like them, see no one "but Jesus alone" (v. 8). By moving so swiftly from glory and theophany back to simple humanity the narrative magnificently reaffirms the sense of divine presence and divine self-gift in the human person of Jesus. Moses and Elijah were the two figures who came closest to God in the biblical tradition, both experiencing theophanies on a mountain (Exod 34:29-35; 1 Kings 19:8-18). The disciples have shared their experience, but they do not have to remain on the mountain to preserve it. Whenever they are with Jesus they are with God—or, rather, God ("Emmanuel" [1:23; 28:20]) is "with" them.

On the way down from the mountain Jesus warns the disciples not to speak of what they have seen "until the Son of Man has been raised from the dead" (v. 9). Glory must not be proclaimed apart from destiny to suffer. The disciples' thoughts, however, are on another issue, raised by the sight of Elijah. If Jesus is the Messiah, where does that leave the scribal teaching, based upon Mal 3:1 and 4:5-6 (cf. Sir 48:10), that Elijah must return

---

[29] But why would heavenly figures require earthly dwelling-places? And would Jesus, who is still "earthly" as well as heavenly, be in need of one in the same way as Moses and Elijah?

[30] A cloud regularly signals the presence of the unseen God in the biblical tradition (Exod 16:10; 19:9; 24:15-16; 33:9).

"to restore all things"? Jesus affirms the scriptural prophecy (v. 11) and then definitively interprets it in reference to John the Baptist (v. 12), whose fate has become a harbinger of his own (v. 13).

The Faith Required for Healing: 17:14-20 (21); a Further Passion Prediction: 17:22-23

As they descend the mountain, Jesus and his three companions are not only literally but also figuratively brought back to earth by the reality that confronts them: a parent's anguish over the desperate state of a child.[31] Matthew's account of the episode greatly scales down the details in Mark to make everything focus on faith. The issue is not whether Jesus can heal the boy—that has been amply illustrated and is presupposed. The problem is that in his absence the disciples have not been able to do so despite the powers conferred on them to deal with afflictions of this kind (10:1). So when Jesus has healed the boy[32] he explains to the disciples that their incapacity was due to the "littleness of their faith" (cf. 6:30; 8:36; 14:31; 16:8). In the time that is coming (that of the Church) Jesus will no longer be physically present with them (as indeed he has been physically absent for a time on the mountain). But he and the divine power that attends him will be "with them" (1:23; 28:20), granted the all-important condition of faith. Faith is the necessary channel through which God's presence and power become effective in the world.[33]

A "gathering" of the disciples in Galilee (v. 22a) leads Jesus to make a further prediction concerning his Passion (17:22-23). Confronted once again with a plain statement of Jesus' fate, the disciples no longer respond with challenge or misunderstanding, but with "great distress" (v. 23).[34] They grieve because they know all too well what lies before them.[35]

---

[31] The condition is identified by Matthew as epilepsy, which the worldview of the time associated with demonic possession (cf. v. 18). This aspect of the episode, now completely outmoded in view of medical science, needs sensitive handling so that interpretation does not add to the distress of sufferers and carers today.

[32] Typically, the Matthean version of the story contains two separates instances of "heal" (v. 16; v. 18).

[33] Cf. Boring, "Matthew," 368.

[34] So Matthew; contrast Mark 9:32 and Luke 9:45, where they still misunderstand what Jesus is saying.

[35] Cf. Davies and Allison, *Matthew* 2:735.

The Temple Tax: 17:24-27

This is surely one of the most curious pieces in the entire gospel tradition. Interpreters and preachers down the ages have grappled with the instruction Jesus gives to Peter at the end (v. 27) to go and catch a fish, adding that the first one to hand will contain in its mouth a coin sufficient to cover the tax for both Peter and himself. Though attention naturally fastens on this final instruction—and the singular miracle it implies (though never narrates!)—it is best to regard it as a folkloric detail that Matthew added to reinforce the special position of Peter.[36] The center of gravity of the episode lies elsewhere, especially the teaching on freedom balanced by concern to avoid unnecessary scandal.

The tax in question is the half-shekel tax that, until 70 C.E., devout Jews sent to the Temple yearly to defray the cost of the sacrifices.[37] At the time the gospel was written, of course, the issue was no longer relevant, as the Temple and its sacrifices were no more. But Matthew records the tradition because of the more generally applicable teaching it contains (cf. 5:23-24). Just as "kings of the earth" do not tax members of their own family, so the King of heaven does not tax members of God's family. Since Jesus and the band of disciples constitute precisely this family of God (12:46-50) they are, therefore, free of such obligation. Freedom, however, does not always need to be exercised. In some circumstances—as, for example, to avoid giving scandal (v. 27)—a deeper exercise of freedom may express itself in the choice to forego exercising one's rights in such external matters (cf. 1 Cor 9:1-23). The final instruction about the fish is probably best taken, then, as a humorous, perhaps even teasing afterthought: the deeper freedom one chooses to exercise responds to the providence members of God's family constantly experience from their heavenly Father, symbolized by the gift of the coin in the mouth of the fish.

---

[36] See especially the excellent discussion by John P. Meier, *A Marginal Jew: Rethinking the Historical Jesus.* Vol. 2: *Mentor, Message, and Miracles* (New York: Doubleday, 1994) 880–84.

[37] The Pharisees seem to have regarded the tax as obligatory in light of Exod 30:11-16. Not all parties in Second Temple Judaism agreed. After 70 C.E. it was replaced by a Roman tax, which was compulsory.

Life in the Community of the Church: 18:1-35

Matthew 18 consists entirely of the fourth discourse given by Jesus in the gospel: the discourse on life in the Church. We have learned of the origins of the Church in the band of disciples selected by Jesus out of a wider Israel that is now largely rejecting his ministry. A seemingly innocuous question from the disciples ("Who is the greatest in the kingdom of heaven?" [v. 1]) prompts an instruction from Jesus on the way members of the community should live in relation to each other (contrast the "Mission Discourse" in chapter 10, which focused on attitude to outsiders). While the instruction is set within the later Galilean ministry of Jesus, it reflects the conditions and challenges facing the community responsible for the gospel in the late first century C.E.—conditions vastly different from those of the Church today. Nonetheless, the instruction touches on issues of power, conflict, scandal, and pastoral concern that permanently stir in Christian communities, some resurfacing with renewed vigor in recent times.

The discourse falls into two main sections. The first, 18:1-14, deals with the humble attitude that should prevail in the community, especially in relation to care for its more vulnerable members; it ends with the parable of the Lost Sheep (vv. 12-14). The second, 18:15-35, sets up a structure for dealing with deviant behavior (vv. 15-19), but sets this within the context of unbounded forgiveness (vv. 21-22), reinforced, again, by a concluding parable, that of the Unforgiving Servant (vv. 23-35). A flow of ideas is discernible in the discourse, but there are also tensions: for example, between the radical forgiveness required at the end and the insistence on acting vigorously, even to the point of expulsion, against those who persist in wrongdoing. While the tensions should not be dismissed, it is possible to discern a pattern in which the sensitive matter of fraternal correction (vv. 15-20) falls within an overall framework advocating humility and radical forgiveness.[1] Only if these attitudes prevail will correction reflect the values of the kingdom.

Humility and Concern for the Little Ones: 18:1-14

The disciples' query about the greatest in the kingdom of heaven (v. 1) doubtless has the future, fully arrived kingdom in mind and presumes their own secure place within it. Jesus subverts the concern for rank by making childlike lowliness an *entrance* requirement for the kingdom (vv. 2-3). In so doing he is not commending qualities supposedly characteristic of children—innocence, simplicity, or the like. He is presumably as realistic about children's capacity for nastiness as any parent. In a culture where children were doubtless loved and valued within their families but had no social value or status whatsoever, he is making a stark challenge to the will to power that flourishes in any community. The humility required for entrance into the kingdom consists in not expecting or demanding to be treated with any more consideration than a child, in that society, could expect (v. 4).

When Jesus goes on to say (v. 5) that "whoever welcomes one such child in my name, welcomes me," the perspective begins to shift from one's personal attitude of humility to the kind of consideration for the lowly *members* of the community that such an attitude would promote. The motivation is profound, anticipating the guiding principle of the judgment in 25:31-46: Jesus himself is present in the lowly person symbolized by the child; in welcoming that person one welcomes the living Lord (cf. also 10:40). This introduces a severe and protracted warning (vv. 6-9) against behavior that would "scandalize any one of these little ones." The exact reference of "little ones" (Greek *mikroi*) is much discussed. The fact that they are vulnerable to being scandalized—that is, seriously led astray so that their adherence to the faith is jeopardized—suggests that the phrase refers to people immature in faith, though the main factor behind the description is probably insignificant social status and/or lack of impressive personal gifts.[2] The "millstone" image (v. 6) and the woes that follow (vv. 7-9) employ exaggeration to underline the gravity of the offense.[3] The

---

[1] So W. D. Davies and Dale Allison, *A Critical and Exegetical Commentary on the Gospel According to Saint Matthew.* ICC. 3 vols. (Edinburgh: T&T Clark, 1988–97) 2:751.

[2] Cf. Davies and Allison, *Matthew* 2:761–62; Daniel J. Harrington, *The Gospel of Matthew.* SP 1 (Collegeville: Liturgical Press, 1991) 267.

[3] The "millstone around one's neck" (v. 6) is a proverbial expression like our sense of "an albatross around one's neck." The warnings in vv. 8-9 seem a bit intrusive to the

threat of future punishment, couched in the worldview of apocalyptic Judaism that Matthew inherited, is not mentioned for its own sake, but to bring out the *value* the "little ones" have in God's sight, something also shown by the fact that each has his or her own angel in heaven—no ordinary angel, moreover, but an "angel of the presence," one of those privileged to look upon God's "face" (v. 10).[4]

The parable of the Lost Sheep (vv. 12-14) reinforces this sense of value. A more accurate title might be the "Devoted Shepherd."[5] The shepherd leaves the ninety-nine sheep and goes in search of the one that has gone astray because of its value in his sight—shown by his "rejoicing" over it (v. 13) when at last it is found. The concluding comment (v. 14: "It is not the will of your Father in heaven that one of these little ones should be lost") and the echoes of Ezekiel 34[6] suggest that the shepherd reflects the attitude and action of God.

It is hardly necessary to dwell upon the painful actuality that texts such as this have acquired in recent years in the context of the sexual abuse scandals that have swept the Church—both in regard to actual abuse of "little ones" (either minors or those entrusted to the care of pastors) and failure on the part of administrators to take effective measures to prevent it.

Dealing with Misconduct in the Church: 18:15-20

From concern for the "little ones" who were in danger of straying *from* the Church, the instruction now moves to consider the person who misbehaves and remains *within* the Church. On the one hand the community must be a place where forgiveness is at a premium (18:22-35). On the other hand, the Church is committed to practicing the "surpassing righteousness" of the kingdom (5:20); like any community, it cannot simply turn a blind eye to one or more members who consistently, either knowingly or

---

sequence between vv. 6-7 and v. 10, since now it is a matter of causing *oneself* rather than another "to stumble." They largely repeat the warning already sounded in 5:29-30. There it was a question of taking radical steps to curtail lust; here it is a matter of controlling the will to power. Cf. M. Eugene Boring, "The Gospel of Matthew," in Leander E. Keck, ed., *The New Interpreter's Bible*. Vol. 8 (Nashville: Abingdon, 1995) 375.

[4] The sense is not so much that of a "guardian angel" (whose ministry would be exercised on earth) but of a heavenly advocate who keeps God informed about the treatment, good or bad, meted out to the "little one" on earth.

[5] The parable occurs in another form in Luke 15:3-7, where the sheep is "lost" rather than "gone astray."

[6] "I (God) will seek the lost and bring back the strayed" (Ezek 34:16).

unknowingly, act or live contrary to the values central to its identity. More-over, no community can simply paper over serious disagreements and re-sentments among its members without serious detriment to communal wellbeing. It must have structures of reconciliation in place to deal with both moral deviance and the injuries that people living together inevitably inflict upon one another.[7]

To deal with this issue the gospel provides a carefully gradated struc-ture of fraternal correction, which has close parallels in Judaism of the time and biblical roots in texts such as Lev 19:17-18.[8] The steps are designed to preserve the errant brother or sister as far as possible from public shame. The goal is to "win" (v. 15) the brother or sister in the sense of bringing him or her to an understanding of the matter that will result in conversion and full reintegration into the holiness of the community—in contempo-rary language, to make the procedure a growth opportunity for all con-cerned. If this does not work, then recourse must be had to more serious steps, bringing in two or three witnesses,[9] then "the church,"[10] and ulti-mately, if the person persists in refusing to listen, proceeding to excom-munication[11]—a last resort that was, on the lines of Paul's instruction in 1 Cor 5:1-5, intended to be remedial and temporary rather than final.

The following assurances (vv. 18-20), while couched in more general terms, give the community the comfort that what they are doing when undertaking grave measures of this kind enjoys heavenly ratification.[12] Pre-supposed (v. 19) is agreement in the decision and recourse to prayer. These transform what could be a purely legal and punitive procedure into an act

[7] Whether the instruction deals with sin in general or with interpersonal injury depends on a textual issue: namely, whether the phrase "against you" (Greek *eis se*) in the opening clause (v. 15) is or is not original. If the phrase is original, then interpersonal injury is meant; if not, then sin in more general terms. On balance the longer text has the edge. Even so, the more general sense can be preserved if the second person singular "you" is taken to refer generically to members of the community.

[8] "You shall not hate in your heart anyone of your kin; you shall reprove your neighbor, or you will incur guilt yourself. You shall not take vengeance or bear a grudge against any of your people, but you shall love your neighbor as yourself. . . ."

[9] The language echoes the legal procedures laid down for court cases in Deut 19:15.

[10] Here, of course, the local community is in view—not, as in 16:18, the wider Church.

[11] "Let such person be to you as a Gentile and a tax collector" (v. 17) clearly means excommunication, at least on a temporary basis. The phraseology reflects the Jewish origins of Matthew's community.

[12] The "binding/loosing" authority, which in 16:19 referred to Peter's authority in regard to teaching that is binding upon the Church, here has more specific reference to the local community's power of excommunication.

of union with God in which the risen Lord himself promises to take part (v. 20), guaranteeing the acceptance of the heavenly Father.

In its original sense, then, the instruction and the assurances that support it are tied to a specific disciplinary procedure—one that could really only "work" in a small local community. This does not mean that the values in question are not capable of far wider generalization. What emerges from the passage is an intense sense of the value Christian community life and interaction have in the sight of God. Particularly striking is the way in which the sense of Jesus Emmanuel, explicit at the beginning (1:23) and end (28:20) of the gospel but pervasive throughout, emerges here in a community context. Where "two or three" (the number states the minimum; no number beyond one is too small) are gathered in Christ's name (that is, because they belong to him)—whether for worship or solemn declaration, or simply for prayer and life together—there the risen Lord is present in community with them.[13] And because he is present, they are present also to the court of heaven, anticipating the union of the kingdom.

Forgiveness: 18:21-22;
Parable of the Unforgiving Servant: 18:23-35

An inquiry from Peter (v. 21) raises the issue of forgiveness. Before letting Jesus respond to his question as to how many times he ought to forgive a brother who sins against him,[14] the impetuous Peter makes his own suggestion: "seven times." The perfect number (7) suggests perfect forgiveness, but Jesus goes to the extreme: "seventy-seven times" (v. 22), echoing—but reversing—the brutal threat of Lamech in Gen 4:24 ("If Cain is avenged seven times, truly Lamech seventy-seven times"). Forgiveness must be uncalculating, limitless.

To justify this call for forgiveness without limit Jesus tells the parable of the Unforgiving Servant (vv. 23-35).[15] The king in question (whom we

---

[13] The Greek expression "in the midst of them" *(en mesōi autōn)* echoes exactly the description of Jesus' "placement" of the child in v. 2, suggesting again his identification with the child as symbol of the "little ones" (cf. v. 5).

[14] The Lukan parallel (17:4) makes the situation more reasonable by specifying that the brother or sister has repented and asked for forgiveness; Matthew, more radically, leaves open whether the offending party has expressed regret.

[15] The basic parable undoubtedly goes back to Jesus, with Matthew, as so often, supplying an allegorical application to life in the community (v. 35). The criticism that the parable responds poorly to the issue raised by Peter since it does not feature repeated forgiveness (so,

should not from the start identify with God) is clearly a Gentile king.[16] The servant would be a high official, probably one in charge of the treasury. The amount owed, ten thousand talents,[17] is astronomical, excluding all prospect of repayment—even over a lifetime. Hence the futility of the servant's plea. Precisely because a *Gentile* ruler is in view, the total remission of the debt is an act of pure grace that is utterly unexpected and striking. The order of justice is overwhelmed by mercy.[18] In contrast, the debt the fellow servant owes, one hundred denarii (v. 26), is not excessive;[19] the man could have paid it off in a comparatively short time. His plea (v. 29), couched in the very same terms as his creditor had used (v. 26), is reasonable; he is not asking for remission, only for patience and more time to pay. Hence the monstrosity of the refusal and the recourse to imprisonment (which in fact renders raising the sum impossible). The unforgiving servant, whose entire existence has been restored through an overwhelming triumph of mercy over justice, now in a case against himself that a little mercy would swiftly resolve, withdraws from the sphere of mercy and reverts, with brutal effect, to a narrow application of justice.

We, the audience of the parable, are meant to feel the outrage of the fellow-servants (v. 31) and the justice of the master's remonstration (v. 33). This is the focal point of the story: the vast measure of remission of debt that the unforgiving servant had received created an obligation for him to act with mercy in the far lesser debt owed to him. He has chosen to revert to the order of justice. Now that order is turned against him. Mercy is withdrawn, the debt reinstated, and he must be handed over to the torturers until the entire debt is repaid. Since the debt is so immense as to be unrepayable,

---

e.g., Bernard Brandon Scott, *Hear Then the Parable* [Minneapolis: Fortress, 1989] 268) fails to see that Jesus' reply has already taken the issue beyond "how many times?"

[16] Jewish law forbade the sale of a debtor's wife into slavery and the selling of children was only countenanced in the case of restitution for theft. Nor was torture (v. 34) practiced in Israel—though Herod, aping foreign rulers, made good use of it. Nor, finally, would "worship" (Greek *proskynein*) of an earthly ruler come into question in Israel. (*NRSV* obscures this detail.)

[17] The sum simply represents the largest monetary unit (talent) multiplied by the largest unit of measurement (10,000). The resultant sum would represent more than the annual produce of most of the Eastern provinces of the Roman empire combined. In the present-day context it is difficult not to think of the vast international debts under which the economies of developing countries labor.

[18] Cf. John R. Donahue, *The Gospel in Parable* (Philadelphia: Fortress, 1988) 77. My overall interpretation of the parable is indebted to Donahue.

[19] Since a denarius was roughly equivalent to a day's wages for a laborer, a few months' work could have realized the sum.

the sentence is in fact eternal. Ironically, the servant gets the "time" he had originally begged for (v. 26), but now he will spend it in torment.

Jesus' proclamation of the kingdom of heaven (v. 23) entails a vast measure of divine forgiveness (release of the "debt" of sin). Hence the summons: "Repent, for the kingdom of heaven is at hand!" (4:17). What this parable brings out is the sense that those grasped by the kingdom must realize that the sea of divine forgiveness in which they have been plunged must now so penetrate and mold their lives that they extend it graciously and without measure to those who offend against them. What God wants from *them* is "mercy, not sacrifice" (Hos 6:6; Matt 9:13; 12:7). If they choose in their interpersonal relations to revert to the order of justice, that order will fall back upon them at the judgment with the consequences the ending of the parable (v. 34) so graphically describes. Punishment is not inflicted upon them; they will have chosen it for themselves.

Matthew (v. 35) rams this ending of the parable home by relating it to the behavior of God at the judgment. What are we to make of it? First of all, we do not have to identify *all* the aspects of the Gentile king's behavior with God. As in all the parables, Jesus takes an example of how things happen in the real world, exaggerating some aspect to shock and surprise (here the king's generosity in wiping out the debt), and then lets this make some point about the kingdom. That the king should rescind his original remission and act in the brutal way described has a kind of rough justice about it and hearers of the parable would probably agree that that is how Gentile rulers behave. That Matthew (or Jesus?) should apply this detail to God comes as a shock and surprise. But the torment to which the unforgiving servant is consigned (v. 34) communicates, in the language of apocalyptic Judaism, a sense of the barrier that unforgiveness creates for human sharing of the life of God. Divine forgiveness in the present is unmerited and total. But full possession of the kingdom is still outstanding and "entrance requirements" apply—the one stressed in this parable being that of having passed on to others the forgiveness we have ourselves received from God.[20] We cannot—and do not have to—earn God's forgiveness, but we can lose it.[21]

Forgiveness, nonetheless, is not easy. For some people—and very understandably in view of things they have suffered—it seems an impossible requirement. Fellow Christians and above all pastors would be foolish

---

[20] We recall the same point made in a comment at the conclusion of the Lord's Prayer (6:14-15).

[21] Cf. John P. Meier, *Matthew.* New Testament Message 5 (Wilmington: Michael Glazier, 1980) 209.

simply to confront such people with the demand for forgiveness in the stark form in which it appears here. The capacity to forgive is itself a grace. For many it will be a lifelong project, to be sought in prayer and supplication from God. What Jesus requires is forgiveness "from the heart" (v. 35), that is, from that radical core of a person that is the domain of God and that only God's grace can ultimately touch and heal. It is well to hear the parable of the Unforgiving Servant alongside that of the Weeds in chapter 13. Forgiveness and unforgiveness may long wrestle in human hearts. But God takes the long view and will never deny the grace necessary for salvation. God writes the final chapter in the human heart.

Costly Values of the Kingdom: 19:1–20:34

Jesus now leaves Galilee for the last time (19:1). Instead of going straight to Jerusalem, he makes the customary Jewish detour around the hostile region of Samaria. This means that the location of the narrative section that follows is the "region of Judea beyond the Jordan."

There, as so often in Matthew's account, Jesus heals the large crowds that follow him (v. 2). But he no longer teaches them. Teaching is now reserved for the disciples, whom he is instructing in the values and ways of living distinctive of the kingdom. At stake is a costly way of life, at odds with prevailing values and expectations, one that will be publicly validated only at the great reversal that will accompany the full arrival of the kingdom.

Save for this general sense of costliness and challenge, it is not easy to find a common theme running through this part of the gospel. Jesus interacts with people in ways that show how the values of the kingdom touch upon key areas of family and personal life. The prospect of end-time reversal, illustrated by the centrally located parable of the Laborers in the Vineyard (20:1-16), underpins all.

Marriage, Divorce, Celibacy: 19:1-12; Children: 19:13-15

Some Pharisees approach Jesus in a testing way, inquiring about the lawfulness of divorce "for any cause" (v. 3).[1] Jesus has of course dealt with this matter before, in the Great Sermon (5:31-32), and ultimately his ruling will be the same (v. 9). But here he sets his ruling within a broader pattern of scriptural witness to what God wants in the matter of relations between

---

[1] The last phrase, "for any cause," differentiates the Matthean from the Markan form of the query (10:2). In Mark, Jesus is being asked about the lawfulness of divorce as such; in Matthew the Pharisees draw him into an intra-Jewish debate concerning what constituted valid grounds for divorce.

man and woman. The combined witness of Gen 1:27 and 2:24 shows that the two are to become "one flesh," and so Jesus concludes: "What God has joined together, let no human being separate" (v. 6a). When the Pharisees bring up the Mosaic provision (Deut 24:1) "commanding" (v. 7) a bill of divorce, Jesus (v. 8a) disputes that this was in any sense a command: it was simply a concession to human weakness in the sinful dispensation ("your hardness of heart") that had come about in human affairs. It does not represent the original intention of God (v. 8b), which is now, with the onset of the kingdom, to be reclaimed. Thus Jesus' reiteration (v. 9) of the prohibition against divorce—in its distinctive Matthean form with the exceptive clause[2]—places marriage among those aspects of human life in which the kingdom reasserts and restores the true order of creation. Lifelong faithfulness in marriage is a sign and manifestation of the kingdom—the basis of the later sense of marriage as sacrament.

This ruling draws from the disciples a rather pessimistic, if not cynical, observation, "If such is the case of a man with his wife, it is better not to marry" (v. 10).[3] Jesus does not dismiss the remark out of hand, but qualifies its sweeping generalization (v. 11). Not all can accept "this teaching," but there are some "to whom it has been given."[4] These are those who, in contrast to two other classes of eunuchs (those born that way and those subsequently castrated) "have made themselves eunuchs for the sake of the kingdom of heaven" (v. 12). With this striking phrase Jesus, like Paul in 1 Cor 7:7, endorses celibacy as a state of life some believers are called and gifted to undertake for the sake of the kingdom. As in the cases of the person who discovered the treasure in the field (13:44) and the merchant who has at last come upon the pearl of great value (13:45-46), a glimpse of the kingdom has set them free from other attachments in order to devote themselves more intensively to its service.[5]

Jesus is not here exalting celibacy at the expense of marriage. Both vocations, when faithfully lived out, are manifestations of the kingdom. Since celibacy is meant for some only, it is inappropriate to place celibacy and marriage "side by side" and ask in an abstract kind of way which is the

---

[2] See on 5:31-32 above.

[3] As formulated, the remark reflects a totally male point of view: "If a man cannot get rid of a wife found to be undesirable. . . ."

[4] "This teaching" could refer to the ruling on divorce in vv. 3-9, but it is preferable to relate it to what the disciples have just said: that "it is better not to marry," understood in the restricted sense (for those who have the gift) that Jesus is now explaining.

[5] Herein lies the problem of *compulsory* celibacy, that is, celibacy *imposed* as a condition of some other calling, such as priesthood, not intrinsically connected with it.

"higher" vocation. Marriage is certainly "higher" for someone not called to celibacy. For all that, there has perhaps been an over-compensatory reductiveness in regard to celibacy in the Catholic tradition in the years since Vatican II. It seems clear that Jesus here in Matthew 19 (like Paul in 1 Cor 7:7-8, 25-35) proposes celibacy, *for those who have the gift,* as the way of life most appropriate in view of the onset of the kingdom.

From the question of marriage the "family" theme proceeds, quite naturally, to that of children (vv. 13-15). In 18:2-4 Jesus had taken a child and made that little one a symbol of the humility that should prevail in the community of the kingdom. Now when children are brought to him he no longer speaks of them symbolically but, in the face of contrary inclinations from the disciples (v. 13b), insists that children have a central place in the community's life and worship.[6] From the children in their midst adult members of the community have much to learn about the true nature of the kingdom and the dispositions required to receive it (v. 14b). Jesus seals his words by performing the action his disciples had tried to prevent: he lays his hands on the children before going on his way (v. 15).

Wealth and the Kingdom: the Rich Young Man: 19:16-29

The "family" theme continues in a loose kind of way with the story of the rich young man (vv. 16-22). Seemingly an idealistic person at the threshold of adult life,[7] he asks (in Matthew's version) "What good thing must I do to have eternal life?" (v. 16b)—as though there was just one clear path this renowned teacher could set him upon that would make the gaining of life absolutely secure. Jesus begins by taking up the idea of "goodness," referring it solely to God. Then he sends the man back to the Torah, summed up in the Ten Commandments (v. 17). When the man presses the point further ("Which ones?"), Jesus quotes the "Second Table" commandments (those dealing with the neighbor), adding to the commandment about honoring one's parents a further positive command, from Lev 19:18: "You shall love your neighbor as yourself" (vv. 18-19). Already, then, he is moving the man away from the rather individualistic concern reflected in

---

[6] The disciples' action may reflect conventions of the time, when children were not customarily brought to worship. Jesus counters this by laying his hands on them and praying (v. 13a; v. 15). Cf. M. Eugene Boring, "The Gospel of Matthew," in Leander E. Keck, ed., *The New Interpreter's Bible.* Vol. 8 (Nashville: Abingdon, 1995) 387.

[7] Only Matthew (v. 20) specifies that he is a young man.

his initial query to a more outward-going view focused on the neighbor. The young man's protestation (v. 20) that he has kept all these, and his persistence ("What do I still lack?") strongly convey the sense of seeking something beyond the Torah way. Jesus seems to agree, because he goes on to issue a majestic invitation: "If you wish to be perfect, go, sell your possessions and give the money to the poor, and you will have treasure in heaven; then come, follow me" (v. 21).

It is not at all clear how we should understand "perfect" (Greek *teleios*) here. What does it add to the keeping of the commandments of the Torah, to which Jesus had pointed as leading to eternal life (v. 17) and to which he had added the command to love one's neighbor as oneself (v. 19), later indicated as the second of the commandments upon which "hang the whole law and the prophets" (22:39-40)? Is a "perfection" being described here over and above that of keeping the Torah, even in this radicalized way? In the Jewish frame of discourse presupposed by Matthew's gospel "perfect" has particular reference to observance of the Torah. By inviting the young man to sell all and "come, follow me" the Matthean Jesus is adding to the essential definition of "perfection" the following of himself in discipleship.[8] Henceforth there can be no Torah perfection that does not include following him in dispossession from all source of security except radical trust in God. The "good thing" the young man should do (v. 16) is to surrender himself totally to the One who alone is good (v. 17a).[9]

For the young man, however, the cost is too high. The grief that accompanies his departure (v. 22) shows that in his deepest self he wants to take up Jesus' invitation, but his many possessions in fact possess him.[10] Unlike the man who found the treasure in the field (13:44), or the pearl-dealing merchant (13:45-46), he lacks the freedom to "sell all" in order to obtain the kingdom.

The young man's dilemma leads naturally into the reflection Jesus puts before his disciples on the blockage wealth creates for entrance into the kingdom of God (vv. 23-26). The saying about the camel and the needle should not be watered down,[11] but understood as comic exaggera-

---

[8] This "christological" definition of perfection corresponds to the "theological" one given in 5:48: "Be perfect as your heavenly Father is perfect."

[9] In this sense the invitation picks up the commandments of the "First Table," focused upon God, that Jesus had not quoted in his earlier reply.

[10] Cf. John P. Meier, *Matthew.* New Testament Message 5 (Wilmington: Michael Glazier, 1980) 220.

[11] For example, by suggesting that there was a small "Needle Gate" in Jerusalem and so forth.

tion meant to shock the hearers out of complacency.[12] When the disciples —indeed shocked—protest that what Jesus has just said would exclude virtually everyone from salvation,[13] he points out that salvation is a divine, not a human achievement. By placing their security in something less than God (namely, wealth) human beings block their access to divine power and goodness. Hence the "difficulty" attachment to wealth creates in regard to salvation.[14] The only wise thing to do with wealth is to give it here and now to the poor, thereby converting it into currency viable in the kingdom ("treasure in heaven" [v. 21]).

Peter's observation that he and the other disciples have in fact done what the young man declined—left everything to follow Jesus—leads Jesus to assure them of their "treasure in heaven" (vv. 27-30). The loss they suffer here and now is relativized by the "hundredfold" that awaits them following the great eschatological reversal.[15] Only in light of that reversal does the kind of life they have embraced make sense. We have returned to the perspective of the Beatitudes (5:3-12).

The age-old question remains as to whether the call to radical discipleship ("perfection") Jesus issues to the young man is something meant for a special category of followers, or whether it applies to all believers without discrimination. Interpreters, Catholic as well as Protestant in recent years, scramble over each other in the race to distance themselves from any suggestion of a special category—the kind of thinking that allowed the Catholic tradition to speak of "states of perfection" (monks, religious, bishops, etc.) distinct from the ordinary mass of the faithful. The discussion needs to recover a bit of balance. On the one hand, the fact that Peter goes on to point out (v. 27) that he and the other disciples have in fact done what the young man declined—left all things and followed Jesus—does suggest that Jesus is speaking more generally. On the other hand, when we look at the list

---

[12] An example of a focal instance—as in taking the beam out of one's own eye first (6:4-5).

[13] Why they draw so sweeping a conclusion is not immediately clear. Jesus had spoken in regard to the rich—a minority, surely, in any society. Were there not plenty of poor people who could still be candidates for salvation? (cf. 5:3).

[14] In v. 23 Jesus speaks of difficulty, not "impossibility"—as Boring, taking the "camel/ needle" statement too literally, maintains ("Matthew," 391, 394).

[15] The reversal, expressed here by the rare Greek word *palingennēsia,* refers to the general resurrection when all, including those who have died, will rise for judgment by the Son of Man; cf. Dan 12:1-2. The reversal will particularly vindicate the disciples when they, now despised and humiliated by those presently in ascendancy in Israel, share in the Son of Man's role by "judging the twelve tribes of Israel" (v. 28).

(v. 29) of what leaving all involves—not only houses, siblings, and parents, but also children—clearly what is in view is the itinerant life of Jesus and his immediate disciples in the towns and villages of Galilee (cf. 10:5-16). There is no way that a community like that of Matthew, which saw itself living for at least some generations as the Church (16:17-20), could require such radical abandonment of family life from *all* its members. Counter to Jesus' own words and actions in the section immediately before (19:13-15), children could have no place in such a community.

My sense, then, is that Matthew sees Jesus' invitation as applying to all in some respects and not in others. It applies to all in the sense that salvation is entirely the gift of God that comes to us in Jesus. It further applies to all in the sense that reliance on wealth for security gets in the way of the radical trust in God incumbent upon all who enter the kingdom. Those who retain some measure of wealth and adopt family life must come to terms in other ways with this inner requirement of the kingdom. But, as the history of Christianity has shown, there will always be some who hear Jesus' invitation to the rich young man addressed to themselves more literally. They take on a form of discipleship more closely patterned upon that of Jesus and his immediate disciples, with its radical poverty and dependence on hospitality for support (10:7-14). Individuals such as Anthony of Egypt and Francis of Assisi come instantly to mind. Such individuals have inspired others to follow them—hence the growth of monastic and other religious orders in the Catholic and Eastern tradition—though, as members of such orders will be the first to agree, it is notoriously difficult to "routinize the charism," to retain on a communal basis the radical actual poverty that an individual can practice in response to the call of Jesus. Some few will feel themselves called to literal poverty in this sense for the sake of the kingdom, just as some feel themselves called to be "eunuchs" in the same cause (19:12). But *all* are called to poverty of spirit (5:3), that radical trust—necessary for salvation—in the "good" God proclaimed and made present by Jesus. In this carefully nuanced sense the "two ways" model remains a valid reading of this section of the gospel.

Parable of the Laborers in the Vineyard: 19:30–20:1-16

As told by Jesus, the parable of the Laborers in the Vineyard—more aptly perhaps "the Generous Landowner"—probably served to defend his association with those conventionally branded "tax collectors and sinners" (cf. 9:10-13). The parable addresses the resentment felt by those who had spent long years in faithful observance of the Torah at the welcome and acceptance Jesus gave to those who appeared to come so late to any sense of conversion. It challenges this complaint by unmasking the image of God that lies behind it (One who acts in strict justice) and throwing up a totally different view of the God in whose name Jesus has issued the summons to the kingdom. Matthew appears to have "interfered" very little with the parable as it came to him from the tradition. But "framing" it at the beginning (19:30) and end (20:16) with almost identical statements of reversal (the first to be last/the last to be first), has the effect of making the parable reinforce theologically the prospect of end-time reversal that is the basis of Jesus' assurance about the value of leaving all things (19:27-22).[16]

The details of the parable reflect the socio-economic situation of Palestine in Jesus' day. The denarius was the basic day's payment for the kind of casual labor involved (*NRSV*: "usual daily wage"); the Torah stipulated payment before sundown (Lev 19:13; Deut 24:14-15). Everything goes according to expectation save that our curiosity is aroused by the landowner's instruction, when the time for payment comes, to begin with those who had begun their work last (v. 8). We share the expectation of the early workers that they will receive more, and we share their resentment when they, who have borne the heat and burden of the entire working day, receive the same remuneration as those who had worked less than an hour (vv. 10-12). The landowner's defense (vv. 13-15)[17] poses a neat dilemma concerning justice. Does justice mean being paid the exact amount agreed upon? Or does it mean being paid what others are paid for the same amount of work? The latter would certainly apply in industrial relations today. But the landowner's defense plucks us out of the sphere of strict equity in the name of his freedom to be generous. The latecomers too had families to support; they needed the denarius subsistence wage. If the landowner, out of wider social concern, chooses to be generous and to pay everyone what social justice today would call a "living wage," have they really grounds for complaint?

The parable dramatically reinforces the sense of a God desirous to be as generous as possible with the gift of salvation, continuing in this way the sense of divine "goodness" that underpinned Jesus' interaction with the

---

[16] Strictly speaking, the idea of reversal applies to the parable only in the sense that the workers get paid in reverse order to their hour of hiring.

[17] It is rather long-winded for an original parable of Jesus. Matthew may have added vv. 14b-15 by way of allegorical application to God.

young man (19:16-22).[18] In the long run God gives salvation as an unmerited free gift. Whether human beings have "worked" long or little for it is not ultimately decisive.[19]

The Costly Following of Jesus Continued: Another Passion Prediction: 20:17-19; Service Rather Than Ambition: 20:20-28; Two Blind Men Healed: 20:29-34.

A further warning about what awaits Jesus in Jerusalem intervenes (vv. 17-19). Communicated privately to the Twelve and very explicit in its details, it forms a striking background for the approach by the mother of two of them, the sons of Zebedee (James and John). Her request is that they be assured of the two leading places in the messianic kingdom.[20] The request shows how little the companions of Jesus had advanced in their understanding since the episode at Caesarea Philippi (16:13-28). They know he is the Messiah, destined one day to be in possession of the messianic kingdom. Despite four clear warnings (16:21-23; 17:12; 17:22-23; 20:17-19), they still cannot or will not grasp that the path to that possession will run through suffering and death. Much of the preceding narrative had dealt with the problems created for discipleship by attachment to wealth. This episode deals with a parallel human tendency, equally contrary to the way of Jesus: the craving for power and prominence.

Jesus does not dismiss the request but, speaking directly to the two disciples themselves (vv. 22-23), puts before them two considerations bound up with its fulfillment. First (v. 22), are they prepared to "drink the cup"—biblical imagery for suffering—that lies ahead?[21] When they reply in the affirmative, Jesus assures them (v. 23) that they will indeed drink his cup, but then goes on to point out that the assigning of places at the banquet

---

[18] Cf. Rudolf Schnackenburg, *The Gospel of Matthew* (Grand Rapids and Cambridge: Eerdmans, 2002) 192–93.

[19] This should be a comfort for those worried about the ultimate fate of loved ones whose pattern of life has shown no outward sign of virtue or respectability.

[20] It is probably to shield these two significant disciples from suspicion that they have entirely misunderstood what Jesus has been saying that Matthew has the mother, rather than the disciples themselves (as in Mark 10:35) make the request. She will be present at the scene of Jesus' death (27:56) when her sons, along with all the other male disciples, have fled.

[21] "Cup" in this sense recurs in Jesus' prayer in Gethsemane (26:39, 42).

of the kingdom belongs to the Father alone. For Jesus—and for those who would follow him—the present task is "to fulfill all righteousness" (3:15): to carry out his messianic mission according to the way marked out in the Scriptures (26:54, 56), trusting simply in the power and faithfulness of the One whose "beloved Son" he knows himself to be (3:17; 17:5); the details of how it will all end remain in the hands of the Father.

The episode moves to a second stage (vv. 24-28) when the remaining ten disciples, uncomprehending of what Jesus is saying, show resentment at the Zebedees' attempt to advance their cause. Aware of the reaction, Jesus brings the issue of ambition and power out into the open, taking the opportunity to explain how authority is to run in the community of the kingdom. Nothing could be clearer than the contrast he draws between the way secular Gentile rulers exercise power[22] and what should prevail "among them." In contrast to those rulers, anyone "who wishes" (the verb picks up the sense of ambition) to be "great among you" must be servant *(diakonos)* and slave *(doulos)*. The Zebedees had wanted to sit in the places of honor at the banquet. Jesus is saying: Leave place allocation to the Father; the task now is to adopt the position of the waiter *(diakonos)* who brings the food to the guests at the table[23] or—even more radically— that of the slave *(doulos)* whose whole person and capacity is totally at the disposition of others.

The climactic statement, "for the Son of Man came not to be served but to serve and to give his life as a ransom for many" (v. 28), makes the practice of the Lord (christology) the pattern for how the way things are to run in the community (ecclesiology).[24] One of the most important sentences in the entire gospel, it sums up the meaning of Jesus' mission and the outcome to which it is now leading. Instead of being the conquering Messiah of conventional expectation, in which he could hope to "be served," Jesus "fulfills all righteousness" (3:15) by placing himself at the service of others. He has done so in his burden-lifting ministry of teaching and healing. He is now to consummate this service by giving "his life as a ransom for many." The final phrase "for many" (to recur in the eucharistic words over the cup [26:28]) once again ascribes to Jesus the role of the Isaianic Servant, this time alluding explicitly to the ending of the Fourth Song

---

[22] The two Greek verbs, *katakyrieuein* and (the rare) *katexousiazein,* convey the sense, not only of exercising authority, but of doing so in an oppressive and exploitative way.

[23] The basic sense of the Greek word *diakonos* is that of one who acts as an emissary or go-between on behalf of another, one who conveys something on behalf of another.

[24] Cf. Meier, *Matthew,* 229.

(Isa 53:10-12), where the Servant's suffering "bears" the sins of others (literally, in Semitic idiom, "of many" [53:10, 12]).[25] As announced at his birth and naming, the Messiah's final "service" will be to "save the people from their sins" (1:21).

The Church uses the language of this passage—"ministry" (the Latinate form of *diakonein*)—to describe its characteristic activity. But it is sobering to consider the extent to which its structures, procedures, and self-presentation developed over its long history reflect those of secular authority rather than what might be suggested by the words of Jesus. Obviously, as a permanent community gathered around certain core values the Church requires formal structures and institutions of leadership. One wonders, however, whether the Church, especially in its more hierarchical order, returns sufficiently often to this passage, to ponder its implications for life and service.

In this difficult area we can draw comfort from the final scene in Jesus' journey: his healing of two blind men as he is leaving Jericho.[26] Twice the men cry out to the Son of David in terms reminiscent of the Christian liturgy: "Lord . . . have mercy on us" (v. 30; v. 31). Finally (v. 33), they ask the Lord that their eyes be opened. "Moved with compassion," he touches their eyes; they regain their sight and follow him (v. 34). The quasi-liturgical appeals and the location of the scene after so many instances of the disciples' "blindness" to the cost of following Jesus suggest that it has an intentional symbolic meaning in regard to the later Church.[27] Jesus' compassion and power are available for all who make their way along the costly path of discipleship.

---

[25] Neither here nor in 26:28 should "many" be understood in a restrictive sense, as though the Servant (and ultimately Jesus) conferred benefits upon a select number only. "Many" stands over against the single one in the sense of "the one and the many." Not all interpreters find allusion to Isaiah 53 here (cf., e.g., Ulrich Luz, *Matthew 8–20. A Commentary.* Translated by James E. Crouch. Hermeneia [Minneapolis: Fortress, 2001] 546), but see the extended discussion in W. D. Davies and Dale Allison, *A Critical and Exegetical Commentary on the Gospel according to Saint Matthew.* ICC. 3 vols. (Edinburgh: T&T Clark, 1988–97) 3:95–97; also Meier, *Matthew,* 229.

[26] The miracle, while based on Mark 10:46-52 (with a typical Matthean doubling of the characters), is also a doublet of the healing described in 9:27-31.

[27] Cf. Luz, *Matthew 8–20,* 459.

4. THE MESSIAH'S MINISTRY IN JERUSALEM: 21:1–25:46

The Contest for Authority in Jerusalem: 21:1–22:46

Jesus' journey from Galilee to Judea has reached its goal. The Messiah, Son of David, is poised to enter and take possession of David's city, Jerusalem. Though he will do so in a way that shows him to be a humble rather than a conquering king, his entrance will shake the city to its foundations (21:10). His presence and activity in the city provoke the conflict with those currently in power that will lead, before the end of the week (Passover week) to his arrest and execution. Physically, then, Jesus will lose out. What the long sequence of conflict stories and judgment parables (21:23–22:46) will show is his moral supremacy. To this his resurrection will give final vindication when, standing on a mountain in Galilee, he will claim: "All authority has been given to me in heaven and on earth" (28:18).

Jesus Enters Jerusalem as Its Messiah, Son of David: 21:1-11

Following Peter's correct identification of him as Messiah (16:16) Jesus had given his disciples strict instructions that they were not to spread this information to anyone else (16:20; cf. also 17:9). This was to dampen any messianic recognition of him not accompanied by awareness of the distinctive way in which he was going to fulfill his mission: serving and giving his life as a ransom for many (20:28). Now Jesus does make an

157

entry into Jerusalem that is clearly messianic and understood to be such by the accompanying crowd.[1] But he carefully stage-manages the entry to make it conform to and signal the kind of Messiah he intends to be.

Jesus achieves this transformation by choosing to enter the city riding not on a white charger like a conquering king, but on a donkey, a symbol of peace and humility.[2] Matthew portrays this as a deliberate intention to fulfill a scriptural prophecy concerning the Messiah (vv. 4-5):

> Tell the daughter of Zion, Look, your king is coming to you, humble, and mounted on a donkey, and on a colt, the foal of a donkey.

The text as quoted from Zech 9:9[3] omits the epithets "triumphant and victorious is he,"[4] so as to focus all attention on "humble" (Greek *praus*) and on the mode of transport. So anxious is Matthew to have Jesus fulfill the prophecy as literally as possible that, ignoring the conventions of Hebrew parallelism (which simply offered two descriptions of a single beast), he has Jesus ride simultaneously on two animals, a donkey and her colt. The resultant, unintentionally comical picture shows that in entering the city in this humble way Jesus fulfills the role marked out for the Messiah in the Scriptures.

The crowds hail Jesus as Son of David (v. 9), transforming the old cry of welcome to pilgrims: "Blessed in the name of the Lord is the one who comes" (Ps 118:25-26) into a messianic acclamation: "Blessed be the one who comes in the name of the Lord" (v. 9). Like the magi's enquiry many years before (2:3), the acclamation causes "the whole city" to "shake" (v. 10).[5] Well might the inhabitants ask, "Who is this?"—even if the response they get from the crowds ("This is the prophet Jesus from Nazareth" [v. 11]) hardly does justice to the stature of the one being acclaimed.

---

[1] The "crowd" in this scene (vv. 8, 9, 11) seems to represent a wider body, distinct from the inner band of Jesus' disciples, that is vaguely enthusiastic about Jesus but not clear about the true nature of his messiahship (cf. v. 11).

[2] The donkey was not an animal of ridicule. In 1 Kings 1:31-32 David gives instructions that his son and designated successor Solomon is to ride to his anointing as future king on the royal donkey.

[3] The quotation is basically from Zech 9:9, though the opening clause, "Tell the daughter of Zion," is taken from Isa 62:11, replacing Zechariah's "Rejoice greatly, O daughter of Zion."

[4] So the Hebrew original. The LXX reads "righteous and saving," which would have been more appropriate.

[5] The Greek word *(eseisthē)* normally describes an earthquake (cf. 27:51 and 28:2). Many translations (e.g., *RSV; NRSV*) mask this strong expression.

The Messiah Reclaims the Temple: 21:10-17

The heart of Jerusalem and source of its holiness was the Temple. It is appropriate, then, that following his festal entry into the city God's Son should enter and assert his authority in his Father's house (v. 12). There (in the Matthean account) he does two things. First, he drives out those who were selling and buying, overturning also the tables of the moneychangers and dove-sellers (v. 12), justifying his action with a composite scriptural appeal in the name of his Father, "My house shall be called a house of prayer (Isa 56:7) but you are making it a den of robbers (Jer 7:11)" (v. 13). The action upholds the sanctity of the Temple while at the same time pointing prophetically to its destruction, since the activities overthrown by Jesus were essential to the sacrificial system. Second, he resumes in the Temple the ministry of healing characteristic of his entire mission.[6] The blind, the lame, and the physically afflicted in general were not supposed to be in the Temple at all, their presence considered incompatible with its holiness (Lev 21:16-24). David had excluded such persons from the Lord's house (LXX 2 Sam 5:6, 8). Now the Son of David attracts the afflicted to the Temple and makes it a place of healing. The two activities of Jesus in the Temple—expulsion and healing—neatly give expression once more to the divine preference: "What I want is mercy, not sacrifice" (Hos 6:6; Matt 9:13; 12:7).

This activity attracts the hostility of the chief priests and scribes, the ones Jesus had already named in the Passion predictions (16:21; 20:18) as the prime agents in bringing about his death. When they react to his healing activity and to the children's crying out in the Temple, "Hosanna to the Son of David" (v. 15),[7] Jesus throws back a further scriptural challenge. Have they never read the words "out of the mouths of infants and nursing babes you have prepared praise for yourself" (Ps 8:2)? The "infants" who recognize him, in contrast to the religious professionals and experts who do not, illustrate the exclamation made earlier in the gospel: "I thank you, Father, Lord of heaven and earth, because you have hidden these things from the

---

[6] Only Matthew mentions Jesus' healing activity (v. 14) and the reaction it provokes (vv. 15-16).

[7] The hailing of Jesus as "Son of David" in association with healing may associate him with Solomon, celebrated in the Jewish tradition for his healing powers and also the builder of the original Temple. Jesus has declared his intention to "build" the Church (16:18) as the place where the afflicted may have access to the healing power of God. Cf. especially M. Eugene Boring, "The Gospel of Matthew," in Leander E. Keck, ed., *The New Interpreter's Bible*. Vol. 8 (Nashville: Abingdon, 1995) 405–406.

wise and the intelligent and have revealed them to infants" (11:25). With this exchange Jesus' visit to the Temple comes to an end. The stage is set for confrontation with those presently in power. They will not easily surrender their hold on the city and the Temple to this kind of Messiah.

A Fig Tree Bearing No Fruit: 21:18-22

What are we to make of the curious episode the following day in which Jesus curses—and blights—a fig tree on which he finds no fruit (21:18-22)?[8] This last miracle, if such it deserves to be called, is exceptional in that nowhere else (save in the Markan parallel, Mark 11:12-14, 20-25) do the gospels portray Jesus using his powers for his own benefit, and especially not in the kind of piqued and vengeful way displayed here. The origins of the tradition are shrouded in mystery,[9] but the image of a fig tree that fails to bear fruit appears in the prophetic literature as an expression of divine disappointment with Israel (Hos 9:10-17; Jer 8:13; cf. Luke 13:6-9). At some stage in the early gospel tradition it was felt appropriate to insert this account of a prophetic gesture on the part of Jesus as a comment on the leaders' critical reaction to Jesus' activity in the Temple and a sign of the judgment to come. Mark, followed by Matthew, retained the prophetic gesture but, perhaps embarrassed by this record of behavior uncharacteristic of Jesus, made it end as a lesson on faith and prayer (Mark 11:22-25; Matt 21:21-22). Jesus had found the Temple wanting as a "house of prayer" (v. 13); the community of the Church he is "building" is to be, in its stead, a "house" of truly efficacious prayer.[10]

The Question of Authority: 21:23-27

Jesus has returned to the Temple (v. 23a). He had made it a base for his ministry of healing (v. 14). Now it becomes the locale of his parallel ministry of teaching (cf. chs. 5–7; 8–9). Those currently in power, the chief

---

[8] Mark distributes this episode in two stages with a night between (11:12-14, 20-25). In Matthew it is a single incident, with Jesus' cursing having instantaneous effect on the tree.

[9] After long discussion John P. Meier (*A Marginal Jew: Rethinking the Historical Jesus.* Vol. 2: *Mentor, Message, and Miracles* [New York: Doubleday, 1994] 884–96) firmly rejects any likelihood that the tradition goes back to an action of Jesus.

[10] Cf. W. D. Davies and Dale Allison, *A Critical and Exegetical Commentary on the Gospel according to Saint Matthew.* ICC. 3 vols. (Edinburgh: T&T Clark, 1988–97) 3:154.

priests and the elders of the people, approach and put to him the question that directly rules the entire section, "By what authority are you doing these things and who gave you this authority?" (v. 23b). Jesus' authority, of course, comes from God. But to claim this directly would place him in their hands on a charge of blasphemy. So, setting a pattern that will run through the sequence, he refuses to answer directly, confronting *them* instead with a question of his own concerning the baptism of John. Trapped, they are forced to feign ignorance (v. 27). Round one to Jesus!

The Two Sons: 21:28-32

Jesus remains on the offensive with the little parable of the Two Sons, one of whom after an initial refusal ended by doing his father's will, while the other failed to carry out what he had initially promised. Forced to the inevitable conclusion that it is the first rather than the second son who does the will of the father (v. 31a), the opponents find themselves exposed to an intolerable comparison with tax collectors and prostitutes. These outcasts, whose lifestyle suggested a complete "No" to God's will revealed in the Torah, eventually carried it out by responding to the preaching of John. The opponents, whose adherence to the Torah seemed to betoken a strong "Yes," frustrated that by resisting his summons to conversion. That is why the tax collectors and prostitutes will gain entrance ahead of them to the kingdom of God.

Though spoken with reference to the ministry of John, the parable applies equally to the ministry of Jesus, who received a more positive response from those on the margins (cf. especially 9:9-12). Toward such people, fidelity to the will of the Father impelled Jesus to act *inclusively* rather than exclusively. At a deeper level the parable makes the point that what God looks to is the final outcome in people's lives. God can put up with an initial "No," and a lot of other "No's" besides, on the way to a final and lasting "Yes." On the other hand, people who appear religious and obedient from the start may never sufficiently plumb the depth of God's mercy to know God as God really is. A judgmental attitude may indicate lack of true conversion and real knowledge of God.

What ultimately determines fitness for eternal life is conformity of the human heart to the heart of God. No human being could ever amass sufficient good works to merit even a second of life with God. The latter will be God's gift in abundance if only we have grown—sometimes in the course of a very winding life journey—into the capacity to receive it.

The Murderous Tenants: 21:33-46

The "vineyard" theme continues in the parable of the Murderous Tenants. While it is not easy to discern the shape of the parable as told by Jesus, we can be fairly sure that he told it against the religious leadership in Jerusalem in his day. Because they had resisted the prophetic messengers sent by God, the last of whom was himself, they have shown themselves to be usurpers, attempting to control and retain for themselves the vineyard (Israel) and its produce (the life of the people). For them the full arrival of the kingdom will mean dispossession and retribution.

Whatever the shape of the original parable, in the accounts we have in the synoptic tradition (Matt 21:33-46; Mark 12:1-12; Luke 20:9-19) allegory has completely taken over, introducing features that make the story quite unrealistic.[11] With the help of allegory the early Christian tradition, followed by Matthew, transformed the parable into a rich account of salvation history. The vineyard is Israel,[12] the landowner God. The slaves sent to collect the produce are the prophets sent to Israel. The son whom the tenants throw out of the vineyard and kill is, of course, Jesus, who died outside the city of Jerusalem.[13] The response the hearers are compelled to give (v. 41) clearly alludes to the destruction of Jerusalem in 70 C.E., while the "other tenants" to whom the vineyard is leased until harvest time would be the community of a reconstituted Israel made up of Jewish and Gentile believers. The reach of the parable extends to take in the resurrection when Jesus directs (v. 42) his hearers to the prophecy about the "rejected stone" that became "the cornerstone" (Ps 118:22-23),[14] while the final comment (v. 43)[15] reinforces the sense of the Church as inheritor of the kingdom removed from the original tenants.

---

[11] Following the murder of two sets of slaves the landowner's sending of his son, in the hope that he would be respected, seems foolish in the extreme. Likewise unreal is the tenants' hope to get control of the inheritance simply by murdering the heir, as also is the landowner's ability to put them to "a miserable death" (v. 41).

[12] Verse 33b contains echoes of Isaiah's "song" of his friend's unproductive vineyard (Isa 5:1-2), which the prophet applied to "unfruitful" Israel (vv. 3-4).

[13] The "vineyard" has at this point become Jerusalem. In Matthew the killing of the son precedes expulsion from the vineyard, matching more closely what was done to Jesus (contrast Mark 12:8).

[14] From "vineyard" the image has become architectural. A stone that because of its irregular shape was initially rejected as unsuitable for inclusion in the main (straight) part of a wall was subsequently found to be just right for a position on a corner or an arch.

[15] The odd sentence appearing in some manuscripts as v. 44 is best seen as an interpolation from Luke 20:18.

This parable, particularly in light of the comment appearing as v. 43, is one of the texts in the New Testament most open to a sense of the Christian Church "superseding" or "replacing" the Jewish people as the people of God. It is important to note, however, that it is the "tenants" who are destroyed, not the vineyard. The parable is targeting the Jerusalem leadership, not the Jewish people as a whole. While "the nation" to whom the kingdom will be given (v. 43) seems unmistakably to be the Church as the mixed community of Jewish and Gentile believers,[16] the parable leaves open the relationship between the Christian Church and that part of Israel (the Jewish people) that did not come to faith in Jesus as Messiah. Moreover, "kingdom" and Church are not simply identified. The kingdom *will* be given to a people *that produces its fruits*. The future reference is to the judgment: possession of the kingdom will be for those whose lives display the "righteousness" God wants. The reconstituted Israel, no less than the old, is a "vineyard" from which God expects to reap the "produce" of good works (cf. 25:31-46). The parable provides no grounds for Christian triumphalism at Jewish expense.

The Spurned Invitations to the Wedding: 22:1-14

The story of declined invitations to a royal marriage feast appears in significantly different form in Luke 14:16-24.[17] While Jesus seems to have told a parable of the kingdom around this image, retrieving its original content through the layers of tradition is not easy. Nonetheless, we can say that central to the parable is the sense of the kingdom as a great banquet of life. Jesus' role is to issue the invitations. The "banquet" still lies in the future, but those who respond positively to his message can live meanwhile in the joy of anticipation and the sense of being valued and wanted that the invitation conveys. In this sense the kingdom, while not yet fully present, can already transform people's lives (cf. 13:44-46). Jesus presumably told the parable as a comment on the lack of response he was getting from the religious establishment (those first invited), contrasted with the positive response from those on the margins. With these he was already celebrating the joy of the kingdom (9:10-17).

---

[16] Attempts have been made to restrict "nation" to the Christian leadership; see Anthony J. Saldarini, *Matthew's Christian-Jewish Community* (Chicago and London: University of Chicago Press, 1994) 58–63; Daniel J. Harrington, *The Gospel of Matthew.* SP 1 (Collegeville: Liturgical Press, 1991) 304. These strain the meaning of the Greek word *ethnos*.

[17] Likewise in the (non-canonical) *Gospel of Thomas* (64).

Where Luke made the parable a reflection upon the way in which absorption in various concerns prevented people from responding to the invitation,[18] Matthew so allegorized it in the direction of the Christian story of salvation as to deprive it of virtually all realism. Matthew also added the denouement about the guest without a wedding garment, placing realism under still further strain. While people still hear the parable as a story, it is probably best to make clear from the start that it is an allegory through and through and that we should not be too dismayed by all the aspects that fail to add up.

In the allegory as it stands in Matthew the king represents God, the son Jesus, and the wedding banquet the time of divine-human celebration symbolized by the kingdom. (The parable continues in this sense the attractive biblical theme featuring relations between YHWH and Israel in terms of spousal and wedding imagery [Hos 2:19-20; Isa 54:4-8; 62:5].) In the social world of Jesus' day it was not uncommon for invitations to be sent out in two stages: first, a general invitation to an event as yet some time off; then, on the day itself or just before, a "reminder" to come since all is ready. The story presupposes that the first invitation has already gone off: "those invited" (v. 3) would represent Israel; those sent to issue the reminder in the first instance would be the biblical (OT) prophets. Those sent following the first rejection would be Christian missionaries devoting their efforts to Israel (10:5); the message they convey—"everything is ready" (v. 4)—reflects the sense of the messianic era *(kairos)* having arrived with the ministry of Jesus. The note of unreality enters with what happens next: the mistreatment of these second emissaries and the king's violent response, destroying the perpetrators and burning their city[19]— clear allusions to mistreatment of Christian missionaries (cf. 10:17-33) and the destruction of Jerusalem in 70 C.E., interpreted by Matthew, along with the wider early Christian tradition, as divine retribution for failure to respond to the Gospel. The story proper resumes (vv. 8-10) with a final invitation, this time going into the streets to draw everyone, bad and good alike,[20] into the wedding hall for the banquet. Clearly in view at this point is the mission of the Church beyond Israel to the nations of the world (28:18-20).

---

[18] See further Brendan Byrne, *The Hospitality of God: A Reading of Luke's Gospel* (Collegeville: Liturgical Press; Strathfield, N.S.W.: St. Paul's Publications, 2000) 123–24.

[19] "While dinner waits, the king wages war . . ." (Boring, "Matthew," 417).

[20] The *NRSV* ("good and bad") reverses the order in the Greek original, masking the way Matthew draws attention to the presence of the "bad" in the community of the kingdom.

Now (vv. 11-13) comes the part of the parable readers find most disturbing: the king's unreasonable treatment of the unfortunate person who, picked up from the street, is faulted—and ejected into outer darkness—for not having a wedding robe. How could he have had time—let alone resources—to get one? Once again we have to keep in mind that what we have here is not something integral to the story but an illustration, within an allegory, of an important truth for the Christian community. Those ultimately invited to the banquet of the kingdom include "bad" as well as "good" (v. 10). The community of the kingdom is a mixed bag—a situation that will persist until the judgment (cf. already 13:24-30, 36-43). The man without a wedding garment represents all those who accepted the invitation but did not, within that calling, undergo the conversion of life required for entrance into the final kingdom. At the judgment—imaged by the king's coming in to see the guests (v. 11)—they will be found lacking the "wedding garment" of good works and suffer the exclusion described (in familiar Matthean terms, v. 13).

Thus this allegorical parable takes a sweep across salvation history extending further than the previous one. Going beyond the experience of Israel's "No" to the Gospel, it challenges members of the Church not to be complacent about their inheritance of the kingdom. "Many" (= "all") are called to the "banquet" of the kingdom (v. 14) but "few" (= not all) are "chosen" (= destined to enter).[21]

Paying Taxes to Caesar: 22:15-22

Following the three parables we have the first of four conflict stories in which representatives of leading parties in Jerusalem struggle with Jesus for moral and social ascendancy. Not only does Jesus in each instance escape the trap; he wrests the issue away from his adversaries, making it an opportunity for significant teaching of his own.

The tax issue offers a perfect stratagem to entrap Jesus. If he supports the payment of the highly unpopular poll tax he will lose standing with the people; if he rejects payment he runs the risk of being identified with

---

[21] The language of v. 14 reflects Semitic idiom, in which "many" can mean "all" and "few" can mean "not everyone." "Chosen" has the sense of those destined to have eternal life. The sentence holds together the truth that both divine grace and human works have a role in salvation. "Salvation history is a web made up of the interaction between God's gracious invitation and man's *(sic)* free response" (John P. Meier, *Matthew.* New Testament Message 5 [Wilmington: Michael Glazier, 1980] 249).

groups (such as those later known as Zealots) who were in more or less perpetual rebellion against Rome, and so presenting himself as a significant threat to peace and public order.

Jesus not only escapes the dilemma but actually goes over to the offensive. By calling for *them* to produce a coin with Caesar's image on it he shows his adversaries up as people who carry around the offensive coinage, while he does not. They are revealed as already collaborating, whereas his own position is not disclosed. His dual "render . . ." instruction (v. 21) goes beyond their terms of reference by setting responsibility to the civil power (which he does not deny) within the broader and higher framework of obedience to God. Members of God's people are summoned to constant discernment as to how, within the overall claim of God, they are to discharge civic obligations. In the matter of relations between Church and state, Jesus bequeaths an ethical task rather than a detailed prescription.

Concerning the Resurrection: 22:23-33

The challenge from the Sadducees arises naturally out of a characteristic tenet of their sect. Accepting only the Five Books of Moses (the Pentateuch) as authentic Scripture and finding in them no trace of life after death, they refused to believe in any kind of human immortality save the continuance of an individual's name in the family line. Hence, from the Torah's prescription requiring a man to raise up offspring for a brother who has died (Deut 25:5-6; cf. Gen 38:8) they have conjured up a quibble (vv. 24-28) that seems to make belief in life after death ridiculous. The quibble rests on a crass assumption that such a mode of existence would simply be a repetition or extension of life in the present time, with the same conditions applying. Jesus attacks this flaw in their argument with a two-stage clarification, displaying both theological and scriptural superiority. First (vv. 29-30), in the case of the risen life we are dealing with a totally new situation brought about by God's power.[22] Since no one dies any more (being in this respect "like the angels in heaven") there is no longer any need for procreation, and hence no need for marriage, the institution designed to supply it.[23] Second (vv. 30-32), the Pentateuch itself has a cele-

---

[22] Cf. Paul's plea for a similarly sophisticated understanding of risen bodily existence in 1 Cor 15:35-53.

[23] We should not look here for a complete theology of marriage. Jesus is responding to the Sadducees on their own terms.

brated passage in which God declares "I am the God of Abraham, Isaac, and Jacob" (Exod 3:6). This description—"I *am*," not "I was"—implies an ongoing divine relationship with the three and hence their continuing personal existence.[24] The relationship God seeks to forge with human beings here and now is one that transcends death; otherwise it would not be truly personal.

The Greatest Commandment of the Torah: 22:34-40

In Matthew's account (contrast Mark 12:28-34) the question about the greatest commandment of the Law comes as a further attempt on the part of the Pharisees to put Jesus to the test. Once again Jesus sails through the trick question to new vistas of understanding. The "greatest command- ment" he takes from a very familiar text: the command in Deut 6:5 to "love the Lord your God with all your heart, and with all your soul, and with all your mind," the commandment that forms the basis of the *Shema* prayer recited by observant Jews several times a day. He goes beyond the original question (v. 39) by placing alongside this command "a second like it," also taken from Scripture: "love your neighbor as yourself" (Lev 19:18), adding (v. 40) the comment, "On these two commandments hang all the law and the prophets."[25] The "second" commandment is "like" the first in the sense of being of equal weight.[26]

The distilling of the Torah to a single, all-embracing command, whether of love of God or of neighbor, was not unknown in the Judaism of the time. The combination is less evidenced and seems distinctive of Jesus.[27] We remember that he had already added the command to love one's neighbor as oneself among the commandments listed for the young man who asked him about eternal life (19:19). More significantly still, we recall two instructions given to the disciples in the Great Sermon: the extension of the "love" command to loving (not hating) one's enemies

[24] Strictly speaking, the argument proves only immortality rather than bodily resurrection but, since the Sadducees rejected any concept of life after death, the point against them stands.

[25] This comment is peculiar to Matthew, for whom "the law" (= the Pentateuch) must always be interpreted in conjunction with "the prophets"—specifically the "mercy" require- ment of Hos 6:6 (Matt 9:13; 12:7).

[26] The "twinning" reflects the "two tables" division of the Ten Commandments, those dealing with God, those dealing with one's neighbor.

[27] See further Boring, "Matthew," 424.

(5:43-48) and the summary of the meaning of the "law and the prophets" as treating others as one would wish to be treated oneself (7:12). Without erasing the distinction between them, Jesus reaches here for a radical unity in the two commandments. To love God with all one's heart and soul and mind (that is, with one's whole being and life-energy) is inseparable from an active love of those whom God loves in the way God loves them, that is, with a love that is compassionate and extends even to the hostile.[28] Jesus does not set aside other commandments of the Torah (cf. 5:17-19) but, as his illustrative rulings (5:21-48) have already shown, he makes love the criterion and the key for interpreting all its other requirements (v. 40; cf. Gal 5:14; Rom 13:8-10 [also citing Lev 19:18]).

The Messiah—More Than "David's Son": 22:41-46

In the fourth and final conflict story Jesus himself goes on the offensive, putting a question of his own to the Pharisees. The question bears upon an issue that has run throughout the narrative and been posed acutely by the manner of Jesus' entry into Jerusalem: can someone who acts in the way Jesus acts be truly the long-awaited Messiah, Son of David? In a final display of his superiority as interpreter of Scripture, Jesus unmasks the inadequacy of the prevailing messianic understanding and in so doing prepares the way for the exalted sense in which messiahship as applied to him must be understood. He does so by putting before the Pharisees an exegetical problem arising out of Ps 110 (LXX 109):1: "The Lord said to my lord. . . ." The problem presupposes the conventional attribution of the Psalms to David and also a messianic understanding of the psalm in question. If, as the Pharisees concede, the Messiah is David's son, and if (as generally held) descendants are inferior, not superior, in status to ancestors, how is it that David, an inspired author ("speaking in the Spirit"), can address his "son" in this psalm as "lord"? The inability of the Pharisees to reply leaves an answer hanging in the air: the Messiah is David's son, yes, but he must also be more than David's son. He must be, as we readers and the disciples know, the Son of *God*.

---

[28] Cf. especially Ulrich Luz, *Das Evangelium nach Matthäus.* 4 vols. Vol. 3: *Mt 18–25* (Zürich: Benziger; Neukirchen-Vluyn: Neukirchener Verlag, 1985–2002) 3:283.

True and False Models for Leadership: 23:1-39

No area of Matthew's gospel presents more difficulty for the modern interpreter than the section (ch. 23) that now lies before us. It consists almost entirely of sustained polemic against the scribes and Pharisees, whose manner of leadership it presents as a negative example of what should *not* prevail in the community of Jesus (see especially vv. 1-12). In the central portion (vv. 13-36) Jesus pronounces a series of seven "woes" directly against the scribes and Pharisees in language of ever-increasing bitterness, portraying the chief accusation—hypocrisy—in vivid and hence memorable imagery. It all ends with a prophetic denunciation of Jerusalem as a city that murders prophets (vv. 37-40), a city Jesus, its Messiah, is about to abandon (24:1). No text in the New Testament has contributed more to the creation in Christian and wider imagination of the stereotype of "the Pharisee" as a byword for hypocrisy, a caricature that inevitably redounds upon Judaism as such. In a post-Holocaust situation the question of responsible reading arises with particular force in connection with this text—not least in the present connection because there are areas in which things it says in positive mode (v. 4; v. 23) contribute significantly to the approach to Matthew I am taking.

Some preliminary remarks: First of all, from what we know of the Pharisees from other sources it has to be said that the presentation of them here is a caricature lacking historical foundation. There were doubtless individuals whose behavior did match the various descriptions in this chapter, but branding the whole class in this generalized way is unhistorical and unfair. The majority of Pharisees, especially in the persons of their rabbinic descendants after 70 C.E., were attempting to recreate and preserve the identity and religious life of the people around the Torah following the

destruction of other national institutions such as the Temple; their own
(later) literature contains self-criticism explicitly directed at the behavior
depicted here. We should not, then, read Matthew 23 as an accurate source
of information concerning representatives of these Jewish groups in the
late first century C.E.—let alone of Judaism as such.[1]

Second, the kind of sustained denunciation appearing here, especially
the vivid imagery in which adversaries are depicted, is typical of polemic
at the time, including intra-Jewish polemic. Matthew 23 in fact can seem
rather mild when read alongside polemic in other sources, such as the
Dead Sea Scrolls, or even the prophetic writings of the Bible.[2] Jesus is not
targeting Israel from outside; in continuity with prophets such as Amos,
Hosea, Isaiah, and Jeremiah, and also like Paul in passages such as Rom
2:17-24; 3:10-18; Gal 5:12; Phil 3:2, 18-20, he is voicing a prophetic critique
against leading groups within Israel. Awareness of this tradition of conventional polemic, both biblical and secular, places Matthew 23 in a wider
context of understanding.

Third, as we have often noted, the sharply polemical tone placed on
the lips of Jesus reflects not so much the conditions of his own time as the
historical situation of the community for whom Matthew was writing
toward the end of the first century C.E. This community had comparatively
recently separated itself—or been forced to separate itself—from the wider
body of Formative Judaism whose leadership is represented here as
"scribes and Pharisees." The polemic reflects both the sense of injury and
an attempt at self-definition, typical of any new religious movement.[3]

Fourth, while rightly recognizing that the depiction of the adversaries
in Matthew 23 is not characteristic of Judaism as such but reflects a particular historical situation toward the close of the first century, we cannot
simply relate it all to the past and leave it there as a now-meaningless
historical relic left in the scriptural canon. Underlying the polemic of
Matthew 23 and emerging expressly in vv. 8-12 is a warning: "This is not
how it must be among you!" The words of Jesus are an admonition to the
Christian community and as such remain addressed by the living Lord to

[1] The heading, "The Judgment Upon Judaism," over the commentary on chapter 23 in
John P. Meier's otherwise admirable work (*Matthew.* New Testament Message 5 [Wilming-
ton: Michael Glazier, 1980] 260) is unfortunate, dating the work to a time of less sensitivity
to Jewish-Christian issues.
[2] We should not leave out of consideration intra-*Christian* polemic at the time of the
Reformation.
[3] Cf. especially Daniel J. Harrington, *The Gospel of Matthew.* SP 1 (Collegeville:
Liturgical Press, 1991) 323.

the Church.[4] Though the chapter must be read with great sensitivity in regard to Judaism, we cannot simply say, "Oh, it's all about back there. It doesn't apply to us!" It may have a great deal of application to "us" at the present time.

Avoiding the style set by the scribes and Pharisees: 23:1-12

Jesus does not at first address the scribes and Pharisees directly, but speaks "to the crowds and to his disciples" about them (v. 1).[5] The instruction begins, curiously, with an acknowledgment of the authority of the scribes and Pharisees (v. 2) and a warning to do what they teach but not to do as they do (v. 3a). It is very unlikely that Matthew's community saw itself as still under the authority of those soon to be termed "blind guides" (v. 16). In light of the gospel's strong emphasis elsewhere on the importance of "doing" rather than just saying or thinking (cf. especially 7:21-27; 21:28-32), the instruction seems to be simply a rhetorical preliminary to the following comment, "For they do not practice what they teach" (v. 3b).[6] This comment neatly sums up and anticipates the whole indictment to follow, in which the central charge is that of hypocrisy: presenting oneself as someone or something that one is not; saying one thing and acting otherwise.

Two particular instances of hypocrisy on the part of the adversaries are indicted: tying onto the shoulders of others heavy burdens that they themselves are unwilling to lift (v. 4) and making a public show of religious observance in order to attract notice and titles of honor (vv. 5-7). The way these experts "lay heavy burdens" (Greek *fortia barea*) on others is presumably through making and imposing interpretations of the Torah in which, contrary to the interpretation of Jesus, priority is not given to mercy or love as the supreme criterion of what God wants.[7] One inevitably thinks

---

[4] Cf. W. D. Davies and Dale Allison, *A Critical and Exegetical Commentary on the Gospel According to Saint Matthew.* ICC. 3 vols. (Edinburgh: T&T Clark, 1988–97) 3:262–63.

[5] The "crowds" would represent people in Jerusalem still positive toward Jesus and hence potential disciples; cf. M. Eugene Boring, "The Gospel of Matthew," in Leander E. Keck, ed., *The New Interpreter's Bible.* Vol. 8 (Nashville: Abingdon, 1995) 430.

[6] Ulrich Luz, *Das Evangelium nach Matthäus.* 4 vols. Vol. 3: *Mt 18-25* (Zürich: Benziger; Neukirchen-Vluyn: Neukirchener Verlag, 1985–2002) 301–302.

[7] The Pharisees extended to the entire community of Israel the purity laws that the Torah enjoined only upon the priests. Keeping all these prescriptions could become an intolerable burden, especially for people who were not, like the Pharisees, expert in casuistic ways around them in situations of necessity.

of Jesus' claim in 11:29 that *his* yoke is easy and *his* burden light. In contrast to his "burden-lifting" interpretation, they offer "burden-imposing" interpretations that, paradoxically, neglect what Jesus will subsequently term "the weightier matters of the Torah (Greek *ta barytera tou nomou*): justice, mercy, and faith" (v. 23). These are the only respects in which the Torah should be "burdensome" or "heavy."

It is in respect to the second manifestation of hypocrisy—attracting notice and titles of rank—that the practice of the scribes and Pharisees explicitly becomes a counterindication of what should prevail in the community of Jesus (vv. 8-10). Where "they" love to have the people call them "rabbi,"[8] no one in the community should have such a title because there is only one Teacher (Jesus) and all others are "brothers (and sisters)."[9] Behind this lies the sense of the community as constituting the "family" of God (12:46-50). Still less, then, should they call anyone on earth "father" (v. 9), because they have only one Father—the one in heaven, whom Jesus called *Abba,* and to whom he taught them to pray with filial love and confidence (6:9-13).[10] The prohibition is reinforced (v. 11) by an echo of the call in 20:26 for the "greatest" to adopt the role of "servant" *(diakonos),* modeled on the pattern established by Christ (20:28).

As is often pointed out, scarcely any injunction of the Lord has been so ignored as this ruling out of titles and, by extension, accoutrements of dress and ceremonial. The very appearance of such an instruction in the gospel suggests an intention to nip in the bud tendencies in this direction already underway in the Matthean community. The instruction to live as brothers and sisters under the one Father in heaven, each striving to emulate the "servant" rank and role modeled by Christ, has fought a losing battle against the tendency to institutionalize and socially elevate leadership figures. One wonders why the Church felt free to ignore literal fulfillment of Christ's clear injunctions in this area, while taking others—for example, the sayings on divorce—with legal rigor. Are fundamental values of the Gospel not as much at stake in the one as in the other?

---

[8] From being a general title of address to a respected person or teacher, toward the close of the first century "rabbi" was on the way to becoming a technical title for a teacher in the Synagogue communities.

[9] The *NRSV* translation "students" rightly picks up the sense of the Greek *adelphoi,* in the sense of the community constituting a "student fraternity" who have only one teacher. However, the sense of "family equality" is probably more significant, especially in view of the following instruction in v. 10.

[10] To complete the triad, the gospel (v. 10) adds a more specific form of the prohibition in v. 8: the community is not to call anyone "instructor" (Greek *kathēgētēs*) because they have one instructor, identified as "the Messiah."

Woes Against the Scribes and Pharisees: 23:13-36

In the context of expectation of a coming great reversal, the "woe" is the opposite of the beatitude.[11] Where the beatitude congratulates those to whom it is expressed because the situation is soon to be radically reversed in their favor, the woe brands as unfortunate and lost those who will be radically *dis*advantaged. Put more colloquially, it says to them, "You're going to lose out!" It is not my intention here to go closely through the seven woes that follow. Most are polemical accusations hurled at the adversaries without further justification. Behind some, however, lurk the positive countervalues that should prevail in the believing community (cf. vv. 8-10).[12] These I shall attempt to winkle out.

The first woe (v. 13) condemns the scribes and Pharisees for locking people out of the kingdom of heaven. "Locking" inevitably recalls by contrast the conferral on Peter of "the keys of the kingdom of heaven" in 16:19. The teaching and example of the adversaries excludes people from the kingdom. The Church, on the contrary, while not itself identified with the kingdom, has the "keys" that give entrance to it in the shape of the teaching and instruction it has received from Jesus.[13]

The second woe (v. 15) suggests that the Matthean community saw itself to be in "missionary" competition with Pharisaic circles for the gaining of proselytes (converts) from the Gentile world.[14] The third (vv. 16-22) at least provides some backing for its critique in that it expounds at length the rabbinic casuistry regarding vows. As in 5:32-37, the critique rests on the point that all oaths made in respect to the Temple and its fittings inevitably entail witness before God.

More interesting for our purposes is the fourth woe (vv. 23-24), where the scribes and Pharisees are castigated for tithing minute agricultural products—herbs such as mint, dill, and cummin—while neglecting "the weightier matters *(ta barytera)* of the Torah: justice, mercy, and faith" (v. 23). The obligation to give a tenth of agricultural produce appears in the Torah (Deut 14:22-29; Lev 27:30-33); its purpose was the support and upkeep of the Temple cult and its officials (the priests and Levites; cf. Num 18:8-32). The general instruction concerning tithing was later extended to

[11] Hence Luke's balancing of four beatitudes with four woes at the beginning of the Sermon on the Plain (6:20-26).

[12] Cf. Harrington, *Matthew,* 323.

[13] Cf. Luz, *Matthäus* 3:322–23 and n. 38.

[14] An intriguing allusion in Gal 5:11 suggests that Paul, in his brief "persecuting career" (1 Cor 15:9; Gal 1:13, 23), may have been a zealous participant in such a mission, when, in contrast to his later policy, he required circumcision of Gentile male converts.

include even small herbs not specifically mentioned in biblical law. Jesus does not necessarily condemn the extension of tithing to such things (cf. the last clause of v. 23). What he criticizes is preoccupation with such minutiae (lampooned in v. 24 as "straining out gnats and swallowing camels") to the neglect of the "weightier matters of the Torah: justice, mercy, and faith." Behind the actual triad listed here, "justice" *(krisis),* "mercy" *(eleos)* "faith" *(pistis),* may lie a similar expression of divine will to be found in the prophet Micah: "What is it that the LORD requires of you except to do justice, and to practice loving kindness (literally 'to love mercy'), and to walk humbly with your God?" (6:8). Similar lists occur in the general prophetic witness to the heart of the Torah (cf. Hos 2:19; 12:6; Jer 9:24; 22:3; Zech 7:9-10; etc.).[15] "Justice" here has its social sense of rendering faithfully to a person what is that person's due; "mercy" (the subject of the fifth beatitude [5:7]) would be illustrated by the kind of actions on behalf of others listed in the evocation of the judgment in 25:31-46; "faith" may have the sense of dealing faithfully with others or else the more God-directed sense expressed in the third member of the triad in Micah 6:8. In view of the function of tithing to support the sacrificial system, we are not at all far here from the sentiment of Hos 6:6 ("What I want is mercy, not sacrifice"), cited twice earlier in the gospel (9:13; 12:7). The sense of mercy *before* (not in place of) ritual observance is of a piece with the priorities running through the six illustrative rulings in the Great Sermon (5:21-48, especially 5:23-24), as also with Jesus' response to the inquiry about the "greatest commandment of the Torah" in terms of the inseparable twin commands to love God and neighbor (22:34-40; cf. 19:19b).[16]

The fifth and sixth woes both target the kind of hypocrisy shown in discrepancy between the front one presents to the world and what one is within. In the fifth (vv. 25-26) Jesus, taking up the Pharisaic concern to preserve ritual cleanliness (cf. 15:1-20), makes the idea of a cup or bowl, clean on the outside but unwashed within, a telling symbol of hypocrisy. The sixth (vv. 27-28) conveys the sense of inner/outer inconsistency more sharply still by drawing attention to whitewashed tombs, which are beautiful on the outside but contain the corruption of death within. All this builds to a shrill and bitter climax in the seventh and final woe (vv. 29-36), which retains the focus on tombs. The adversaries show themselves to be hypocrites in that, while keen to preserve and decorate the tombs of prophets

---

[15] Cf. Luz, *Matthäus* 3:332.
[16] Cf. ibid. 332–33.

slain of old (vv. 29b-30), they make themselves the true descendants of those who slew them by being ready to shed the blood of the prophets ("and sages and scribes") of the new era. Jesus foresees here (vv. 34-36; cf. 10:17-23) the mishandling and bloodshed his own emissaries will suffer at the hands of "this generation" (v. 36).[17]

This climactic seventh woe, with its chilling evocation of the fate of Christian missionaries sent to Israel, shows the extent to which the whole set of denunciations reflects the recent experience of the community behind the gospel. The community—or at least its evangelist—is depicting the scribes and Pharisees as a paragon of all that it does not want its own leadership to be. Provided we remain conscious of its historical context and its debt to rhetorical conventions of the time, we need not banish this text completely from Christian reading and preaching. There is some "gold" to be mined from it, especially from the fourth woe with its indication of the "weightier matters" of the Torah.

Lament over Jerusalem: 23:37-39

The tone of denunciation turns to that of a lament directed more broadly to the city of Jerusalem as a whole. Jesus utters a divine complaint embracing in one great sweep the long history of Jerusalem's rejection of the prophets sent to it by God, culminating in the mistreatment of those sent more recently by him as risen Lord. This final appeal to Israel (cf. 10:5) was simply the last in a long divine attempt to gather a scattered and threatened people under the "wings" of the divine presence *(Shekinah),* expressed in the image of the mother hen (v. 37b).[18] As a result of its failure Jerusalem's "house" will be left desolate (v. 38). The "house" refers to the Temple, which, of course, at the time of writing of the gospel has been

---

[17] Verses 34-36 belong to the seventh woe (not the following lament [vv. 37-39]) in that they provide "the evidence" (the persecutions experienced by the emissaries) for the hypocrisy involved in claiming to venerate the prophets of old while persecuting those sent to them. The identity of "Zechariah son of Barachiah" (v. 35) is uncertain. Matthew seems to have invested the fate of a worthy figure of that name murdered early in the First Jewish Revolt (cf. Josephus, *Jewish War* 4.334-44) with the colors of an earlier Zechariah stoned to death in the Temple under King Joash (2 Chron 24:20-22). This enabled him to portray the recent Zechariah as the very last in a series of murdered prophetic figures reaching right back to Abel, son of Adam.

[18] For the idea of sheltering under the "wings" of the divine presence see Pss 36:7; 57.1; 61:5; cf. also Isa 31:5; Deut 32:11.

rendered desolate by the Romans, a fate that, as we have noted, the gospel attributes to Jerusalem's rejection of its Messiah. In the action of the narrative, however, the "desolation" refers more immediately to the fact that Jesus Emmanuel, the incarnation of the divine *Shekinah* (1:23), is now about to depart from the Temple (24:1), no more to appear in Israel until his end-time return as Son of Man and Judge.[19]

What are we to make of the response attributed to Jerusalem—and by extension to all Israel—when, at the end of time, it will again see the Lord (v. 39)? Is the cry "Blessed is the one who comes in the name of the Lord" (the same acclamation [Ps 118:26] as that of the crowds accompanying Jesus' messianic entry a few days before [21:9]), an expression at last of recognition of the Messiah, the result of conversion? Or is it a cry preparatory to judgment, wrung from a people who have recognized the truth, but too late? If the former is correct, then Matthew, like Paul in Rom 11:25-32, would envisage a positive outcome in regard to Israel and Messiah Jesus.[20] If the latter, then the Son of Man will bring nothing but judgment, an outcome already sealed by Jerusalem's rejection of its Messiah (27:25).[21]

It is hard to hear the acclamation in beatitude form based on Ps 118:26 as something wrung from a people about to face judgment. It seems more reasonable to interpret it in a more positive sense, as an expression of hope. Throughout the long indictment Jesus has spoken in the denunciatory tones of the prophets of Israel. The prophets denounced Israel's unfaithfulness, indicated the punishment it would endure as a result, and pointed to a restoration to come because of the saving faithfulness of God.[22] Within such a tradition even the woes, for all the sharpness of their expression, can be understood as warnings rather than condemnations.[23] By the same

---

[19] The "departure" of the divine presence recalls Ezekiel's dramatic vision (11:22-24) of the departure of the divine glory from Jerusalem to the "mountain east of the city," that is, the Mount of Olives—the location from which Jesus will deliver the Discourse on the Future (chs. 24–25).

[20] So Davies and Allison, *Matthew* 3:323–24, interpreting "until" (Greek *heōs an*) in a conditional sense: "the text means not, when the Messiah comes, his people will bless him, but rather, when his people bless him, the Messiah will come" (323). While in one sense more positive, such an interpretation presupposes a conversion on the part of Israel to Jesus as Messiah—not something at all congenial to Judaism.

[21] So Meier, *Matthew*, 274–75; Luz, *Matthäus* 3:384–85.

[22] See Antony F. Campbell, *The Study Companion To Old Testament Literature* (Wilmington: Michael Glazier, 1989) 393–410.

[23] For this reason I do not go along with Luz's judgment on this section of the gospel as a "betrayal" of the values of the Sermon on the Mount—especially the injunction to love enemies (*Matthäus* 3:398–99).

token, in the sense explained above, they are warnings the Christian Church cannot simply deflect back upon Israel, away from itself. Hypocrisy and the imposition of burdens upon others that one is unwilling to bear oneself are failings from which no religious tradition can think itself exempt.

The Challenge and Hope of the Future:
24:1–25:46

The fifth and last of the great discourses Jesus gives in the Gospel of Matthew presents difficulties for readers and interpreters on at least two grounds. First, it projects a vision of the future within the worldview, language, and imagery of Jewish apocalypticism, much of which makes little sense to people today.[1] Second, the motif of the final judgment, never far from view in Matthew's gospel, comes particularly to the fore in this section and in fact forms the climactic scene: 25:31-46. No one is comfortable with judgment—unless perhaps it is being given against the enemy. But in this part of the gospel members of the Church face the prospect of judgment, alongside the wider surrounding world. The challenge is to interpret the discourse in a way that remains faithful to Matthew and yet allows it to be "good news" for today.

Again, I do not propose to go through the discourse in detail, though I shall linger somewhat on the two parables and the judgment scene in chapter 25. But first let me offer some more general considerations by way of introduction to the kind of material Matthew has gathered into this long discourse.

As just remarked, in reading and hearing this discourse we are in the realm of Jewish apocalyptic eschatology. Let us be clear about these two terms. Eschatology refers to teaching or speculation about what is going to happen in the future, the final future, in fact (the Greek word *eschatos* means "limit"), the last act in the cosmic drama. "Apocalyptic" is an adjective describing a cast of thinking or mode of literary expression in which or through which some content, usually about the future, is expressed. Strictly speaking, what makes a text "apocalyptic" is the presentation of its content

---

[1] Nevertheless, the popularity of *The Lord of the Rings* saga (J.R.R. Tolkien) and the *Harry Potter* (J. K. Rowling) phenomenon suggests a continuing capacity to enter alternative imaginative worlds.

as something received by "revelation" (Greek *apokalypsis*) given to some privileged person (a prophet or seer) through interviews with angels or by being taken on a heavenly tour. Characteristic of apocalyptic discourse is vivid imagery depicting upheavals and calamities on a cosmic scale. The conflict between good and evil appears in starkly dualist mode. A profound pessimism reigns concerning human possibility in the present era, where sin is pervasive; hope for improvement rests entirely on direct intervention by God. The purpose of apocalyptic discourse is to give encouragement to the faithful now suffering the evils of the present age. It does so by imparting privileged and prior information concerning the divine plan and program whereby God or God's agent(s) will soon intervene. A moment of reckoning and judgment will arrive, which will mean exposure and condemnation for the wicked, vindication and reward for the faithful, who will then share the final triumph of God's rule (the kingdom of God).

The discourse Jesus speaks here is "eschatological" in that it treats of what will take place leading up to and including the final transformation. It is "apocalyptic" in its imagery, its tone, and its purpose. It is not strictly apocalyptic in its mode of communication, since there is no angel or heavenly transport involved, but direct instruction from Jesus concerning the future and his own coming as Son of Man. In this sense the discourse, while having apocalyptic features, is more akin to another literary genre found in the Bible, that of a farewell testament: an address or instruction a significant teacher or leader gives to his or her disciples just before death.[2] In such testaments the revered teacher or patriarch looks beyond his or her own death to the future awaiting the disciples, foreseeing the troubles and temptations that will inevitably arise and offering appropriate warning and encouragement. This is very much what Jesus does in the discourse we are now considering. It is best described, then, as an "eschatological testament."[3]

For most Christians today the expectation of Christ's return in glory ("Second Coming"), though still proclaimed in liturgy and creeds, is hardly a daily preoccupation. We "look back" to his life, death, and resurrection as the chief elements of his saving work. For the early generations, however, the emphasis was the other way around. It was as the Son of Man returning in glory that Christ would perform his principal messianic role:

---

[2] The entire book of Deuteronomy is a farewell discourse given by Moses just before he dies on the threshold of the Promised Land; so also Jesus' discourse at the Last Supper in John 13–17 and Paul's address to the elders of Ephesus in Acts 20:18-35.

[3] So W. D. Davies and Dale Allison, *A Critical and Exegetical Commentary on the Gospel According to Saint Matthew*. ICC. 3 vols. (Edinburgh: T&T Clark, 1988–97) 3:326.

to be the agent of the final victory of God. Cohabiting with a lively faith in the risen Lord was a strong sense of "unfinished business." Because they believed that the messianic age had "dawned" in the ministry and resurrection of Jesus there was impatience—and doubtless increasing dismay—that the conditions of the pre-messianic era (sinfulness, suffering, and death) lingered on. When would the Lord return to deal with all these things and finally institute the rule of God?

In the mode of a "farewell testament," the discourse on the future addresses this situation by showing that Jesus had accurately foreseen the trials the community is experiencing or has just experienced in the recent past. The community is to draw comfort and encouragement from the fact that he has foreseen these trials and has located them within an unfolding divine "program" leading, inexorably, to the final triumph of God. The discourse also had to dampen false hopes and expectations arising out of events that might reasonably have been seen as signs that the final days were at hand, leading to disillusionment and loss of faith when these expectations were not met. Within the community such misleading events could be the appearance of persons claiming to be the returned Messiah Jesus (those who come in his name saying: "I am the Messiah!" [24:5]). On a wider scale, events such as wars, famines, earthquakes, and other calamities could be taken as indications that the final cosmic upheaval was underway (vv. 6-7). Above all, the catastrophe represented by the fall of Jerusalem and destruction of the Temple (70 C.E.) was surely an occasion, appropriate as no other, for the arrival of the Son of Man. In regard to all this the discourse communicates a two-pronged message: (1) Maintain your hope. Don't be dismayed that the Son of Man has not yet arrived and if he delays a little longer. All these things—the calamities that have occurred and even worse—must take place before "the end" (v. 14). (2) But come he will, as judge as well as deliverer, and so be vigilant and watchful in your pattern of life.

In Matthew's form of the discourse this second aspect of the message runs like a counterwave across the message of hope—not washing it away entirely, but bringing the aspect of exhortation and warning strongly to the fore. Uncertainty as to when the Son of Man will arrive is a reason for vigilance and appropriate use of the time remaining. Whereas Jewish apocalypses devoted a good deal of space to indicating signs by which the likely time of arrival of the end-time events could be calculated, in Matthew—despite the question from the disciples that sparks off the whole discourse ("Tell us, when will this be, and what will be the sign of your coming?" [v. 3b])—Jesus counters any interest in signs pointing to the time of the

Son of Man's arrival. There will not be any signs save that of the arrival itself
(v. 30), the time of which is unknown—even to Jesus! (v. 36). The possibility that the Son of Man could arrive at any moment—probably when
least expected—becomes a key motivating force for the attitude of watch-
fulness and proper use of the time that the final parables, in particular, seek
to commend.

The upshot is that the discourse communicates a somewhat mixed
message to the believing community: on the one hand, comfort and consolation because trials, including even increase of lawlessness and cooling
of love *within* the community (24:10-12), have all been foreseen by Jesus;
on the other hand, warning *to* members of the community that such developments place one in danger of the greatest loss.

The discourse on the future in Matthew[4] falls into two main sections:
(1) a more expository part (24:4-35) deals with the "program" of events
leading up to the coming of the Son of Man; (2) a sentence (v. 36) dis-
claiming knowledge as to when that will take place then serves as a bridge
to a longer second half (24:37–25:46) commending the behavior appropriate in view of that uncertainty.

Discourse Part 1: All That Will Take Place Up to and
Including the Arrival of the Son of Man: 24:1-36

The prelude to the discourse is Jesus' definitive departure from the
Temple (24:1a). Jesus' prediction of its destruction (v. 2) leads to the question from the disciples that sparks the discourse: "Tell us, when will this be
. . . ?" (v. 3c). The discourse begins, then, with a question about the time
of the destruction of the Temple, but this specific issue rapidly falls from
view. (For the Matthean community it had of course been answered by the
all-too-familiar events of 70 C.E.) The bulk of Jesus' response addresses
the second part of the disciples' question: "what will be the sign of your
coming (Greek *parousia*) and the end of the age?"

The response seems to envisage a course of events unfolding in four
stages of ever-increasing suffering and distress. First (vv. 4-8) there is the

---

[4] Matthew adopts all of Jesus' discourse in Mark 13 (except for Mark 13:9, 11-12,
already incorporated into the Missionary Discourse in 10:17-21) and supplements this with
eschatological material from Q (placed by Luke in an earlier and separate discourse [17:20-
37]), thereby creating a single composite discourse, further extended by the two parables and
the judgment scene that make up chapter 25.

era dubbed "the beginning of the birth pangs" (v. 8). This is a time when false messianic pretenders will arise in the Jewish world outside the community and lead many astray (vv. 4-5).[5] There will also be other dismaying external events: wars, famines, and earthquakes.[6] But none of this should signal the arrival of "the end." Then (vv. 9-14a) the discourse moves to a second stage, not necessarily distinct in time from the preceding one but with the focus not on external events but on what the community itself has to endure. Some of this trouble comes from outside in the shape of persecution and hatred, leading even to death (v. 9). More poignant, however, in a way Matthew particularly emphasizes,[7] is the suffering caused from within: intra-community betrayal (v. 10), false prophecy (v. 11), and the "increase of lawlessness" that will cause "the love of many to grow cold" (v. 12). The last two problems (peculiar to Matthew) reflect the Evangelist's keen sense of the Church as a far from perfect body. "Lawlessness" refers, presumably, to failure to keep the Torah in the sense of its interpretation by Jesus in which "justice, mercy, and faith" are the determining or "weightier" matters (23:23) and the "greatest commandment" is the double commandment of love (22:34-40). It is not surprising, then, that lawlessness should lead to a cooling of love.

Dismaying as such failings may be—then as now—they are developments foreseen by Jesus and gathered into his overall vision of how things were to unfold before his return as Son of Man. Faced as we are today with so much evidence of moral failure within the Church, we can be grateful that Matthew so explicitly built inner-ecclesial failure into his depiction of the trials the community would endure in the time—now vastly extended —before the full arrival of the kingdom.

A hint of that extension appears in the final comment dealing with this stage: the reference to the worldwide proclamation to the nations of "this good news of the kingdom" (v. 14a). For all its trials and wounds, both those stemming from without and those that are self-inflicted, the Church remains the vehicle of "this good news," the good news of the final triumph of God. The time for that universal proclamation has been extended far

---

[5] The Jewish historian Josephus mentions the prevalence of such figures in the years leading up the great revolt (*Jewish War* 6.288).

[6] Such phenomena—particularly the civil strife within the Roman world following the death of Nero in 68 C.E.—are well attested in the same period.

[7] Matthew's earlier location in the Missionary Discourse (10:17-20) of the prediction in Mark 13:9, 11-12 about being dragged before religious and civil courts leaves room for greater concentration on the inner-community problems.

beyond anything Matthew could ever have imagined. But the inclusion of this note about its proclamation "throughout the world" before the coming of the end inserts into the discourse a kind of wedge that, retrospectively at least, frees it from its original narrow time-span and gives it a flexible and potentially indeterminate application. What Jesus foresees in the discourse will apply as long as the Gospel is still to be proclaimed—that is, up to our time and, indefinitely, beyond.

The third stage envisaged by the discourse (vv. 15-28) is the time of "the great affliction" immediately preceding "the end" (v. 21; cf. v. 29)[8]— a time when evil would in a sense boil over before finally giving way. Matthew, following Mark (13:14-20), has Jesus paint a picture of the future distress in language and allusions largely taken from Daniel. Interpretation is difficult because the allusions (e.g., "desolating sacrilege" [v. 15])[9] and warnings (vv. 16-22) have lost any original reference to historical events and serve simply as pieces of tradition that readers are called upon to discern and relate to distress in their own times (v. 15c).[10] False messianic claimants and prophets—active within rather than outside the community (contrast v. 4)—will put on a great display of signs and omens (vv. 23-25). Yet no signs will be given for calculating the time of the Son of Man's arrival (vv. 26-28).[11] That moment, when it comes, will be as sudden, as obvious, and as totally illuminating as the lightning that flashes from east to west (v. 27).[12]

The Son of Man's arrival is, of course, the fourth and final stage (vv. 29-31) of the program envisaged by the discourse. His coming "on the clouds of heaven" (Dan 7:13) will throw the observable heavenly powers—sun, moon, and stars—into confusion (v. 29) and "all tribes of the earth will

---

[8] Verse 14b says, "and then the end will come," but the following material up to v. 28 clearly describes what will happen *before* "the end," that is, the arrival of the Son of Man.

[9] The "desolating sacrilege" (v. 15a) referred in Dan 9:27; 11:31; 12:11 to a pagan image set up in the Temple in 167 B.C.E. by the Seleucid Greek king Antiochus IV Epiphanes. Early Christian tradition seems to have related the Danielic phrase to a series of subsequent notorious sacrileges culminating (according to Mark 13) in the desecration of the Temple by the Romans in 70 C.E. In Matthew, for whom of course this event lay in the past, the expression serves simply as a vague biblical marker signaling the onset of great distress.

[10] If the cataclysm that is coming is cosmic in scale (cf. v. 29), what would be the point of physical flight (vv. 16-22)?

[11] Matthew here introduces for the first time material from Q; cf. Luke 17:23-24, 37.

[12] The mysterious statement in v. 28 seems to make the same point: the Son of Man's coming will be as sudden and obvious as eagles (or vultures) circling over carrion; for further suggestions see Davies and Allison, *Matthew* 3:55–56.

mourn" as they recognize[13] in the appearance of the Son of Man the One to whom all authority for rule and judgment on the earth has been given (Dan 7:14).[14] Why do all the nations "mourn"? Is it because they now realize the judgment to which they are summoned? Or does the "mourning" contain an element of repentance and conversion?[15] The text seems to leave this open (cf. 23:39).[16] Summoned also (v. 31) by angelic trumpet blast[17] from the four corners of the earth are "the elect," the faithful destined to share the life of the kingdom. What will take place at the judgment—and specifically the two outcomes to which it will lead—is left to be described in detail at the climax of the discourse (25:31-46).

Four rather difficult comments conclude this first part of the discourse (vv. 32-36). The fig tree, unlike most trees in Palestine, is deciduous and puts out new leaves only at the very end of spring. Hence its leaf signals the immediate onset of summer—an image applied to the imminent arrival of the Son of Man (vv. 32-33). The statement about this generation not passing away until all these things have taken place (v. 34), underlined by the added comment about Jesus' words not passing away (v. 35), had surely been rendered inaccurate at the time of composition of the gospel. Matthew preserves this traditional material to reinforce the sense that the events spoken of will most certainly—and very soon!—take place. Finally, the confession of ignorance on Jesus' part of the actual timing (v. 36) has caused problems for christology down the ages. It is best interpreted as part of Jesus' complete surrender of his entire fate into the hands of the Father. As he goes obediently to his death, the time of his return to claim the world for the kingdom, no less than his being raised from death, rests completely with the Father.

---

[13] They do not see the sign *of* the Son of Man, which is what the disciples originally asked about (v. 3), but the sign that the Son of Man *is*: his arrival is the sign that judgment is about to take place.

[14] Cf. Davies and Allison: "When the Son of man finally appears, all will recognize what the church even now confesses: that he has all authority in heaven and earth (28:18)" (*Matthew* 3:358–59).

[15] A hint of conversion may come from the fact that "mourn" and the use of "tribes" (Greek *phylai*) alludes to Zech 12:10-14, where it is said the inhabitants of Jerusalem will mourn "when they look upon the one they have pierced" (a text cited explicitly with reference to the crucified Christ in John 19:37 and Rev 1:7).

[16] See M. Eugene Boring, "The Gospel of Matthew," in Leander E. Keck, ed., *The New Interpreter's Bible*. Vol. 8 (Nashville: Abingdon, 1995) 444.

[17] A standard apocalyptic image for the summons to judgment: cf. 1 Cor 15:52; 1 Thess 4:16; Rev 8:2.

Discourse Part 2:
Living Appropriately in the Time of Waiting: 24:37–25:46

The long second part of the discourse derives the strength of its warning from the sense of uncertainty about the time of the Son of Man's coming just expressed by Jesus (v. 36). Since he will most certainly come and very soon, but not at an hour one can foresee, the only attitude to adopt is one of constant vigilance and care to be living the way of life that will lead to inclusion among those destined for the kingdom. The discourse promotes this exhortation through a series of parables—three short (24:37-51)[18] and two long (25:1-30)—and the concluding evocation of the final judgment (25:31-46).

The three short parables—really extended images rather than parables proper—communicate a sense of salutary fear at the prospect of being caught off guard by the Son of Man's sudden arrival. The generation of Noah provides a biblical example (vv. 37-41): people were carrying on life as usual, oblivious to the fate (the Flood) that was so swiftly to overwhelm them. Just so, of two pairs of persons presently at work—two men in a field, two women grinding meal—the judgment will swiftly come and disclose what is now hidden: that one is destined for life, one for loss.[19] Likewise, a householder who has received a tipoff that his house is going to be burgled would be extremely foolish to go to sleep and not keep watch to ward off the thief (vv. 42-44). Finally (vv. 45-51), a slave left in charge of his master's household, since as a slave he will not be informed about his master's movements (cf. John 15:15), cannot afford to behave in a dissolute and irresponsible way. If he does so he is likely to be caught out by the master's sudden return and consigned to the fate described (v. 51) in exaggerated but typically Matthean tones.[20]

These short but telling images stressing the uncertainty of the coming of judgment could convey the sense of a God just waiting for the opportunity to spring and catch people. That would not respond to the image of God behind the whole economy of salvation revealed in the gospel: the God who sent the beloved Son precisely to save rather than condemn humankind. The future, however, is not in our hands. Attempts to crack the code, so to speak, of apocalyptic books like Daniel and Revelation are

[18] Matthew incorporates here material from the Sayings Source ("Q") shared with Luke.
[19] Here I follow Boring, "Matthew," 446.
[20] "Cut in pieces," a Persian form of execution, probably represents a proverbial threat of punishment: "Just try that and you'll end up in pieces!"

futile and contrary to the spirit of trust commended by the gospel. Eugene Boring puts it well:

> We are called to be agnostics about the time of Jesus' return. We simply do not know. What we do know is what we are supposed to be doing in the meantime . . . the deeds of mercy, forgiveness, and peace that characterize kingdom people.[21]

The Ten Bridesmaids: 25:1-13

Interpretation of the parable of the Ten Bridesmaids[22] is difficult because we lack sufficient knowledge of the wedding customs of the time, a problem exacerbated by the allegorical form in which the parable now appears. What the story seems to presuppose is a wedding custom whereby unmarried young women wait with the bride at her family's house for the arrival of the bridegroom.[23] When he appears they go out to meet him with blazing torches[24] and escort the couple back to his house where the marriage feast has been prepared and the guests have been waiting for the couple's festal entry.[25] The parable further presupposes a late-arriving bridegroom, though whether this is due simply to unpunctuality or some custom unknown to us is not clear. In the present story, however, when notice of the bridegroom's approach is given, five of the young women dis-

---

[21] "Matthew," 448.

[22] The Greek word *parthenos* denotes a young woman (more rarely a young man) of marriageable age who is still virginal—though virginity as such plays no part in the story. The description of the ten young women as "bridesmaids" has to be supplied from the context. See n. 25 below.

[23] The reference to their "going out" in v. 1 is best understood not as part of the story (which would have the young women asleep at night on the public street!), but as a title for the whole parable: "The kingdom of heaven is like ten maidens who have been deputed to welcome the bridegroom with torches"; cf. Ulrich Luz, *Das Evangelium nach Matthäus.* 4 vols. Vol. 3: *Mt 18–25* (Zürich: Benziger; Neukirchen-Vluyn: Neukirchener Verlag, 1985–2002) 3:472, 474.

[24] "Torches" is the proper translation of the Greek word *lampas.* Luz, *Matthäus* 3:469–71, suggests that we should think of rods with a vessel containing oil-soaked rags attached on top. Early Christian depictions of the parable show young women holding blazing torches of this kind. Lamps were for indoor use; outdoors a puff of wind would swiftly extinguish their flame.

[25] Alternatively, the young women could be thought of as waiting at the bridegroom's house for his return with his bride. In this case, since they wait upon the bridegroom, they are not properly described as "bridesmaids."

cover they are not in a position to carry out their welcoming role.[26] Their
going off to buy oil for their torches means that they are not there at the
crucial moment. When they return and make their way belatedly to the
feast they find the door shut in their faces and the bridegroom, angry at
their failure, refusing to know them.

Jesus probably told the parable to address, as so often, the tension
between the future status of the kingdom, symbolized by the wedding banquet, and the need to make preparations now for its coming (cf. 4:17).
Since the precise time of its realization is not certain, how foolish to be
found unprepared and so in a situation that might lead to missing out on it!
The parable vividly communicates the sense of "Can you imagine what
those five young women must have felt—their panic at realizing they had
no oil, their anguish and shame on arriving back too late and finding the
door barred in their faces and harsh words from the groom? Would you like
to be in that situation in regard to the kingdom?"

As recorded by Matthew and placed at this point in the gospel, the
parable has become an allegory addressing life in the Church as it awaits
the return of its Lord, clearly to be identified with the bridegroom for
whom the young women keep watch (cf. 9:14-15). The detail that five of
them are wise and five foolish reflects the mixed nature of the Church in
which, as so often in Matthew (13:36-43, 47-50; 18:6-14; 22:11-14; 24:9-
14), fervent and not so fervent exist side by side; at present they are not all
that distinguishable from one another (perhaps we are to think of bridesmaids all wearing a similar dress), but the bridegroom's arrival as judge
will show the difference between them.[27] The supply of oil that the five
wise young women were sensible enough to bring would then be the "surpassing righteousness" (5:20) commended in the gospel—the performance
of Torah according to the interpretation of Jesus in which love is the "chief
commandment" (22:34-40) and deeds of "justice, mercy, and faith" are
"the weightier matters" (23:23; cf. 25:31-46). The plaintive cry of the five
foolish bridesmaids ("Lord, Lord, open to us") represents the kind of believer who cries out, "Lord, Lord" but has no good works to accompany
this confession of faith (cf. 7:21-27). The wise may "sleep" (in death) before the coming of the Lord, but when he does come they will go out to

---

[26] Verse 7b does not refer to the "trimming" (of wicks) of lamps that, previously alight,
have since gone out, but to the moment when the women first attend to their torches and the
foolish discover that they have insufficient oil to keep them alight; cf. Luz, *Matthäus* 3:472.

[27] Cf. especially Boring, "Matthew," 450.

meet him, their "torches" brightly ablaze (cf. 5:16) because of the "oil" (good works) they have in sufficient measure.

The final warning about "staying awake" because neither "the day nor the hour" is known (v. 13) really means "be prepared," rather than "stay awake." It is not falling asleep that is reprehended; all ten, both the wise and the foolish, fall asleep. The difference between them is that the wise have made sure to have sufficient oil to kindle their torches when they are roused, while the foolish have neglected this precaution. Those who have always with them the "oil" required for salvation can "sleep" without anxiety about being caught short by the sudden arrival of their Lord.

The Talents: 25:14-30

The parable of the Talents presents difficulty on two fronts. First, it seems to endorse a highly capitalistic mode of proceeding in regard to the use of wealth, which sits ill with Jesus' instruction on the use of money elsewhere. Second, if the reckoning the returning businessman makes with his servants has allegorical reference to the final judgment, a none-too-attractive image of the deity seems to emerge. Does Jesus—or God—conform to the master as described by the unhappy third slave: a harsh man, reaping where he did not sow and gathering where he did not scatter seed (v. 24)?

Once again we have to keep in mind that Jesus took parables from life as he saw it lived, without necessarily commending or reproving the be-havior described. He used the way people acted in situations of crisis in everyday life to illustrate—not model—appropriate behavior in view of the kingdom.

Can we discern behind the allegorical parable appearing in Matthew a form of the story that Jesus might have told?[28] If we strain out the evident Matthean accretions[29] we can perhaps recover a parable of the kingdom

---

[28] The Parable of the Pounds in Luke 19:12-27 has sufficient features in common with Matthew's Parable of the Talents to suggest that both draw upon a form in Q, to which already the saying in v. 29 had been attached. I offer an interpretation of the Lukan parable in *Hospitality of God,* 152–53.

[29] Such accretions would include: the consignment of the third slave to "outer darkness" in v. 30; the "inflation" of the gifts from "pounds" (as in Luke 19:12-27) to the virtually un-realistic "talents" (on "talent" see above on 18:23-35); "after a long time" (v. 19)—to account for the delay in the *parousia;* "enter into the joy of your master" (vv. 21, 23)—to

along the following lines. Presupposed is the fact that in the ancient world—the Gentile rather than the Jewish world is in view[30]—slaves could exercise great responsibility. A wealthy man about to go on a long journey takes the opportunity to test the capacity of three of his slaves in handling wealth. Making a shrewd appraisal of the personal capacity of each, he entrusts different sums to each one accordingly.[31] His trust in the first two turns out to be well founded and he rewards them with still higher responsibility. The third slave, however, has done nothing to increase the sum entrusted to him; fear of his master (a fear he foolishly explicitates when making excuses [v. 24]) has led him simply to preserve the sum given him by burying it in the ground[32] so that when a reckoning is called for he can simply return it intact; he will not be rewarded but at least he hopes not to be punished. Whether or not the master is actually the kind of person this fearful slave describes him to be and whether he accepts the description (which he himself repeats [v. 26]) we do not know. The master simply takes the description at face value and points out how, in view of it, the slave ought to have acted: if he was incapable of trading with it, as the other two appear to have done, he could at least have let the bankers take care of it so that some interest might accrue. Then to some extent the master would have "reaped where he did not sow" (v. 27). But the slave did nothing, and so loses everything: even the little he had is taken from him and given to the one with the highest amount (v. 27).

This last detail is the surprise element in the parable. It tells us that from the start the master intended the amounts assigned to the slaves to be gifts for them to keep; he was not looking to get his money back; his interest lay in seeing how well the slaves traded with what had been given to them. The first two slaves seemed to have understood this. Appreciating their master's generosity, they felt free to take risks and use the sum given them creatively. The third slave cannot conceive that his master could be

---

express entrance into the banquet of the kingdom. The maxim in v. 29, which may go back to Jesus himself (cf. Mark 4:25; Matt 13:12; Luke 8:18), probably had an independent existence in the tradition until it became attached to the parable in its Q form.

[30] Shown by the keeping of slaves and the taking of interest on a loan; cf. Luz, *Matthäus* 3:502.

[31] The Lukan reference to the sums in terms of "pounds" *(minas)* is more probably original than "talents" (a very large sum), which would be an instance of Matthean "inflation." The later use of "talent" to describe personal qualities or skills is derived from this parable on the basis of the comment in v. 15: "to each according to his capacity."

[32] A regular way of preserving treasure in the ancient world; see above on the parable of the Discovered Treasure (13:44).

otherwise than as he describes him; he reckons that reliance on a pattern of strict justice will allow him at least to save his skin. But, trapped in this image, he loses all.

Jesus may have told the parable to illustrate varying human capacities in relation to God's gift of the kingdom. Those who understand that it is the pure gift of a boundlessly generous God—to be received unearned as little children receive gifts from those who love them (19:14)—ready themselves for its full reception by living in the free, creative way illustrated by the first two slaves. Those who are crippled by a restricted idea of God and the way God operates with human beings run the risk of missing out on the kingdom altogether.[33] Understood in this way, the parable does not endorse the view of the master described by the third slave. In fact, it refutes it.

Incorporating the parable into the discourse on the future, Matthew has related it to the judgment and made it again a warning to the community about profitable use of the present time. Has he in so doing, contrary to the tendency of the original parable, applied to Jesus as judge the characterization of the master given by the third slave? I do not believe this to be the case.[34] True, we do have at the end of the allegory (v. 30) a consignment of this slave to eschatological punishment described in characteristically Matthean terms (cf. 8:12; 13:42, 50; 22:13). But the Matthean allegory, no less than the original parable, lays the blame for the slave's unproductiveness precisely on his limited—and false—image of God. As in all the parables in this discourse, there is indeed great stress upon right use of the time. However, the chief point seems to be this: Some, through fear, may think they can get by simply by avoiding wrongdoing and giving back to God what they have received on a basis of strict justice (cf. the third slave). But those who appreciate God as Jesus reveals God to be have the freedom to live in the creative and adventurous way that is truly appropriate (cf. the first two). They seek to carry out "what God wants": an enterprising, even

---

[33] In this sense the parable does bear out the maxim (v. 29) about more being given to those who have (much) and about those who have nothing (= no capacity to understand) losing all.

[34] Contrary to John P. Meier, who speaks of the "fierce demands of Jesus" and finds here that "stringency of judgment" has replaced "imminence of judgment" (*Matthew*. New Testament Message 5 [Wilmington: Michael Glazier, 1980] 300). This sets the parable—unnecessarily in my view—at odds with the image of Jesus presented elsewhere in the gospel: e.g., in 11:28-30. Cf. Rudolf Schnackenburg: "The dialogue belongs to the logic of the narrative, and does not authorise a harsh picture of God" (*The Gospel of Matthew* [Grand Rapids and Cambridge: Eerdmans, 2002] 254).

risk-taking practice of the "weightier matters of the Torah: justice, mercy, and faith" (23:23). Hence they stand to receive at the judgment the invitation "Enter into the joy of your master" (vv. 21, 23). In this way, with its emphasis on action and enterprise, the parable prepares the way for the centrality of works of mercy in the great judgment scene that now follows as the climax of the discourse.[35]

The Great Judgment: 25:31-46

Here, undoubtedly, we stand before one of the defining texts of the Christian faith. It is often classed among the parables of Jesus, but the only element of parable is the image of the shepherd separating sheep from goats, which soon falls away. What we really have is a dramatic evocation of the last judgment that will determine who gets entrance into the kingdom. Earlier (24:29-31) the discourse gave a description of the Son of Man's arrival. Now we learn what is to take place as he discharges his appointed role.

From what has been said before in this gospel and from the tenor of Jewish apocalyptic expectation in general we might expect to learn about the long-awaited sorting out of good and evil—the weeds from the wheat (13:36-43), the bad fish from the good (13:49-50)—and the assignment of outcomes, negative and positive respectively. In a sense this is what does happen. But what is truly remarkable—and at least for the initial reader completely unexpected—is the criterion on which judgment is given: judgment according to works, yes, but not works in general. Rather, judgment rests on the performance/non-performance of works of *mercy*. The only ethical area raised by the Judge is that illustrated by the six corporal works of mercy, which are cited again and again.

What we hear, moreover, is not in fact a process of judgment but a pronouncing of sentence. Judgment is already over and done with before the great assize begins. Members of the human race have determined the outcome for themselves according to whether they have acted or neglected to act on behalf of those in need. So while it is true that the scene does take us to the final act, it is of a piece with the preceding parables in the sense that everything depends on how one acts or fails to act here and now in the time before the judgment. We are told about it in order to communicate the

[35] Here Meier's comment is very apt: "God's grace is like our physical limbs and intellectual talents: exercise brings greater strength; neglect brings atrophy" (*Matthew,* 300).

message: "The outcome—after grace—is in your hands, in what you choose to do or fail to do in the present. Do you want to be relieved of the fear of judgment? Well, then, dedicate yourself to this kind of life. Then the judgment will be already behind you."

This is why, presumably, the actual separation of the two classes, symbolized within the "shepherding" image by the sheep and goats, is over very quickly (v. 32b). The rest of the story simply highlights what emerges over and over in the lengthy dialogue between the Son of Man—now become "the King" (v. 34)—and the two groups he addresses. This is his personal identification with those ("the least of my brothers and sisters") who stood in need of various ministrations of mercy, and the shock and surprise of members of both groups at this identification, which neither of them suspected. The fourfold reiteration of the six works[36]—feeding the hungry, giving water to the thirsty, hospitality to the homeless, clothing the naked, caring for the sick, visiting the imprisoned—underlines the Son of Man's identification with the needy. It also makes this scene a powerful reinforcement of Jesus' interpretation of the Torah according to what God wants—mercy, not sacrifice (9:13; 12:7; cf. 5:17-48; 7:12; 23:23).

The scene also reveals a new dimension in the "Emmanuel" theme running through the gospel (1:23; 18:20; 28:20). On the one hand Jesus is the exalted Lord who comes in glory attended by the whole court of heaven, possessing and about to exercise all power and authority in heaven and on earth. On the other hand we hear this exalted heavenly personage publicly owning and declaring his identification with the disadvantaged of the world ("*the least* of my brothers and sisters"), among whom he came not to be served but to serve (20:28) and who himself had nowhere to lay his head (8:20).[37] In this self-identification, spanning the "distance" between the divine and "the least" of the human, Jesus' two-part response to the question about which commandment of the Torah is the "greatest" (22:34-40) acquires new depth. In loving and serving one's neighbor in the way described here one is actually loving and serving Christ, and in loving and serving Christ one is loving and serving "God with us." The two commandments making up the "greatest commandment of the Torah" come together on this christological base.[38]

---

[36] The narrative lingers expansively on the account of what the just *have done* (vv. 34-36, vv. 37-39). At the end (v. 44), in regard to what the unrighteous have *omitted,* the actions are simply listed; cf. Davies and Allison, *Matthew* 3:341.

[37] Cf. Luz, *Matthäus* 3:537–38.

[38] Cf. Meier, *Matthew,* 305.

While this is the general sense of the scene, quite a number of questions remain. Two in particular stand out and largely determine interpretation. (1) Who is included among "all the nations" summoned for judgment? (all humankind? all nonbelievers? all Gentiles [non-Jews]?) (2) Who is meant by "the least of my brothers and sisters"? (the needy of the world in general? all believers? a particular group of believers [missionaries of the Matthean community]?). Traditionally, both questions have been answered in a more universal sense: humankind will be judged according to the way it has treated its most disadvantaged members—a criterion that will apply equally, or even *a fortiori* to members of the Christian community, who are, of course, principally in view across the discourse as a whole. Recently a narrower view, at least as regards the strict meaning of the Matthean text, has been favored by exegetes. On this view the "nations" are the members of the nonbelieving world and "the least" are members of the Matthean community or, more specifically, the missionaries sent out to "make disciples" of the nations (28:19-20). In other words, the nations are being judged not according to how they have treated the needy of the world in general but with regard to their treatment of this particular group. The scene is not, then, a warning to believers but rather, in the spirit of apocalyptic literature generally, a comfort and assurance to missionaries that the reception or non-reception they receive from those to whom they are sent is being noted in heaven and will receive eschatological requital.

Though this "particularist" (or "exclusivist") interpretation is not without exegetical grounding in the text[39] it does not, to my mind, find sufficient support there to oust the more traditional view, which is so much more theologically and ethically satisfactory. I set out my reasons for this in the Excursus at the end of this chapter. The idea of "brothers and sisters," which in first place applies to members of the believing community, is here in the context of world judgment widened to include all humankind.[40] Christ does not identify only with the "least" in the believing community. He identifies with them on the basis of a prior identification with the needy of all humankind, a universal identification that itself lies behind his entire mission to be not only Messiah of Israel but the Messiah in whose "name the nations (= all humankind) will hope" (12:21). Hence the same criterion of judgment applies to all, both those who are believers

[39] Perhaps the best exposition of it is that of Graeme N. Stanton, "Once More Matthew 25:31-46," in idem, *A Gospel for a New People: Studies in Matthew* (Edinburgh: T&T Clark, 1992; Louisville: Westminster John Knox, 1993) 207–31.
[40] Cf. Schnackenburg, *Matthew,* 258.

and those whom the Gospel will not have reached. Believers, who do know Christ and call him "Lord," will have to have gone beyond this acclamation and recognized and served him in the poor and needy. Nonbelievers, who by definition have not known him as "Lord," but who have treated their fellow human beings with decency and mercy, will find themselves welcomed into the banquet of life by One who, unawares, they were serving.

We might ask then: Why bother about the Christian mission (28:18-20) if the nations can be saved without explicit knowledge of Christ? The scene undeniably gives rise to a tension here, one prominent in theological discussion today. Confronted with the tension, the Evangelist might respond: yes, members of the nations *can* be saved through their works of mercy but, granted the human propensity for selfishness and exploitation of others, how many will exercise such mercy without a sense of the preciousness of human life communicated by the Gospel? Hence the validity of the appeal to as many as possible to become disciples of the One who came not to be served but to serve and give his life as a ransom for many (20:28).

A final comment: the scene once again features the Matthean apocalyptic eschatology that so many find disturbing. In accordance with the fifth beatitude ("Blessed are the merciful, for they will have mercy shown to them" [5:7]), those who have shown mercy are invited to "inherit the kingdom prepared for them before the foundation of the world" (v. 34). Those who have not shown mercy will be banished to "the eternal fire prepared for the devil and his angels" (v. 41a). In contrast to the positive statement about the kingdom, it is not said that that punishment was "prepared" for human beings; it was not meant for human beings at all. But unmerciful human beings have ranged themselves on the side of the counter-kingdom (the rule of Satan) and now, at the overthrow of that counter-kingdom, they will have to share the lot of those who have been its agents. We may not embrace literally the depiction of eschatological rewards and punishments in the form Matthew derived from the apocalyptic worldview of his time. But the the truth that mercy leads to life while its opposite leads to exclusion from the banquet of life emerges from this text as an inescapable aspect of the Christian Gospel.

Excursus: Interpreting Matthew 25:31-46

A. The "inclusive/universalist" interpretation appeals to the following considerations:

1. The interpretation coheres best with the location of the judgment scene as the climax of a long series of parables all designed to warn *believers* concerning appropriate behavior in the present in view of the coming judgment. The particularist interpretation excludes believers from the judgment process; they become simply "spectators" of the judgment of others.

2. The exclusivist interpretation implies a separate judgment for believers and unbelievers. This runs counter to 16:27, which seems to presuppose a single all-embracing judgment.

3. That the criterion of judgment should be performance/non-performance of the works of mercy listed is far more understandable on a universalist understanding. In particular, it seems highly incongruous that nonbelievers should be expected to visit Christian missionaries in prison.

B. The "exclusivist" interpretation appeals to the following considerations. (I add after each, in italics, the counter-considerations, which to my mind refute them.)

1. The Missionary Discourse in chapter 10 seems to anticipate the vindication of Christian missionaries at the judgment (vv. 11-15). Christ tells them (v. 22) that they will be "hated by all" (the nations) and assures them that "whoever welcomes you, welcomes me" (v. 40; cf. vv. 41-42).

The early part of the Missionary Discourse (ch. 10), including vv. 11-15, refers to the disciples' mission to Israel (cf. v. 5), not to the nations of the world. The references to "welcome" in vv. 41-42 add specifically "Christian" tags ("in the name of a prophet . . . righteous person . . . disciple") that are missing in 25:36-41. Thus the evidence adduced from chapter 10 is not at all as cogent as that stemming from the immediate context of the judgment scene (cf. A 1, above).

2. The "least of my brothers (and sisters)" is more naturally referred to members of the believing community in accordance with Jesus' use of "family of God" language (12:46-50; 18:15, 21-22, 35) and references to "little ones" (10:42; 18:6, 10, 14) and "least" (11:11) in their regard.

Though the language "least"/"little ones" sounds very similar in English translation, the Greek words being used are different: mikros in 10:42; 18:6, 10, 14, elachistos in 25:40, 45. "Sibling" language ("brother" ["sister"]) occurs in a more general sense in passages such as 5:22-24; 7:3-5 and we should note that "brothers (and sisters)" is not mentioned in the second reference (v. 45: "least of these") to the (non)recipients of mercy.

3. The Greek word *ethnē* appearing in v. 32 usually has the specific meaning "Gentiles" (non-Jews) in biblical literature rather than "nations."

But ethnē does not always have that sense in Matthew: cf. 24:9, 14.

4. There are impressive parallels in contemporary Jewish literature in which the nations of the world (Gentiles) are judged according to their treatment of Israel or the righteous within Israel.[41]

Yes, but in such cases the nations are being judged for positively persecuting Israel, not for the simple omission of deeds of mercy. The parallels are not really close at all.

5. The idea that the nations could be saved or not saved simply according to their works of mercy without explicit faith in Christ undercuts the mission of "making disciples" of all the nations.

This tension remains in Matthew. But, other things being equal, it is more advantageous for salvation to become a disciple; hence the rationale for the mission.

6. Only nonbelievers would be surprised to learn that in showing or not showing mercy to fellow human beings they were doing so to the Judge. If believers are included among those being judged, they should have learned this already from the Gospel!

The first statement does not really hold up since even nonbelievers who reacted positively or negatively to Christian missionaries would also at the same moment be reacting to their message, which proclaimed Christ. They would have "known" Christ in this sense. If the second statement were true, it would be better not to preach to believers this part of the Gospel, since then their motives would be purer in the sense that they would be serving for pure love of others without any sense of doing good to the One who is going to be their Judge. Both the objection and these responses rest upon a false "testing" of the text against what might happen in reality, whereas the whole "non-recognition" motif really has a literary function: to bring home, especially to believers, what they will continuously tend to forget: that Christ is present, waiting to be served, in the persons most likely to be passed over.[42]

---

[41] For this see especially Stanton, "Once More Matthew 25:31-46."
[42] Cf. Luz, *Matthäus* 3:536–37.

5. THE MESSIAH'S ULTIMATE "SERVICE": 26:1–28:15

Passion I:
Jesus Confronts His Death: 26:1-56

Jesus has been speaking of his future coming as Son of Man to bring the whole world to account before God. Rounding off this last discourse in the usual way (27:1a), he brings the disciples—and us—sharply back to the reality of the present: "You know that after two days the Passover is coming, and the Son of Man will be handed over to be crucified" (v. 2). The One who is going to judge all human beings on the sole basis of whether they have served their brothers and sisters through works of mercy (25:31-46) stands now before his own supreme service to his brothers and sisters as the Son of Man who came "not to be served but to serve and to give his life as a ransom for many" (20:28). The long Passion narrative tells the story of that service in which, as the obedient Son in whom the Father is well pleased (3:17; 17:5), the Messiah will "fullfill all righteousness" (3:15) to the end.

Matthew's Passion Narrative

We begin with some general remarks about the nature of the Passion narratives of the gospels and that of Matthew in particular. Understandably, the memory of what happened to Jesus in the last days of his life left a vivid impression on the disciples. Nowhere else are the four gospels so preserving of detail and so coherent among themselves as in their Passion stories. But from the start a very strong impress of interpretation accompanied what memory there was of the historical details. The disciples had to make some sense of the catastrophic fact that the one whom they believed to be God's chosen Messiah had suffered so appalling and degrading a death at the hands of the authorities.

Central in the process of finding meaning was the task of searching the Scriptures (the Old Testament) to see if they contained any indication that this would be how things would go. According to a very early credal fragment cited by Paul, "Christ died for our sins *according to the scriptures . . .* and was raised on the third day *according to the scriptures*" (1 Cor 15:3b-5). A concern to unpack that expression "according to the scriptures" has left its mark on all the Passion narratives—none more so than that of Matthew. That the First Evangelist should be foremost in this regard comes as no surprise, granted the concern evident from the beginning of the gospel to indicate again and again how some particular aspect of Jesus' life "fulfilled" what had been written in the prophets. In connection with the Passion above all, tracing the scriptural predictions and echoes communicated the sense that the death Jesus suffered and his being raised from the dead were all part of a divine plan for the Messiah set out long before. The coherence between what had been predicted and what had happened lent meaning to otherwise calamitous events. On the surface Jesus goes to his death the passive victim of the human authorities who have become his enemies. At a deeper level, in his submission to violence and condemnation he actively fulfills a divine design to strike the decisive blow against the rule of Satan in the world and establish once and for all in its stead the rule of God. It is to this deeper subtext that the scriptural quotations and allusions call our attention, even as Jesus dies a human death devoid of "supernatural" alleviation.

Matthew's Passion narrative follows very closely that of Mark, reproducing its content entirely save for a few small details. But Matthew has made significant additions. Chief among them are the following:

The singling out of Judas as the betrayer: 26:5

Judas' remorse: 27:3-10

Pilate's wife's warning: 27:19

Pilate's attempt to exculpate himself and the crowd's acceptance of responsibility for Jesus' blood: 27:24-25

Earthquake and appearances of dead persons immediately following upon Jesus' death: 27:51b-53

Placing of a guard at the tomb: 27:62-66

The account of Judas' remorse and what it drives him to in the end; the concern of the chief priests not to put the "blood money" he had returned into the Temple treasury; the anxiety of Pilate, warned by his wife, to rid himself of guilt: all these introduce into the Matthean Passion what Raymond Brown has called "a haunting issue of responsibility."[1] Innocent blood is being shed and, according to biblical tradition (cf. especially Deut 21:1-9), when innocent blood is shed the guilt must fall somewhere. The question, "where will this guilt fall?" becomes a leading issue in the narrative. Judas tries to escape it (27:4); the chief priests are anxious to keep it away from themselves and their treasury (27:6); Pilate seeks to evade it by washing his hands (27:24). Finally, and in response to Pilate's empty gesture, the people as a whole make their terrible bid: "His blood be on us and on our children" (27:25). The responsibility has been accepted. The acceptance will have its outcome when "the children" of the generation that cried for Jesus' death (that is, the next generation—*and only that generation*) suffer the destruction of their city and their Temple in 70 C.E.

This leads us straight into the most troubling feature of Matthew's Passion narrative: its accentuation of the Jewish contribution to the condemnation and death of Jesus.[2] The outcome of Judas' attempt to return the money of betrayal to the chief priests and elders shows them up as more concerned about not polluting the sanctuary over which they preside than listening to his protestation of Jesus' innocence (27:3-7). They confer together on the morning after Jesus' arrest precisely, as Matthew indicates, "to bring about his death" (27:1). They incite the crowd to ask for Barabbas and "to have Jesus killed" (27:20)[3] so that, following Pilate's protestation (v. 24), the people as a whole take on responsibility for the blood of Jesus (27:25). Joseph of Arimathea, who sees to Jesus' burial, is not said in Matthew to be a sympathetic member of the (Jewish) council but "a disciple of Jesus" (Matt 27:57; contrast Mark 15:43; Luke 23:50). Finally, peculiar to Matthew is the request on the part of the "chief priests and Pharisees" to have a guard set at Jesus' tomb (27:62-66) and the subsequent bribing of the soldiers to establish the explanation of the empty tomb that, the Evangelist notes, "is still told among the Jews to this day" (28:11-15).

This accentuation of Jewish complicity in the death of Jesus is simply the culmination of a tendency that has run throughout the gospel. It reflects

---

[1] Raymond E. Brown, *The Death of the Messiah.* 2 vols. (New York: Doubleday, 1994) 1:29.

[2] Ibid. 61–62.

[3] Neither of these phrases is in the Markan parallels (Mark 15:1, 11).

the recent history of the Matthean community and its situation *vis-à-vis* the dominant leadership in Formative Judaism at the time of writing. It is a fact of the gospel that we cannot argue away but have to accept, along with the baleful influence it has had on Christian attitudes to Jews and Judaism down the ages. What is crucial in interpretation is to recognize the accentuation, understand why it is there, and deal with it appropriately. Awareness of it should provide impulse and opportunity to point to other voices in the New Testament—notably that of Paul in Romans 11—expressing a more positive attitude to Judaism, as also to the record of anti-Semitism that all Christians must acknowledge and of which they must repent. The Matthean Passion narrative, no matter how sublime its positive message for Christian faith, remains a "text of terror" for Jews and Judaism.[4] To read or proclaim it without consciousness of this is to place oneself in line with those guilty of shedding blood, the same Jewish blood as that which ran in the veins of the One whose unjust and cruel death it narrates with such dramatic power.

The long Passion-Resurrection narrative may be broken into four major sections:

The Events Leading up to Jesus' Arrest: 26:1-56

Jesus on Trial: 26:57–27:26
    1. Before the Jewish Authorities: 26:57-75
    2. Before the Roman Governor: 27:1-26

The Crucifixion, Death, and Burial of Jesus: 27:27-66

The Third Day: Empty Tomb and Risen Lord: 28:1-15

As elsewhere, my intention is to move swiftly over the long narrative, dwelling on those features peculiar to Matthew, in line with the emphases of this study.

Events Leading Up to the Arrest of Jesus: 26:1-56

An unnamed woman anoints Jesus for burial: 26:6-13

The dramatic action of the Passion is set in motion by the plot on the part of those named as Jesus' chief opponents in Matthew's account: "the

---

[4] The phrase comes from Phyllis Trible, *Texts of Terror: Literary-Feminist Readings of Biblical Narratives* (Philadelphia: Fortress, 1984).

chief priests and the elders of the people." They want to bring about his death, but face a blockage: a public arrest at the time of the looming festival (Passover), when Jerusalem was swollen with visitors and pilgrims, might cause a riot (vv. 3-4). As we already know (10:4), one of Jesus' closest associates, Judas, will solve that problem for them.

As a countercurrent to this murderous threat and hint of betrayal, an unnamed woman disciple performs a gesture that demonstrates both love and genuine appreciation of the "service" Jesus is about to enact. While he is at table in a safehouse among friends at Bethany, she brings a costly ointment in an (equally costly) alabaster jar and pours it over his head. The (male) disciples angrily protest: this is a waste of money that could more usefully have been spent on the poor. Granted what Jesus is about to undergo, something he has attempted to make clear to his disciples (v. 2b), the protest is callous. It throws into higher relief the devotion of the woman, who does clearly understand that Jesus is going to his death. As he himself explains, she has in this anticipatory way anointed his body for burial.[5] His description of her action as *kalos* (v. 10) indicates not only something "beautiful" but a gesture that is truly fitting and appropriate for the time.[6] She has understood, as the disciples have not, that he is about to perform an infinitely costly "service" for herself and all humankind. In the name of all who will benefit (the "many" [20:28; 26:28]) she performs this costly gesture of gratitude and appreciation, one that is possible now but will not be when the community no longer has Jesus physically among them.

Jesus' final comment (v. 13) binds the memory of the woman's gesture forever into the Passion story. Wherever *his* story is told, her story will be part of it. Her otherwise puzzling anonymity allows her perhaps to be a point of insertion into the story for all, women and men alike, who seek to respond appropriately to Jesus. How contrastive then is the action of Judas (vv. 14-16), who resolves the chief priests' problem by arranging, for thirty pieces of silver,[7] to betray Jesus in a way that will not cause public commotion (26:14-16; cf. v. 5).

---

[5] In Matthew's gospel, when the women come to the tomb on Easter morning (28:1), they do not bring spices to anoint Jesus' body (contrast Mark 16:1; Luke 24:1); that service has already been performed—by this woman.

[6] The *NRSV* translation "a good service" is lame.

[7] Only Matthew specifies the amount; cf. 27:9 and Zech 11:12.

The Passover Meal and Eucharistic Institution: 26:17-29

Later in the week (Thursday),[8] the disciples remind Jesus concerning the celebration of the Passover meal. As in the case of his entry into the city (21:1-4), the directions he gives suggest that all has been foreseen and prearranged (26:17-19).

As the meal itself gets under way Jesus makes the devastating announcement that one of them is about to betray him (26:20-25). In Matthew's account Jesus explicitly identifies Judas as the betrayer (v. 25). His awareness of being betrayed and by whom further communicates the sense that all is proceeding according to a divine plan laid down in the Scriptures. But that does not relieve the human agent of responsibility ("Woe . . .!" [v. 24]).

This note of betrayal goes along with Matthew's constant depiction of the Church as a mixed community containing both saints and sinners. It is to such a community and for such a community that Jesus now remolds the Passover ritual (26:26-29). He does so to specify the meaning of the death he is about to undergo and to draw the disciples and their successors in the Church into its saving effects. Jesus takes a loaf of bread and, in conformity with Jewish custom before eating, blesses God for the gift of food. Instead of eating it himself, however, he breaks the loaf into pieces, telling his disciples to take and eat it, adding in explanation, "This is my body" (v. 26). Taking into themselves the pieces broken from the one loaf forges for the disciples a profound union with Jesus, since the loaf represents his very person.[9] The words and action with the cup (v. 27) follow in parallel manner,[10] save that this time a string of qualifying phrases completes the meaning (v. 28): "This is my blood of the covenant, which is poured out for many for the forgiveness of sins" (v. 28). "Blood of the covenant" alludes to a ritual act recorded in Exod 24:4-8, when Moses sealed the Sinai covenant by sprinkling the blood of sacrificial animals on the Israelites, saying to them: "See the blood of the covenant that the LORD has made with you in accordance with all these words" (Exod 24:8; cf. Zech 9:11); at this point the Israelites became the covenant people of God. Jesus' words

---

[8] M. Eugene Boring, "The Gospel of Matthew," in Leander E. Keck, ed., *The New Interpreter's Bible*. Vol. 8 (Nashville: Abingdon, 1995) 461, sets out the sequence of the days of the Passion in a helpfully schematic way.

[9] My overall interpretation here is indebted to that of Rudolf Schnackenburg, *The Gospel of Matthew* (Grand Rapids and Cambridge: Eerdmans, 2002) 267–68.

[10] With "giving thanks" (Greek *eucharistēsas*) replacing "blessing," and so creating the name "Eucharist" for the rite being instituted.

over the eucharistic cup reflect the early Christian tradition (seen also in Rom 3:25; Heb 9:11-14), which interpreted the shedding of his blood on Calvary as the inauguration of a new covenant for a renewed people of God.[11] The phrase "poured out for many" applies to Jesus in his death the role of the Servant figure of Isa 53:12,[12] already alluded to in Matt 20:28.[13] As the Servant "bears the sins of many" (Isa 53:12; cf. v. 10), so Jesus' blood is shed "for the forgiveness of sins." In adding this last phrase to the Markan formula, Matthew indicates that in his death Jesus fulfills the role announced for him at his naming: "to set the people free from their sins" (1:21).[14] When disciples, then, partake of the cup they become one with Jesus specifically in respect to all these saving benefits associated with his death. They are the nucleus of a covenant people set free from the enslavement of sin. On the model of the yearly Passover celebration this people will reenact these eucharistic gestures and so draw new generations into the same sphere of salvation.

Jesus' final comment (v. 29) about not drinking "this fruit of the vine" until that day when he drinks it new with the disciples in the kingdom makes clear that the present meal is the last he will share with them before his death. It also makes this supper and every subsequent eucharistic celebration an anticipation of the hospitality that redeemed humanity will experience in the banquet of the kingdom. In this way the Eucharist touches no less than five "moments" in time. (1) Looking "backward," so to speak, it recalls and renews the covenant made with the original people of God and the manna with which they were fed in their desert wandering. (2) Less remotely, it recalls the meals in which Jesus celebrated the mercy of God (9:10-13; 11:19) and especially the two occasions when he multiplied the loaves to ensure that the people did not go away faint and hungry (14:13-21; 15:32-39). (3) Now, on the eve of his death, he transforms the Passover, in order that (4) throughout its life the Church may experience saving

[11] In contrast to Paul (1 Cor 11:23-25) and Luke (22:20), Mark (14:22-24) and Matthew do not mention "new covenant" (cf. Jer 31:33). But the thought of a new covenant is implicit in the very mention of covenant.

[12] Matthew secures the allusion to the Servant by changing the preposition in the phrase "for many" (*peri pollōn* instead of *hyper pollōn,* as in Mark 14:24), so that it conforms exactly to the LXX of Isa 53:4, 10.

[13] As in 20:28, "many" is Semitic idiom and should be understood in a universal, not a restrictive sense: i.e., "for all."

[14] When reporting the preaching of John the Baptist (3:1-2), Matthew omits Mark's notice (1:4) that John's baptism was "for the forgiveness of sins"; Matthew associates that function strictly with the death of Jesus.

union with its Emmanuel Lord, as a foretaste and anticipation of (5) union with him in the banquet of the kingdom.[15]

The Mount of Olives: Jesus' Prayer and Arrest: 26:30-56

The supper concluded, Jesus returns with his disciples to the Mount of Olives (26:30; cf. 24:3). On the way he foretells his disciples' coming desertion, but encompasses it within the divine plan by quoting a form of Zech 13:7: "I will strike the shepherd, and the sheep of the flock will be scattered" (v. 31).[16] The gospel has portrayed him as Israel's compassionate shepherd king (2:1-6; 9:36).[17] Now the Shepherd will indeed be struck and the flock scattered. But, raised from the dead, he will "go ahead" of them (in the way of Palestinian shepherds) to Galilee (v. 32). There they will gather around him once more (28:16-20). Peter's protestation that *he* at least will never be a deserter draws from Jesus a further prophecy: that very night, before the cock crows to announce the dawn, the "Rock" one will have denied him three times (vv. 33-35).

Jesus' anguished prayer in Gethsemane (26:36-46), when he shrinks before the prospect of death and seeks the support of three disciples, is perhaps the most poignant episode in the entire gospel tradition. The tenacity of its hold in the tradition and its widespread attestation (besides Mark 14:32-42 and Luke 22:40-46, cf. John 12:27; Heb 5:7-8) was doubtless due to the precious witness it gave to the cost to Jesus of his sufferings and death, and hence to the extremity of the love and obedience that held him to his purpose. The account takes us into the heart of his relationship to the Father, as it also has him turning constantly for support to his three closest disciples, Peter and the sons of Zebedee (James and John).[18] The same three disciples caught a glimpse of his heavenly status at the Transfiguration (17:1-8). Now "God with us" (1:23) implores them—in vain—to watch "with" him (26:38, 40).[19] There they heard the Father's voice declare him

[15] The "Emmanuel" sense comes through in the Matthean addition "with you" to the Markan original in v. 29.

[16] The quotation is altered so as to make God the agent, expressing the sense that all that is happening is ultimately the work of God.

[17] Cf. Boring, "Matthew," 474.

[18] By referring to James and John in this way (contrast Mark 14:33) Matthew reminds us of the episode in 20:20-21 where the same two had boldly declared their readiness to drink the "cup" before which Jesus now shrinks.

[19] The phrase "with me" in both places is peculiar, typically, to the Matthean account (contrast Mark 14:34, 37).

to be the "Beloved Son" (17:5). Here they see him struggling in a prayer to which the Father makes no response. In contrast to Mark's more summary report (14:35-40), Matthew twice gives us the wording of Jesus' prayer (vv. 39, 42). This allows us to discern a progress in his acceptance of the "cup" (20:22).[20] The "possibility" that it might be removed slips away as Jesus aligns his will completely with that of the Father in words that echo the third petition of the Lord's Prayer (6:10b).[21]

There is perhaps no place in the gospel where Jesus' capacity to bear humanity's burdens is more personally apparent than in this scene. Though never ceasing for a moment to be God's Son, he wrestles with the prospect of death in utter loneliness: a seeming abandonment by God (which will endure to the end: 27:46) and total absence of comfort on the human side. Nothing communicates so powerfully as this scene that we have, in the words of Heb 4:15 (cf. 5:7-10), a High Priest who can feel for us in our weakness, who in every respect has been tested as we are. Here the compassionate Shepherd (Matt 9:36) is "God with us" in the deepest degree.

Matthew's account of Jesus' arrest (26:47-56) brings out two things in particular: the treachery of Judas and the complete rejection of violent resistance on the part of Jesus, now perfectly composed, as he will be to the end. Accompanied by armed men, Judas gives Jesus a treacherous kiss. His cold, outsider's greeting, "Rabbi" (v. 49; cf. already in v. 25) receives a similar response from Jesus: "So, friend, you have come for this!"[22] The brief flurry of violence following Jesus' arrest, when one of those with him draws a sword and cuts off the ear of the high priest's slave (v. 51), allows Jesus to make clear his complete renunciation of that path. They have come to arrest him with swords and clubs *as though* he was a violent revolutionary,[23] whereas he has been a peaceful teacher (v. 55). He *could* resist their attempts, armed not with the weapons of this world but with those of heaven ("twelve legions of angels" [v. 53]). But that is not his choice. He has committed himself—not without struggle, as we have just seen—to

[20] Cf. Ulrich Luz, *Das Evangelium nach Matthäus.* 4 vols. Vol. 4: *Mt 26–28* (Zürich: Benziger; Neukirchen-Vluyn: Neukirchener Verlag, 1985–2002) 137.

[21] As Jesus' later (v. 41) warning to the disciples about praying lest "they enter into temptation" corresponds to the second-last petition (6:13a).

[22] "Friend"—"a politely cool generic form of address to someone whose name one does not know" (Boring, "Matthew," 477); cf. 20:13 and 22:12. The rest of the sentence offers a translation of a highly elliptical phrase, *eph' ho parei;* cf. Luz, *Matthäus* 4:164–65.

[23] The primary meaning of the Greek word *lēistēs* is that of an armed person who commits robbery with violence ("bandit"). Later, particularly in connection with the Jewish revolt of 70 C.E., it gained the connotation of violent revolutionary.

fulfill the costly path laid down in the Scriptures (vv. 54, 56): to be the Servant Messiah who does not "break a bruised reed or quench a smoldering wick" (Isa 42:3, quoted Matt 12:19-20). Following this path, he had often "withdrawn" (Greek *anachōrein*) in the face of hostility and gone another way. Now he neither withdraws nor confronts, but freely surrenders to violence, to overcome it in the way laid down by the Father.

Passion II:
Jesus on Trial: 26:57–27:26

Before the Jewish Authorities: 26:57-75

Abandoned by all the disciples (v. 56b), save for Peter who follows at a distance (v. 58), Jesus is now brought by his captors before Caiaphas the high priest, and the Council (v. 59).[1] The hearing is a "show trial" in the modern sense of the term. The aim is not to discover the truth, but to pin on Jesus the kind of accusation that will serve as grounds for demanding his punishment by death—an outcome already determined (26:3-5). Ironically, the two witnesses who eventually come forward and accuse Jesus of claiming to be able to destroy the Temple of God and to build it in three days (v. 61) do, in a fashion, speak the truth. Jesus had not made such a claim in so many words, but readers of the gospel know that he, the One who is "greater than the Temple" (12:6), had foretold its destruction—something that had actually occurred by the time the gospel was written.

Jesus' continued silence (like that of the Servant in Isa 53:7) leads the High Priest to solemnly place him under oath in regard to the messianic claim: "Tell us whether you are the Messiah, the Son of God" (v. 63). That both titles apply to Jesus in a unique sense has long since been known to the disciples in the gospel (cf. 14:33; 16:16). Now, in this climactic confrontation with the Jewish authorities, the time has come for him to own them openly before the world. Jesus does so (v. 64)[2] and then adds a further claim. In language taken from Ps 110:1 ("seated on the right hand of the

---

[1] Historically, it is most unlikely that a full meeting of the Council (Sanhedrin) to hear a capital charge would have been convoked (1) in the High Priest's house, (2) at night, (3) on *this* particular night (Passover eve). What is described is more likely an informal arraignment prior to handing Jesus over to the Roman authorities.

[2] The reply "You have said so" is affirmative but, in line with the instruction in 5:33-37, throws the oath back upon the priest.

209

power") and Dan 7:13 ("coming on the clouds of heaven"), he proclaims before this worldly tribunal his future coming as Son of Man (24:30). The next time[3] those who are now his judges will see him is when—the situation precisely reversed—they stand before him, the Judge of the world, clad with all authority in heaven and on earth (Dan 7:14; Matt 25:31-46; 28:18b).

The immediate condemnation of Jesus on the charge of blasphemy (vv. 65-66) and the violent mockery of him by those present (vv. 67-68) represent the formal rejection of Jesus as Messiah by the leaders of his people. For Matthew's community the rejection Jesus experienced at his trial anticipated their own experience of rejection at the hands of the Synagogue. With their witness to his unique status continuing to be dubbed blasphemy, they could draw comfort from his steadfast claim of final vindication. That claim and the titles that accompany it make this scene one of the high points of the gospel's presentation of Jesus. At the same time, we have here a passage requiring sensitive interpretation and preaching if anti-Jewish attitudes are not to be promoted. The Jewish authorities acted for themselves, judging one of their own in their own generation. Jesus represents all those unjustly put on trial down the ages. With tragic irony, these include those countless numbers of his fellow-Jews who have suffered through false and blasphemous Christian appeal to his memory and his name.

Meanwhile, out in the courtyard, his leading disciple, who once through divine revelation confessed him to be "the Messiah, the Son of the Living God" (16:16), has three times denied his Lord (vv. 69-74). The "Rock" foundation of the Church (16:18) is also, in his failure, his repentance ("weeping bitterly" [v. 75]), and his eventual restitution, representative of all members of the mixed community that is the Church.

Before the Roman Governor: 27:1-26

For the chief priests and elders of the people there is nothing further to do other than to make a case for Jesus' execution before the Roman governor, the one who alone has the power to bring it about. After a brief morning meeting to confirm this plan (27:1), they bind Jesus and hand him over to Pilate (v. 2).[4]

---

[3] I am interpreting the Greek phrase *ap'arti* in this sense and, with most scholars, relating the "Son of Man" statement to Jesus' end-time coming as Son of Man (16:27-28; 24:30).

[4] The phrase "in order to bring about his death" is a Matthean addition to Mark. The action confirms exactly the details of the third Passion prediction (20:19).

Before proceeding to the Roman trial Matthew inserts the story of the remorse and tragic death of the betrayer (27:3-10). We have already noted how this addition highlights the sense of responsibility for the shedding of innocent blood that (in the words of Raymond Brown) "haunts" the Matthean Passion. Judas at least recognizes and owns Jesus' innocence—though his reaction is more one of guilt-ridden remorse than genuine repentance,[5] and his tragic end fulfills Jesus' dire prophecy in 26:24.[6] The rest of the episode further highlights the callous indifference of the priests. While scrupulous about not polluting the Temple treasury, they have no concern to help Judas rid himself of his guilt; no mercy before sacrifice here! What they do eventually decide to do with the money—buy the potter's field as a burial ground for strangers (vv. 7-8)—enables Matthew to present the episode as a fulfillment of Scripture and so as something at least foreseen by God and encompassed within the wider divine plan (vv. 9-10).[7]

The actual trial before Pilate (27:11-26) falls into three stages. First (vv. 11-14) the governor interrogates Jesus, asking whether he is "the King of the Jews"—in this gospel the Gentile (non-Jewish) way of referring to "Messiah" (2:2; 27:29, 37). As he had done earlier before the High Priest (26:64), Jesus returns an ambiguous answer: "As you say" (v. 11). He is the Messiah but in a different, less political way than Pilate's formulation suggests. For the rest Jesus remains silent, continuing as before to adopt the demeanor of the Servant (Isa 53:7). With the Barabbas episode (vv. 15-24) the trial moves to a second stage. Pilate, clearly unconvinced of any wrongdoing on Jesus' part, seizes upon this stratagem of releasing a prisoner at festival time as a way of ridding himself of the dilemma of conscience he now faces—something greatly heightened by the message from his wife (v.19; unique to Matthew). All the stratagem serves to accomplish, however, is to heighten the malevolence of the chief priests and scribes.

---

[5] The Greek term is *metamelesthai*, as in 21:29, 32, not *metanoiein*, the usual expression for repentance.

[6] The description of Judas' end seems to be modeled on that of Ahithophel, David's betrayer, in 2 Sam 17:23. The rather different account in Acts 1:18-19 at least agrees (1) that Judas died a violent death and (2) that he was connected with the place known as the "Field of Blood."

[7] This last of Matthew's "fulfillment" quotations owes much more to Zechariah (11:12-13) than to Jeremiah, to whom it is attributed (cf. Jer 32:6-15; also 18:2-3) on the basis of a highly complex and contrived association of the two texts. The more impersonal expression of fulfillment used here (cf. also 2:17) suggests something merely allowed by God rather than intended; cf. Donald Senior, *The Passion of Jesus in the Gospel of Matthew* (Wilmington: Michael Glazier, 1985) 107.

They incite the crowd (v. 20) to make a clear choice for Jesus Barabbas,[8] a notorious criminal (cf. v. 16), over Jesus the Messiah and Son of God.[9] When Pilate pathetically asks what he should do with "Jesus, who is called the Messiah," the crowd, now one with the leaders,[10] suggests both the verdict and the penalty: "Let him be crucified" (v. 22). When Pilate makes a last protest, "Why, what evil has he done?" they simply repeat the same cry (v. 23), their refusal to answer the question indirectly providing yet another testimony to Jesus' innocence.

The trial reaches its third and climactic stage (vv. 24-26) when Pilate, forced to act by the threat of a riot,[11] washes his hands in front of the crowd, declaring his innocence "of this man's blood" (v. 24). The gesture reflects a ritual for turning aside the guilt of innocent blood recorded in Deut 21:6-8. The remark that accompanies it, "See to it yourselves," echoes that of the priests when dismissing the attempt of Judas to return the money of betrayal (v. 4). So now we have three parties complicit in the fate of Jesus—Judas, the chief priests and elders, and Pilate—all of whom try to shift the guilt of shedding innocent blood away from themselves and place it on others. How dramatic then, by contrast, the cry that now breaks out from "the whole people": "His blood upon us and upon our children" (v. 25).[12] This acceptance of responsibility for the shedding of Jesus' blood frees Pilate (at least in his own mind) from his dilemma. It allows him to release Barabbas for them[13] and hand Jesus over to be scourged and crucified (v. 26).

---

[8] Despite the lack of "Jesus" in the main manuscripts, with most scholars I take the full name "Jesus Barabbas" as original in v. 17; see W. D. Davies and Dale Allison, *A Critical and Exegetical Commentary on the Gospel According to Saint Matthew.* ICC. 3 vols. (Edinburgh: T&T Clark, 1988–97) 3:584, n. 20.

[9] If, as seems likely, Jesus addressed God as *Abba* (cf. Mark 14:36), there may be an ironic play on the patronymic: "Bar Abbas"—"Bar Abba(s)." But Matthew nowhere records the Aramaic form of Jesus' address to God.

[10] Matthew adds "all" to the Markan narrative.

[11] The mention of a riot developing, another Matthean addition, enhances the dramatic tension.

[12] This is a literal translation of the Greek sentence, which lacks any verb ("be"). There is no suggestion, then, of the crowd calling down a curse upon themselves; they are simply accepting responsibility for the shedding of Jesus' blood. For parallel biblical formulas of acceptance or disclaimer see Senior, *Passion of Matthew,* 117–18; Raymond E. Brown, *The Death of the Messiah.* 2 vols. (New York: Doubleday, 1994) 1:837–38.

[13] The phrase "for them" conveys the sense of cementing their choice for the disreputable Jesus (Barabbas) they had chosen over against the Jesus sent by God to "save the people from their sins" (1:21).

There is no denying the climactic nature of this cry that has echoed down the ages with such terrible consequences for Christian attitudes to Jews and Judaism. Where Matthew has till now referred to the "crowd(s)" (*ochlos, ochloi* [27:15, 20, 24]), he now speaks of "the whole people" *(pas ho laos),* a term regularly used in the gospel for the nation as a whole. It is hard to escape, then, a sense that the perspective at this point extends beyond the hundreds or so present in Pilate's court to encompass, at least symbolically, the entire people.[14] Writing in the last decade or so before the end of the first century C.E., Matthew is conscious of two undeniable facts: that over two generations the bulk of the Jewish people has said "No" to the Christian missionary preaching of the messiahship of Jesus; second, that the Temple and much of Jerusalem have been destroyed by the Romans in response to the Jewish revolt. In the light of these realities the Evangelist seems to make the cry of "the whole people" here a symbolic anticipation of that sustained "No" to Messiah Jesus and, with Luke (23:27-31) and the author of the Fourth Gospel (11:47-48), sees the destruction of 70 C.E. as a divine punishment for that rejection.[15]

By the same token, allusion to the events of 70 C.E. instructs us on how to interpret the final phrase "and on our children"—that is, to interpret it as referring strictly to the succeeding generation—the generation that was to witness and suffer the events of 70 C.E.—*and to stop there!* There is no foundation in the Matthean formulation for the lamentable extension of that phrase in the Christian tradition to encompass all subsequent generations of the Jewish people to the end of time.[16] No more than anywhere else in the gospels do we have here the record of an actual historical event—a moment when the Jewish nation as a whole took upon itself responsibility for the death of Jesus. We have the climax of a theological drama created to explain theologically two historical phenomena that left a deep—and in

[14] Cf. Ulrich Luz, *Das Evangelium nach Matthäus.* 4 vols. Vol. 4: *Mt 26–28* (Zürich: Benziger; Neukirchen-Vluyn: Neukirchener Verlag, 1985–2002) 277–81, 283; for a more restricted view see Davies and Allison, *Matthew* 3:592.

[15] As Brown, *Death of the Messiah* 1:831–32, points out, such a view is an established biblical category, reaching right back to the understanding of the destruction of the First Temple by the Babylonians in the sixth century B.C.E. as a divine punishment for Israel's sins (Ezek 9:8-11). It is found in other (non-Christian) Jewish interpretations of the destruction of 70 C.E., as, for example, Josephus, *Jewish War* 4.386-88; 6.109-10, 118-28; *Testament of Levi* 16:1-2, 4-5.

[16] I take issue with Meier's addition of "forever" in the statement: "the whole people of Israel . . . take upon themselves and their children forever the responsibility for Jesus' death" (*Matthew,* 342).

one case extremely painful—impression on the early Christian community: Israel's "No" to the Gospel and the destruction of the Temple.[17]

This Matthean text has had terrible effects in its historical interpretation, fanned by currents of anti-Semitism and anti-Judaism emanating from other factors. But such go well beyond the intention of the narrative. It can be argued that they go not merely beyond but counter to the basic direction of the entire gospel. Why should the Evangelist have held Jews exempt from the touchstone command of Jesus that his disciples should "love their enemies" (6:43-45)? And, granted that the acceptance of responsibility in 27:25 ceases with the immediately following generation, why should Matthew, in line with the biblical tradition that sees God's punitive action followed by salvation, not have shared Paul's hope for a latter-day inclusion of Israel within the scheme of salvation (Rom 11:25-32)?[18]

Matthew 27:25 remains, then, a very dangerous text—one that, granted its historical legacy and position in Christian imagination, should never be allowed to go without comment in preaching and proclamation. But precisely as such it provides opportunity for the expression of Christian repentance, on the one hand, and for a deeper appreciation of the need to interpret particular passages in the light of the total gospel, on the other.

[17] Cf. Brown, *Death of the Messiah* 1:832–33, 839.
[18] We recall also the possibility of a positive interpretation of Matt 23:39; see above p. 176.

Passion III:
Jesus Crucified, Buried, and Raised:
27:27–28:15

In a sense the execution of Jesus has already begun with the flogging (v. 26), since in Roman practice this was a customary prelude to death by crucifixion. It begins the terrible physical sufferings of Jesus. This aspect of Jesus' Passion, so much to the fore in later Christian meditation, is something upon which Matthew, like the other three evangelists, does not dwell. Even the actual process of crucifixion is referred to simply in an introductory participial phrase (v. 35). The evangelists presumed that their original readers were all too familiar with the terrible mode of execution the Romans reserved for runaway slaves and rebels. What was far more important—and especially for Matthew—was to bring out the theological meaning of the event. Jesus, the Son of God, dies a human death totally unrelieved by any heavenly assistance or alleviation of suffering. Just before he dies Jesus even gives utterance to a sense of abandonment by God (v. 46). Was God absent, indifferent? No, says Matthew: multiple echoes of Scripture—especially of Psalms 22 and 69[1]—show that Jesus continues at this extreme moment to fulfill a divine script set out in the Scriptures for the Messiah and his saving work.[2] God lets Jesus die, but Jesus in dying

---

[1] Arrived at Golgotha, Jesus tastes the wine mixed with gall offered him to drink; cf. Ps 69:21. His clothes are divided in accordance with Ps 22:18. The head-wagging mockery of the passersby (v. 39) fulfills Ps 22:7, while their taunts and those of the chief priests echo the next verse (Ps 22:8), refracted through phrases from Wis 2:10-20 ("He trusts in God; let God deliver him now, if he wants to; for he said, 'I am God's Son'").

[2] Cf. Ulrich Luz, *Das Evangelium nach Matthäus*. 4 vols. Vol. 4: *Mt 26–28* (Zürich: Benziger; Neukirchen-Vluyn: Neukirchener Verlag, 1985–2002) 322; Donald M. Senior, *The Passion of Jesus in the Gospel of Matthew* (Wilmington: Michael Glazier, 1985) 127–30, 134–37.

does not cease to be what he has been throughout the gospel: Emmanuel, "God with us." The death of Jesus is no less a revelation of God than any other scene in his life.

Jesus Mocked and Crucified: 27:27-45

Intimately connected with this revelation is the second feature running through the account of Jesus' execution and death: irony. If the narrative makes no comment on the physical suffering, it dwells at length on the mockery he endures: first, at the hands of the (Gentile) soldiers before he is led out to execution (27:27-31); then, while he hangs on the cross, from the passersby (vv. 39-40), the chief priests, scribes, and elders (vv. 41-43); finally, from the two bandits crucified alongside him (v. 44). In all cases the mockery imposes on Jesus titles and roles that are profoundly true: he *is* "the King of the Jews" (vv. 29, 37)—though in a way very different from what the foreigners who mock and crucify him suppose. He *is* "the Son of God" (vv. 40, 43), who could "save himself" (vv. 40, 42). But precisely as God's Son he remains obediently upon the cross to "save others" (v. 42), leaving the saving of himself to God.[3] They mock his supposed claim to destroy the Temple and rebuild it in three days (v. 40; cf. 26:61); in reality it is they who are bringing about its eventual destruction (70 C.E.) by encompassing his death. Thus through force of irony the narrative compels *them* to reveal the truth of what is going on, the truth they scoff at and reject.

The truly terrifying thing—a terror no amount of familiarity with the narrative can dull—is that, granted the high christology of Matthew, all this is a human mockery of God. Human beings are tormenting the One who embodies the presence of God in their midst. The three-hour darkness that comes upon the whole earth (v. 45) could, in biblical understanding (cf. Amos 8:9-10), be an indication of God's final destructive wrath, of creation going into reverse, the return of the primeval darkness (cf. Gen 1:2).

Jesus Dies on the Cross: 27:46-50

For three hours the narrative leaves us in suspense concerning the divine response. Then at last (v. 46) Jesus, who has been silent since his

---

[3] Senior, *Passion of Matthew*, 136–37.

response to Pilate (v. 11), utters in the opening words of Ps 22:1 the terrible cry of dereliction. He has been abandoned by his people, he has been deserted by his companions; now he gives utterance to a sense of abandonment by the God whose very will he is carrying out. Son of God though he is, he plumbs to the depths the terrible sense of God's absence that so often accompanies human suffering. As with physical suffering, his divine status spares him no measure of spiritual and psychological distress; the darkness without is matched by an intense darkness within. It is not a cry of despair—because Jesus still calls upon God. But it is a cry of dereliction because no answer from God will come until he has shared the lot of all human beings in death.[4]

It is only at the very moment of death that a suggestion of something beyond the ordinary human course enters in. Following the curious episode in which some of the bystanders misinterpret Jesus' cry as a calling for help from the prophet Elijah (vv. 47-49),[5] Jesus cries out again with a loud voice and then expires. Human beings cannot utter a loud cry just before dying of asphyxiation. Moreover, Matthew has altered the Markan description in such a way as to suggest a more controlled, voluntary expiration.[6] Something of the Johannine "It is accomplished" (John 19:30) attends the Matthean description of Jesus' death, and the final cry seems to be at least a signal, if not a trigger, for the cataclysmic events that follow (vv. 51-53).

[4] With most scholars (e.g., W. D. Davies and Dale Allison, *A Critical and Exegetical Commentary on the Gospel According to Saint Matthew.* ICC. 3 vols. [Edinburgh: T&T Clark, 1988–97] 3:624–25; M. Eugene Boring, "The Gospel of Matthew," in Leander E. Keck, ed., *The New Interpreter's Bible.* Vol. 8 [Nashville: Abingdon, 1995] 492; Luz, *Matthäus* 4:342–43), I reject the view (cf. Rudolf Schnackenburg, *The Gospel of Matthew* [Grand Rapids and Cambridge: Eerdmans, 2002] 289) that eases the sense of Jesus' dereliction by taking the text to mean that Jesus recited the entire psalm, including its positive, hopeful ending.

[5] It is not at all clear why the belief that Jesus is calling on Elijah prompts one of the bystanders to place a sponge dipped in vinegar on a reed and offer it to Jesus to drink (a further fulfillment of Ps 69:22 [cf. v. 34]), or why another should say, "Wait, let us see whether Elijah will come to save him" (v. 49). Matthew has eased the tortured syntax of Mark 15:35-36 by making the person who says "Wait" distinct from the one who offers the drink. Whereas in Mark the action seems to arise more out of curiosity than hostility, Matthew has turned at least the final comment (v. 49) into a further instance of cynical mockery; cf. Davies and Allison, *Matthew* 3:627.

[6] Mark (15:37): *exepneusen;* Matthew: *aphēken to pneuma* (literally: "he yielded up the spirit"). This is masked in the *NRSV* translation, which simply reads for both "he breathed his last" (a note in the margin records a more literal translation for Matthew).

The Aftermath: 27:51-66

Those events, beginning with the rending of the Temple curtain (v. 51), signal God's response to the obedient death of Jesus. God, whose "absence" had seemed so palpable, letting the Son die without intervention of any kind, now through phenomena (earthquake and splitting of rock) associated in Scripture with divine revelation (Exod 19:18 [Sinai]; 1 Kings 19:11 [Elijah]; Ps 18:7),[7] makes clear, in the face of the sustained mockery (vv. 39-44), that this is indeed the beloved Son in whom the Father is well pleased (3:17; 17:5). The mockers wanted Jesus to demonstrate that he was Son of God by using his own power to save himself. Now the soldiers who had themselves mocked Jesus, seen to his crucifixion, and watched by his cross are led by the earthquake and all that took place to confess, "Truly this was the Son of God" (v. 54).[8] These representatives of the Gentile world—to whom the disciples will soon be sent (28:18-20)—declare the truth that the divine voice had twice earlier proclaimed (3:17 [Baptism]; 17:5 [Transfiguration]). The Jesus who submitted to death *is* God's Son and the saving effects of his obedient "service" (20:28) are already beginning to stir.

The first of those effects is hinted at in the tearing of the Temple curtain. Neither Mark nor Matthew explains the meaning of this event, and it has been variously interpreted. If the inner curtain is meant, the one screening the sanctuary (Holy Place) from the innermost Holy of Holies, then it is likely that we have an allusion to the crowning ritual of the Day of Atonement. Once a year on this day (Leviticus 16), the High Priest entered behind the curtain and sprinkled the blood of a slain animal on the "mercy seat" (originally a cover over the long-lost Ark of the Covenant; cf. Exod 25:17-22). The ritual enacted God's covenant renewal through the wiping away of the sins and offenses committed in the preceding year. As we have noted in connection with the words over the eucharistic cup (Matt 26:27-28), the early Christian tradition interpreted the saving effects of the shedding of Christ's blood in the light of this ritual.[9] The same understanding

---

[7] The sequence of four verbs in the passive ("divine passive") across vv. 51-52 indicates the action of God; cf. Luz, *Matthäus* 4:369–70.

[8] Along with most scholars, I interpret the soldiers' cry as a positive indication of change of heart (conversion) rather than a cry of terrified acknowledgment wrung from still-hostile representatives of the Gentile world (so David C. Sim, *The Gospel of Matthew and Christian Judaism: The History and Social Setting of the Matthean Community* [Edinburgh: T&T Clark, 1998] 225–26).

[9] Cf. especially Rom 3:25; for this see Brendan Byrne, *The Letter to the Romans*. SP 6 (Collegeville: The Liturgical Press, 1995) 126–28.

likely applies to the rending of the curtain. The shedding of Christ's blood has rendered obsolete the yearly ritual performed by Jewish high priests in the Temple. What was there done in secret behind the curtain, God has now achieved once and for all on Golgotha through the selfless obedience of the Son. Jesus has performed the role signified by his name ("to save the people from their sins" [1:21b; cf. 26:28]) not only for Israel but for the entire world, represented here by the Gentile soldiers, who are the first to acknowledge his true identity as disclosed by the supernatural events. The rending of the curtain symbolizes the end of the Temple sacrifices, presaging the destruction (70 C.E.) of which Jesus himself had been accused (26:60-61; 27:29). The outpouring of mercy occurring here is the crowning instance of the divine preference: "What I want is mercy, not sacrifice" (Hos 6:6; Matt 9:13; 12:7).

At the same time, the earthquake and the splitting of the rocks leads to the opening of tombs and the raising of the bodies of holy ones, who subsequently emerged from their tombs and appeared to many in Jerusalem (vv. 52-53). This curious Matthean detail calls for theological rather than historical interpretation.[10] It gives narrative expression to the fulfillment of Jesus' words that in giving up his life the Son of Man would become a "ransom for many" (20:28). As Jesus pours out his lifeblood, the process of freeing people from the sin-created bondage to death begins. These Jewish holy ones are the forerunners of a renewed covenant people, destined to share the risen life of the Lord in the banquet of the kingdom.

Just as all these events relieve the seeming abandonment of Jesus by God, so also the note (vv. 55-56) about the presence of "many women" looking on from a distance relieves the otherwise total abandonment of Jesus by members of his new human "family." At the beginning of the Passion a loving gesture from an unnamed woman disciple had shown capacity to appreciate and accept the suffering destiny of Jesus (26:6-13). So now, the presence of these women—three of whom are singled out for mention (Mary Magdalene, Mary the mother of James and Joseph,[11] and the mother of the sons of Zebedee[12])—shows their capacity to be with

---

[10] Cf. Davies and Allison, *Matthew* 3:632; Boring, "Matthew," 493. Particularly odd is the implication (cf. v. 53) that the raised holy ones waited around in their tombs for three days before making their move into the city to appear "after his (Jesus') resurrection." The statement is best interpreted as an attempt within Matthew's tradition to safeguard the priority of Jesus' own resurrection.

[11] Hardly Mary the mother of Jesus, who would surely be identified through him rather than through these other two sons.

[12] The same mother who had earlier (20:20-23) put forward her sons for places on Jesus' right and left in the kingdom.

Jesus in his suffering when all the male disciples have fled. As true disciples they complete their "following" of him from Galilee and the "service"[13] they have rendered.[14]

The terrible day closes with two contrasting scenes. Joseph of Arimathea, a rich man who was also a disciple, with courage and fidelity attends to the burial of Jesus' body (27:57-60). He offers to Jesus, the author of life, the new tomb he has prepared for himself, sealing it with a great stone, while the two Marys, continuing their witnessing role, remain sitting opposite the tomb (v. 61). The other action (27:62-66), peculiar of course to Matthew's account, is that of the chief priests and Pharisees. Like Joseph, they approach Pilate, but with a very different request: for a guard to secure the tomb lest Jesus' disciples attempt, through stealing the body, to render believable his pledge to rise again. This relic of anti-Jewish propaganda emanating from the Matthean community paves the way for the bribing of the soldiers after Jesus' resurrection (28:11-15) and the statement that "this story is still told among the Jews to this day" (28:15). Along with that later story, it has no place in any credible Christian apologetic and no place, consequently, in responsible proclamation of the Gospel.

The Third Day: Empty Tomb, Risen Lord: 28:1-15

It is of course natural for us to regard the events of the third day as marking a completely new development. But Matthew portrays it as strictly continuous with the Passion. We have noted how, as soon as Jesus breathes his last, the earthquake and associated events signal new life breaking forth. Continuity is also clear in the depiction of the women disciples. They are witnesses to Jesus' death (27:56); to his burial and sealing in the tomb with a large stone (27:61); to the earthquake, the angelic appearance, and the emptiness of the grave (28:1-6); finally, to an appearance of the risen Lord himself (28:9-10). Likewise, the "counter" story—the guard at the tomb (27:62-66), the experience of the guards (28:4), their bribing (28:11-15a)—spans the Passion and resurrection. It is all one story. The Easter part of it is not a "happy ending," but the emergence into day-

---

[13] *NRSV*'s "provided for him" obscures the nuance contributed by the appearance here of the same term *(diakonein)* used of Jesus' "service" in 20:28; cf. also 8:15 (Simon's mother-in-law).

[14] In the absence of the male disciples these women are the "link-persons" and witnesses to the entire series of saving events: that Jesus died (27:55-56), that he was buried (27:61), and that he was raised (28:1-10); cf. Davies and Allison, *Matthew* 3:637; Luz, *Matthäus* 4:371.

light of what had been running below the surface all along: namely, that though the Passion was something malevolent human beings did to Jesus, it was also something that God was doing, in the person of the obedient Son, for humankind. The resurrection story is the unveiling of this truth.

Matthew tells the story in four scenes: the women's experience at the tomb (28:1-7); their brief encounter with the risen Jesus (28:8-10); the Jewish leaders' attempt to suppress the story (28:1-15); the appearance to the disciples in Galilee (28:16-20). This final scene, ending with the Great Commission (vv. 19-20), stands apart as the programmatic conclusion to the entire gospel.

At the Empty Tomb: 28:1-7

Matthew presents the women—Mary Magdalene and her companion —at the tomb on the first day of the week in very contemplative mode. They come simply to "see" the tomb of Jesus (v. 1)—just as they had "seen" his death and burial. They do not come to anoint his body because that has already been done by an unnamed member of their company (26:6-13). After the Sabbath rest they simply resume their faithful, silent vigil.

Their fidelity is soon rewarded. Following yet another earthquake (cf. 27:51b), a heavenly appearance irrupts upon the scene in the shape of an angel, who rolls back the great stone that had been sealed upon the tomb and sits on it (vv. 2-3)—a picture of divine triumph over all human attempts to seal the Son in the realm of death. The apparition paralyzes the guard with fear (v. 4). For the women, however, the angel has nothing but reassurance and a message of joy (vv. 5-7). With the "courtesy" characteristic of the resurrection stories across the gospels, the angel first acknowledges the women's emotions and their experience, then points them to the reality before them: the crucified Jesus they are looking for is not here (in the tomb), and the reason he is not here is that he has been raised, exactly as he had foretold. They are invited to verify the "emptiness" themselves and then commissioned to take the news to his disciples,[15] adding that he has gone ahead of them to Galilee, where they will see him.

---

[15] Differently from Mark 16:7 there is no singling out of Peter here, reflecting possibly the early tradition of a separate initial appearance to him: cf. 1 Cor 15:5; Luke 24:34; John 21:1-19).

The women do not, of course, witness the resurrection. What they experience—the earthquake, the angelic appearance, the emptiness of the tomb—are the signs or traces of the divine activity that has brought it about.[16] There is, in fact, a remarkable coherence between their experience and that of Joseph at the very beginning of the gospel, when an angel told him not to be afraid and assured him that the "fullness" of Mary's womb meant not infidelity but a similar "invasion" of divine grace and power into the world (1:18-21). The "emptiness" of the tomb points to a divine raising of Jesus' body that corresponds, at the end of the gospel, to the divine "placing" of that body in Mary's womb at its beginning. The one, no less than the other, facilitates God's being "with us" to the end of the age (1:23; 28:20).

Encounter with the Risen Lord: 28:9-10

With mingled emotions of fear and great joy[17] the women run from the tomb on their errand (v. 8). On the way Jesus himself meets them and greets them,[18] whereupon they fall at his feet and worship him (v. 9). This encounter with the risen Lord is peculiar to Matthew, though it shares some features with the appearance to Mary Magdalene in John 20:11-18. In some respects it seems superfluous since Jesus basically repeats the reassurance and instructions already given by the angel, and a vision of the risen Lord at this point to some degree blunts the impact of the climactic vision to take place for all the disciples in Galilee (28:16-20). Nonetheless, it completes the continuity of the women's faithful witness: they have seen Jesus die, seen him buried, and kept vigil at his tomb; they have seen the emptiness of his tomb and heard the news of his rising; now they take hold of the feet of the one they had seen nailed to the cross. Jesus adds something, too, to the angel's instruction: "Go, tell his disciples" (v. 7) has become, "Go tell my brothers . . ." (v. 10). From the lips of the risen Lord the message has an overtone of healing and reconciliation. The disciples who had abandoned him and fled are still "his brothers." The scattered and terrified flock is to be reconstituted as the family of God (cf. 12:49-50; John 20:17), the nucleus of the Church.

---

[16] Luz, *Matthäus* 4:402–403.

[17] They experience fear as the human response to heavenly presence, joy because of the message they have heard.

[18] The sense of the Greek verb is that he goes out of his way to meet them and accompany them on their errand.

The Bribing of the Soldiers: 28:11-15

The "shadow" side of the Matthean Passion makes a final appearance with the episode of the bribing of the soldiers who had stood guard over the tomb and the counter-story to which, according to the narrative, it had given rise. As the fears that led to the chief priests and elders seeking a guard over the tomb (27:62-64) appear to be realized, they meet to deal with this fresh development. Once again money features. Ironically, it costs more ("a large sum" [v. 12]) to suppress the story of Jesus' raising than to bring about his execution.[19] The episode, of course, is almost certainly a creation of the Matthean community, designed to explain and counter Jewish rejection of the central Christian tenet that Jesus was raised from the dead (v. 15b). Doubtless it played its part in the apologetic of a community struggling for survival in a hostile environment. Responsible interpretation today will recognize it for what it is and leave it in the past where it belongs.

That said, we can at least recognize one point it clarifies. All players in the narrative are agreed that the tomb was empty. The explanations for that emptiness narrow down to two: either the disciples stole the body and based their claim on a deception, or divine power intervened to vindicate Jesus by raising him from the dead as the first fruits of the kingdom. The fact of the empty tomb by itself does not create the latter conviction. For that, heavenly prompting was necessary, together with the realization that what had happened fulfilled earlier prediction. Full faith in the resurrection dawns when both come together—and faith, as we see in the case of the women, turns immediately to mission.

---

[19] Cf. Boring, "Matthew," 501.

THE CHURCH ON MISSION
TO THE NATIONS: 28:16-20

We arrive now at the climactic scene of the entire gospel. Here the Church receives from its Lord the instructions and assurances that are to define its identity and mission until the end of time. All that has gone before—the account of Jesus' origins, birth, ministry, Passion, and death—has been leading up to this. We know that the reason Jesus can claim "all authority in heaven and on earth" is that he has fulfilled "all righteousness" as obedient Son to the end. We know that the reason the disciples must turn to the Gentile world is that Israel, having experienced the ministry of its Messiah, has largely said "No" to his call. Now the preaching of the Church is to ensure that Jesus becomes, as the prophet foretold, the Messiah in whose "name the Gentiles will hope" (Isa 42:4, quoted in Matt 12:21).

From the beginnings of the story, when the family of Jesus, fearful of the hostility of Herod's son in Judea, chose not to return to Bethlehem but to "withdraw" to Galilee (2:22), that region has been the place of refuge. After the arrest of John the Baptist, Jesus again "withdrew" to Galilee (4:12), "Galilee of the Gentiles," causing the people who had sat in darkness to see a great light (4:16)—a pattern of "withdrawal" in the face of hostility (from Jewish leaders) set to recur again and again in his public life (12:15; 14:13; 15:21). His appearance as risen Lord on a mountain in Galilee, following his rejection by the Jewish leadership and execution in Jerusalem, is simply the last instance of this pattern of "withdrawal" and the one to which all the earlier ones had pointed. "Galilee of the Gentiles" has become a symbol of the entire Gentile world, now sitting in darkness but awaiting the "great light" of the gospel.

The disciples, obedient to the word of Jesus (26:32) and the report of the two Marys (28:9-10), have gone to Galilee to meet their risen Lord (28:16). They have gathered on a mountain. The unidentified mountain has

225

theological rather than geographical significance.[1] Important things happen on mountains in Matthew: Jesus' rejection of Satan's offer of world authority (3:8-9); his transfiguration and acknowledgment as God's beloved Son (17:1-8); above all, before a great multitude of afflicted humanity, Jesus' solemn communication to his disciples of the interpretation of the Torah that would make them "salt of the earth" and "light of the world" (5:3-16). Now, on a mountain in Galilee, the disciples are to be commissioned to take that instruction to the nations, "making disciples" of them so that the Church may realize Israel's role to be "light of the nations" (Matt 5:14; cf. Isa 42:6; 49:6; 51:4; 60:3).

For all the solemnity of the occasion, there is great simplicity and humanity about it as well. The risen Jesus bears no title nor, in contrast to the description of the angel at the tomb (v. 3), does he appear in heavenly light or splendor. As in the earlier appearance to the women (vv. 9-10), he is simply "Jesus," the one they have known and followed all along. When the disciples see him they fall to the ground in worship (v. 17; cf. 2:11 [magi]; 14:33). Some, we are told (v. 17c), hesitated or doubted (Greek *edistasan;* cf. Peter in 14:31).[2] We are not told why they did so. Was it disbelief that Jesus really was raised and that this was he? Was it hesitation stemming from lingering guilt for their recent desertion? Whatever the cause, we have again, in this climactic scene, Matthew's acknowledgment of the persistence of weakness and failure in the community. It is such a community that Jesus, again with divine "courtesy," approaches and to whom he begins his great commission (v. 18).

Earlier (4:9) Satan had offered Jesus an easy path to world power—at the price of falling down and worshiping him. Faithful to his messianic mission as determined by the Father—that he should enter into the suffering of the world and give his life as a ransom for many (20:28)—Jesus had swiftly rejected that suggestion. Now that he has at great cost fulfilled his mission in the divinely appointed way, Jesus claims that "all authority in heaven and on earth" has been "given" to him (v. 18). The passive con-

---

[1] Cf. M. Eugene Boring, "The Gospel of Matthew," in Leander E. Keck, ed., *The New Interpreter's Bible.* Vol. 8 (Nashville: Abingdon, 1995) 502.

[2] There is a longstanding controversy as to whether the Greek phrase means (1) that all worshiped but some of them also doubted; (2) all worshiped but all also doubted; (3) the eleven worshiped but there were others present who doubted. Greek usage and overall sense favor the first explanation; see further W. D. Davies and Dale Allison, *A Critical and Exegetical Commentary on the Gospel According to Saint Matthew.* ICC. 3 vols. (Edinburgh: T&T Clark, 1988–97) 3:681; Ulrich Luz, *Das Evangelium nach Matthäus.* 4 vols. Vol. 4: *Mt 26–28* (Zürich: Benziger; Neukirchen-Vluyn: Neukirchener Verlag, 1985 2002) 4:438–39.

struction denotes divine agency. God's raising of Jesus from the dead has been at one and the same time his exaltation to the right hand of the Father and installation with the world authority conferred upon the "one like a Son of Man" in Dan 7:13-14, a text to which Jesus alluded in his trial before the High Priest (26:64).[3] Though Jesus does not speak of himself as "Son of Man" here, the authority he claims is that which will pertain to him in his coming role as world judge (24:29-31; 25:31-46). He stands here before the disciples in the role he will play for all—believers and unbelievers alike—at the end of time.[4] The Church is to summon all nations to conform in the time remaining to the way of life that he has commended, in order that they may experience him then not as judge but as the Savior who welcomes them into the kingdom (25:31-46).

It is in virtue of this authority and in view of this role that Jesus commissions the disciples to "go and make disciples of all nations" (vv. 19-20a). His own personal mission had been to Israel. Now, following the very partial success of that mission, the appeal is to be extended, through the members of the Church, to the nations of the world.[5] In this worldwide mission the disciples are commanded to do four things: to go out, to make disciples of the nations, to baptize, and to teach.[6] The central command is that of making disciples; baptizing and teaching are means to that end.[7] This means that the goal of the enterprise is that members of the nations undergo the formation the original disciples have undergone as told in the

---

[3] Daniel 7:13-14 seems to have provided the chief biblical model for the present passage. The same sense of Christ's exaltation to universal dominion after suffering features in many hymnic passages across the New Testament: Phil 2:6-11; 1 Cor 3:21-23; Eph 1:20-23; Col 1:15-20; 1 Pet 3:18-22; see further W. Cotter, "Greco-Roman Apotheosis Traditions and the Resurrection Appearances in Matthew," in David Aune, ed., *The Gospel of Matthew in Current Study: Studies in Memory of William G. Thompson, s.j.* (Grand Rapids and Cambridge: Eerdmans, 2001) 127–53.

[4] Cf. John P. Meier, *Matthew.* New Testament Message 5 (Wilmington: Michael Glazier, 1980) 370.

[5] In principle there is no reason why "all nations" should not continue to include Israel. However, the overall impression gained from the gospel is that, for the Matthean community, the mission to Israel is factually finished; cf. Luz, *Matthäus* 4:447–51. This surely has some bearing upon the controversy as to whether Christians should continue to attempt to "convert" Jews—or, like Paul in Romans 11, leave their salvation to the mysterious designs of God.

[6] The disciples have been sent out on preaching and healing missions before (10:1) but only now are they commissioned to take up Jesus' teaching role.

[7] Cf. Rudolf Schnackenburg, *The Gospel of Matthew* (Grand Rapids and Cambridge: Eerdmans, 2002) 299.

gospel: being called personally by Jesus, inducted by him into the "family of God," learning both from his teaching and his example as healer and instrument of God's mercy, schooled in the way of service in imitation of the Son of Man who came not to be served but to serve and give his life as a ransom for many (20:28). They are to make of the nations scribes "dis-cipled for the kingdom of heaven" (13:52) who know how to bring out of the treasure chest things new (the instruction of Jesus) and things old (the Torah and scriptural treasury of Israel). The Gospel of Matthew, with its constant concern to portray the life and ministry of Jesus as the fulfillment of scriptural promise, is the "handbook" for that process of formation.

Baptism "in the name of the Father and of the Son and of the Holy Spirit" is the initiation into that process.[8] The formula recalls inevitably the "trinitarian moment" at the outset of Jesus' public life. Following his bap-tism at the hands of John "to fulfill all righteousness" (3:15), the Spirit de-scended upon him and he heard the Father's affirmation, "This is my beloved Son, in whom I am well pleased" (3:17). To be baptized "into the name of the Father and of the Son and of the Holy Spirit" is to be drawn into that same divine-human communion; it is to become a beloved son or daughter upon whom the Father's favor rests. This is not a status earned through personal merit. It is a gift that comes through intimate association with the One who is in a transcendent way God's Son.

The final element of "discipling" the nations is teaching them to "ob-serve" all that Jesus has commanded his own disciples (v. 20a). One thinks here especially of the teaching contained in the Great Sermon, that is, of the Torah as authoritatively interpreted by Jesus, where the supreme crite-rion is what God wants: "mercy, not sacrifice" (Hos 6:6; cf. Matt 9:13; 12:7), where "justice, mercy, and faith" are the "weightier matters" (23:23) and where love, in its "double direction" (love of God/love of neighbor) is the "greatest commandment" of the Torah (22:34-40).[9] Those who have lived according to this standard will have nothing to fear and much to hope for when they come before the Son of Man for judgment according to works of mercy (25:31-46).

Last of all, comes the solemn assurance (signaled by the Greek *idou*, "behold") of the Lord's presence in the community to the end of the age

---

[8] We hear nothing of circumcision. Matthew appears to be at one with Paul that Gentile converts do not need to become Jews first in order to enter the renewed People of God.

[9] Cf. Meier's apt formulation in regard to the Mosaic Law: "This teaching of Jesus . . . encompasses much of what was in the Mosaic Law. But the church teaches these commands not because they come from Moses but because they come from Jesus" (*Matthew*, 372).

(v. 20b). An angel had pronounced Jesus' birth to be the fulfillment of God's promise to be personally "with us" (1:23). His ministry has been a continual enactment of that divine presence in Israel. Now the Church is assured that, to the end of time, it is to be the instrument for the realization of the divine presence in the nations of the world. The account of Jesus' teaching and healing ministry to Israel told in the gospel is no simple record of something accomplished in a special time that is now over. It is a paradigm of a teaching and healing ministry the risen Lord continues in the Church on a worldwide scale. In the stories of the disciples with the earthly Jesus the Church is to recognize its own experience with the risen Lord.[10]

For the same reason too there is no mention here (contrast Luke 24:31; Acts 1:9) of a departure or ascension of Jesus. Matthew avoids any suggestion that the risen Lord does not continue to be "Emmanuel," God "with" the Church. The gospel concludes, then, in an extremely open-ended way. Jesus has been raised and exalted to God's right hand, where he enjoys "all authority in heaven and on earth," but he is no absentee lord. His struggle to displace the grip of Satan and reclaim the world for the rule (kingdom) of God continues as, clad with his authority, the disciples go out on their mission to the nations of the world.

It is hard to think of any way in which the Evangelist could have provided a more effective climax for his story than this final scene setting out a program for the future, whose only limit is "the end of the age." When we think of the likely actual composition of the community responsible for the gospel, of its precarious social position in a remote province of Rome's vast empire, the boldness and *élan* of the vision here set forth is stunning. The fact that just over two centuries later the Christian Church was to become the official religion of the empire probably owes much to the impulse its members drew from this text.

Today the Church undertakes mission in a less triumphant way. We have recognized that far too often the "authority" with which missionaries and others have gone out, appealing to this text, has been an authority modeled on and associated with the authority of colonial power, insensitive to other cultures and religious traditions. We need to revisit the "all authority" claim Jesus makes in this text and recognize that it is an authority to be understood in the light of the total gospel: an authority Jesus enjoys as the Son of Man who came not to be served but to serve and to give his life as a ransom for many (20:28). It is an authority, then, designed to liberate rather

---

[10] This, presumably, is why Jesus remains in his risen life simply "Jesus"; his death and resurrection have brought continuity, not rupture; cf. Luz, *Matthäus* 4:456.

than to dominate, an authority that makes its claim principally through the suffering and plight of those whom Jesus called "the least of my brothers and sisters" (25:31-46). It is their claim—which the judgment will unveil as *his* claim—that will determine who gets entrance to the banquet of the kingdom.

Conclusion

I have tried to cull from Matthew's gospel a sense of Jesus as One who lifts humanity's burdens. Readers who were prepared to go along with such a reading for a good part of the gospel may have sensed it slipping away in light of the emphasis on judgment emerging toward the end of the narrative. Even if the terminology in which Matthew describes negative judgment ("weeping and gnashing of teeth," etc.) be explained and interpreted symbolically, can the prospect of judgment ever be anything but burdensome?

Interpreters of Matthew have long wrestled with this issue that arises so centrally out of the gospel.[1] Having struggled with it throughout this book, I do not claim to have made much advance in the direction of its resolution. I have simply tried to draw attention to aspects of the gospel that balance the emphasis on judgment and, I would maintain, place it within a wider, relativizing context. Let me, in conclusion, recall and review some of those aspects.

At the beginning and again in the all-important exit-scene the gospel presents Jesus as "Emmanuel" (1:23; 28:20). He is "God with us" in a unique sense throughout his human life and remains "with" the Church as risen Lord to the end of time. The Son of Man who will appear in judgment (16:27-28; 24:29-31; 26:64) is the One who has been "with us" as the embodiment of God's mercy. In this light the revealed identification of the Lord with "the least" of his brothers and sisters in the judgment scene (25:31-46) is not all that surprising. In fact, the purpose of the evocation of the judgment is to get believers to turn from fixation on his future presence

---

[1] Most impressive to my mind is the discussion by Ulrich Luz in the Excursus: "Zusammenfassung und Exkurs: Das Gerichtsverständnis des Matthäusevangeliums," appearing in the (as yet untranslated) fourth volume of his commentary: *Das Evangelium nach Matthäus.* 4 vols. Vol. 4: *Mt 26–28* (Zürich: Benziger; Neukirchen-Vluyn: Neukirchener Verlag, 1985–2002) 544–61.

as Judge to recognize his presence here and now in the world's afflicted and needy. It is not that future judgment falls away. It is simply that the best way to ensure a welcome into the kingdom is to act mercifully toward the afflicted in the present.

The whole gospel seems designed to create in its readers that merciful vision: to know Jesus as the One through whom I am enveloped and liberated by God's mercy, and through whose example and teaching I can myself become an instrument of mercy. Hence Matthew's emphasis on Jesus as healer, burden-lifting Servant, and Shepherd, alongside portrayals of him as authoritative teacher and judge.[2] Granted the Jewish matrix from which the gospel emerged, it was inevitable that so much would revolve around the Torah and its proper interpretation. Matthew, as we have seen, builds that into his overriding concern by having Jesus interpret the Torah authoritatively and definitively according to the prophetic criterion of mercy (Hos 6:6). All other legal considerations yield first place to this supreme canon.

What then of Jesus' invitation, "Come to me, all you that are weary and are carrying heavy burdens. . . . Take my yoke upon you, and learn from me; for I am gentle and humble in heart, and you will find rest for your souls. For my yoke is easy, and my burden is light" (11:28-30)? I have argued that Jesus is here portraying himself as "burden-lifting" in contrast to rival Torah interpreters (scribes and Pharisees) whom he sees as "burden-imposing" (23:3-4). The ease and lightness do not stem from the requirements of mercy, which in fact remain very demanding. They can only stem from the relationship with Jesus ("Come to me . . .") and the "knowledge" of the Father that relationship imparts (11:27). Those who truly know themselves to be drawn into the life of the Trinity (3:16-17; 28:19) can find their lives built into that outreach of mercy to the world that Jesus Emmanuel embodies.

The drama of the gospel, as we have seen, revolves very much around the rejection that Jesus, as embodiment of that mercy, experiences from those—especially the leaders of his people—whose ideas of what was needed in the shape of divine visitation were very different from his and whose hold on the allegiance of the people Jesus' words and actions threaten. Ultimately at stake are two different visions of God: the God who

---

[2] It is salutary to read through the text of the gospel and experience the cumulative effect of all the places, in addition to the healing stories proper, where this portrayal of Jesus explicitly emerges: 2:6; 4:12-16; 4:23-25; 8:16-17; 9:10-13; 9:35-36; 11:28-30; 12:5-7; 12:15-21; 14:13-15; 15:29-32; 18:33; 20:28; 21:14; 23:4, 23.

reaches out to and *serves* sinful human beings in the person of the Son, or the God to whom only the virtuous have access and whose principal function is to judge. Undeniably, there are aspects of the latter vision preserved in Matthew. The gospel never lets its readers stray far from the prospect of final accountability, and those who seek to frighten people into virtue will find in it some support for their cause. They can do so, however, only by isolating certain sections from the full sweep of the narrative and the overall vision of God it reveals: the God who has forestalled the judgment by coming among us in the burden-bearing person of the Son.

Bibliography

Commentaries

Boring, M. Eugene   "The Gospel of Matthew," in Leander E. Keck, ed., *The New Interpreter's Bible*. Vol. 8. Nashville: Abingdon, 1995, 87–505.

Davies, W. D., and Dale Allison
A Critical and Exegetical Commentary on the Gospel According to Saint Matthew. ICC. 3 vols. Edinburgh: T&T Clark, 1988–97.

Harrington, Daniel J.   *The Gospel of Matthew*. SP 1. Collegeville: Liturgical Press, 1991.

Luz, Ulrich   *Das Evangelium nach Matthäus*. 4 vols. Vol. 1: *Mt 1–7;* Vol. 2: *Mt 8–17;* Vol. 3: *Mt 18–25;* Vol. 4: *Mt 26–28*. Zürich: Benziger; Neukirchen-Vluyn: Neukirchener Verlag, 1985–2002.

———.   *Matthew 1–7: A Commentary*. Translated by Wilhelm C. Linss. Minneapolis: Augsburg, 1989.

———.   *Matthew 8–20: A Commentary*. Translated by James E. Crouch. Hermeneia. Minneapolis: Fortress, 2001.

Meier, John P.   *Matthew*. New Testament Message 5. Wilmington: Michael Glazier, 1980.

Schnackenburg, Rudolf   *The Gospel of Matthew*. Grand Rapids and Cambridge: Eerdmans, 2002; original *Das Evangelium nach Matthäus*. 2 vols. Wurzburg: Echter, 1985, 1987.

Studies on Matthew

Aune, David, ed.   *The Gospel of Matthew in Current Study: Studies in Memory of William G. Thompson, s.j.* Grand Rapids and Cambridge: Eerdmans, 2001.

235

Balch, David L., ed.   *Social History of the Matthean Community.* Minneapolis: Fortress, 1991.

Byrne, Brendan   "The Messiah in Whose Name 'the Gentiles Will Hope' (Matt 12:21): Gentile Inclusion as an Essential Element of Matthew's Christology," *AusBR* 50 (2002) 55–73.

Cotter, W.   "Greco-Roman Apotheosis Traditions and the Resurrection Appearances in Matthew," in David Aune, ed., *Gospel of Matthew in Current Study,* 127–53.

Deutsch, Celia   "Wisdom in Matthew: Transformation of a Symbol," *NovT* 32 (1990) 13–47.

Gerhardsson, Birger   *The Testing of God's Son (Matt 4:1-11 & Par.).* Lund: Gleerup, 1966.

Good, Deirdre   "The Verb *anachōreō* in Matthew's Gospel," *NovT* 32 (1990) 1–12.

Hare, Douglas R. H.   "How Jewish Is the Gospel of Matthew?" *CBQ* 62 (2000) 264–77.

Kingsbury, Jack Dean   *Matthew: Structure, Christology, Kingdom.* Philadelphia: Fortress, 1975.

———.   *Matthew as Story.* Rev. ed. Philadelphia: Fortress, 1988.

Matera, Francis J.   "The Plot of Matthew's Gospel," *CBQ* 49 (1987) 233–53.

Overman, J. Andrew   *Matthew's Gospel and Formative Judaism: the Social World of the Matthean Community.* Minneapolis: Fortress, 1990.

Saldarini, Antony J.   *Matthew's Christian-Jewish Community.* Chicago and London: University of Chicago, 1994.

Senior, Donald M.   *The Passion of Jesus in the Gospel of Matthew.* Wilmington: Michael Glazier, 1985.

———.   *What Are They Saying About Matthew?* 2nd ed. New York: Paulist, 1996.

Sim, David C.   *The Gospel of Matthew and Christian Judaism: The History and Social Setting of the Matthean Community.* Edinburgh: T&T Clark, 1998.

———. "The Magi: Gentiles or Jews?" *Hervormde Teolo-giese Studies* (Pretoria) 55 (1999) 980–1000.

Snodgrass, Klyne "Matthew and the Law," in David R. Bauer and Mark Allan Powell, eds., *Treasures New and Old: Recent Contributions to Matthean Studies.* SBL Symposium Series 1. Atlanta: Scholars, 1996, 99–127.

Stanton, Graeme N. *A Gospel for a New People: Studies in Matthew.* Edinburgh: T&T Clark, 1992; Louisville: Westminster John Knox, 1993.

Other Literature

Arrupe, Pedro "The Eucharist and Hunger" (Address at Philadelphia, August 2, 1976), in *Justice with Faith Today* 2. St. Louis: Institute of Jesuit Sources, 1980, 171–81.

Brown, Raymond E. *The Birth of the Messiah: A Commentary on the Infancy Narratives in Matthew and Luke.* Rev. ed. New York: Doubleday, 1993.

———. *The Death of the Messiah: From Gethsemane to the Grave: A Commentary on the Passion Narratives in the Four Gospels.* 2 vols. New York: Doubleday, 1994.

Byrne, Brendan *The Hospitality of God.* Collegeville.: The Liturgical Press; Strathfield, N.S.W.: St. Paul's Publications, 2000.

———. *'Sons of God' — 'Seed of Abraham.'* AnBib 83. Rome: Biblical Institute Press, 1979.

———. "'To See with the Eyes of the Imagination . . .': Scripture in the Exercises and Recent Interpretation," *Way Supplement* 72 (Autumn 1991) 3–19.

Campbell, Antony F. *The Study Companion to Old Testament Literature.* Wilmington: Michael Glazier, 1989.

Charlesworth, James A. "Exploring Opportunities for Rethinking Relations among Jews and Christians," in idem, ed., *Jews and Christians: Exploring the Past, Present and Future.* New York: Crossroad, 1990, 35–53.

Donahue, John R. *The Gospel in Parable.* Philadelphia: Fortress, 1988.

Garcia Martinez, Florentino   *The Dead Sea Scrolls Translated: The Qumran Texts in English.* 2nd ed. Grand Rapids: Eerdmans, 1996.

Hellwig, Monica K.   *The Eucharist and the Hunger of the World.* New York: Paulist, 1976.

Hughes, Gerard J.   *The God of Surprises.* London: Darton, Longman and Todd, 1996.

Meier, John P.   *A Marginal Jew: Rethinking the Historical Jesus.* Vol. 1: *The Roots of the Problem and the Person.* Vol. 2: *Mentor, Message, and Miracles.* Vol. 3: *Companions and Competitors.* New York: Doubleday, 1991, 1994, 2001.

Scott, Bernard Brandon   *Hear Then the Parable.* Minneapolis: Fortress, 1989.

Segal, Alan   *Rebecca's Children: Judaism and Christianity in the Roman World.* Cambridge, MA: Harvard University Press, 1986.

Talbert, Charles H.   *Reading Luke: A Literary and Theological Commentary on the Third Gospel.* New York: Crossroad, 1989.

Trible, Phyllis   *Texts of Terror: Literary-Feminist Readings of Biblical Narratives.* Philadelphia: Fortress, 1984.

Scripture Index

Modern Author Index

Subject Index

Parables Index